Socio-Economic Review 2006

Socio-Economic Review 2006

DEVELOPING A FAIRER IRELAND

Policies to Ensure
Economic Development,
Social Equity and
Sustainability

CORI
Justice

CORI

ISBN No. 1 872 335 640

First Published August 2006

Published by
CORI Justice
Bloomfield Avenue
Dublin 4
Ireland

www.cori.ie/justice

Tel: 01- 6677363
Fax: 01- 6689460

e-mail: justice@cori.ie

TABLE OF CONTENTS

1.	**INTRODUCTION**	1
2.	**IRELAND IN 2006: The Context**	2
	2.1 Economy	2
	2.2 Society	3
	2.3 Meeting Commitments	5
	2.4 Establishing Priorities	6
	2.5 NESC Report – Developmental Welfare State	16
	2.6 Developing a Fairer Ireland	18
3.	**DEVELOPING A FAIRER IRELAND:**	
	Objectives, Analysis and Policy Proposals	20
	3.1 Income	20
	(a) Poverty	20
	(b) Income Distribution	42
	(c) Achieving an Adequate Level of Social Welfare	48
	(d) Basic Income	52
	3.2 Taxation	62
	3.3 Work	93
	3.4 Public Services	113
	3.5 Housing and Accommodation	120
	3.6 Healthcare	139
	3.7 Education	154
	3.8 Migration and Interculturalism	164
	3.9 Participation	171
	3.10 Sustainability	179
	(a) Promoting Sustainable Development	179
	(b) Environmental Issues	184
	3.11 Rural Development	197
	3.12 The Developing World	211
4.	**VALUES**	224
5.	**CONCLUSION**	227
	REFERENCES	228

INTRODUCTION

Irish society is faced with substantial opportunities, challenges and choices at this time. The future that emerges will result from the decisions taken now. In the context of our growing national prosperity it is time that we gave greater focus to the need to develop a fairer Ireland. The details of such an agenda are spelt out in this socio-economic review. In presenting our analysis and proposals we pay special attention to how Ireland is experienced today by those who have not done so well from the economic growth of recent years. All our proposals are presented within responsible fiscal policy parameters.

In this review we also include the major commitments on social policy contained in the new national social partnership agreement *Towards 2016*. Of particular significance is the fact that the new agreement acknowledges that economic policy and social policy are two sides of the one coin. This is a welcome development and suggests Ireland's social provision deficits will be comprehensively addressed in the years immediately ahead.

Likewise, we welcome the ten-year framework of the new agreement. Many of Ireland's infrastructural and social deficits cannot be effectively addressed within a two or three year time-frame. The agreement to develop a ten-year framework provides the opportunity to deal with both the infrastructure and social deficits in an integrated and timely manner.

We do not claim to have all the answers. However, we present our analysis and make our proposals as a contribution to the public debate on what the key priorities in the socio-economic arena should be in the years ahead. All responses are most welcome.

IRELAND IN 2006: THE CONTEXT

2.1 Economy

Growth prospects, employment and the public finances

Ireland has achieved enormous progress throughout the last decade. Sustained economic growth coupled with very significant job creation has transformed the country. Most significantly, unemployment has fallen to low levels and the era of forced emigration has ended. In 2006 this trend of high economic growth is expected to continue, such that Ireland will continue to outperform the rest of the Europe and the Developed World. In 2006 the Department of Finance expects Ireland to achieve a GDP growth rate of between 4.5 and 5 per cent, making this economy the fastest growing in the EU (Department of Finance, 2005:A8). Looking to the future, the recent ESRI Medium Term Review has projected an average GNP growth rate of 4.6 per cent for the period 2007-2012 (FitzGerald et al, 2005:43).

Employment continues to grow at a very significant pace with the Department of Finance anticipating that Ireland will create 60,000 additional jobs during 2006 (Department of Finance, 2005:A8).

The public finances also remain in good shape. On a day-to-day basis the exchequer continues to collect more taxation revenue than it is spending in the current account. Detailed projections from the Department of Finance for the next three years indicate that the state will record current account surpluses averaging €4.5 billion annually; the 2006 figure being just under €4.4 billion. When expenditure on Ireland's large capital investment programme is taken into account the government will have an overall budget deficit of €952 million in 2006 (Department of Finance, 2005:D5).

2.2 Society

The dramatic economic successes of recent years have changed Ireland. We are now regarded as a very rich country and major progress has been achieved in many areas, particularly employment. Another reflection of this fact is that our population now exceeds four million for the first time since 1871 and the CSO has recently projected that it will climb to five million people over the next 15 years (CSO, 2004:26.32).

However, it would be wrong to judge Ireland using traditional economic measures alone. On closer examination, Irish society still has many problems, some of which persist almost as if they were acceptable. These include sustained levels of poverty, an unequal income distribution, high levels of illiteracy including high rates among young early school-leavers, homelessness, growing social exclusion and problems of racism and discrimination. In no way is this list complete; however, it underscores the necessity to look more broadly at our recent success and assess just how extensive it has been.

United Nations Human Development Report

The United Nations Development Index presents the best available comparative measurement of the quality of life offered in countries across the world. It assesses countries on a range of socio-economic indicators including life expectancy, education, literacy and adjusted real income. The accompanying report also contains tables of other indicators such as economic growth, health status, poverty, personal distress and information flow. For the first time Ireland entered the top ten countries in the world according to the 2004 index; it is in eighth position in the 2005 report (UN, 2005:219). However, a more detailed assessment of the index's components reveals contrasting progress within Ireland.

Ireland performs well according to the economic indicators, and records the second highest GDP per capita in the world (UN, 2005:219). However, the social indicators record a noticeably poorer performance[1]. A total of 22.6 per cent of the Irish population are identified as being functionally illiterate, meaning that they are unable to read basic texts or a newspaper. Similarly the provision of healthcare in Ireland compares poorly with that of other countries.

---

[1] The United Nations Development Index includes poverty indicators (see 2005:230-231 and 334). On this measure Ireland continues to be ranked 16th out of the 18 industrialised countries reviewed. A full discussion of these figures and of poverty may be found in section 3.1(a)

The proportion of GDP spent on healthcare (public) by the Irish government is 5.5 per cent. This compares with 6.6 per cent in the USA, 8.6 per cent in Germany, 7.8 per cent in Sweden, 7.4 per cent in France, 7.3 per cent in Denmark, 6.5 per cent in Belgium, 5.8 per cent in the Netherlands and 6.4 per cent in the UK. Throughout Europe, the governments of countries such as Norway, Italy, Portugal, Slovakia, Croatia, Hungary and Slovenia all allocate a greater proportion of GDP to health expenditure. Consequently it is of no surprise that the health status of the Irish population compares unfavourably with that of other developed countries. Life expectancy at birth in Ireland is 77.7 years, compared to 80.1 in Sweden, 79.5 in Spain and 79.3 in Norway and 78.3 in the UK (UN, 2005: 236, 250).[2]

Perspectives on Irish Society

During the last year a number of published reports and books have given interesting insights into the nature of modern Irish society. However, the contrast between their findings is interesting and reflects the emergence of an ever more prosperous, yet unequal, Ireland.

During the last year the OECD (2006), The Economist Magazine (2005) and the ESRI (2005) all identified Ireland as one of the most successful economies in the world. The OECD classified Ireland as one of the worlds "high income economies" alongside countries such as Luxembourg, Norway, USA and Switzerland. Concurrently, the CSO reported that 19.4 per cent of the Irish population are at risk poverty (see Section 3.1(a)). The Society of St Vincent de Paul also reported during the year that the scale of poverty in Ireland has resulted in the society spending €33 million a year in assisting those in need; this is equivalent to almost €90,000 per day. They also noted that calls for help from members of the public had increased between 10 and 15 per cent during 2005. Both these facts reflect the on-the-ground reality of Ireland's high and sustained levels of poverty.

One interesting reflection on the current socio-economic position of Ireland is the parallel between where we as a country are going and where the United States currently is. Commenting on this at the CORI Justice's 2003 social policy conference, David Begg stated: "it is to European values that I look when seeking to promote the type of Ireland I want to see. In forming these opinions I have been, paradoxically, influenced by the writings of one of the greatest American thinkers, John Kenneth Galbraith. Forty years ago he wrote about his

---

[2] A more comprehensive assessment of Ireland's healthcare performance is presented in section 3.6.

country degenerating into a state of 'Private Affluence and Public Squalor'. In 1998 the United Nations Development Programme invited him to revisit this topic for the Human Development Report. He wrote that there was one significant change he wished to note; whereas there was a sense of guilt about this condition of growing inequality when he first wrote about it, now it is seen as acceptable" (2003:10).

2.3 Meeting Commitments

Throughout the last number of years the government has made a series of commitments regarding socio-economic policy and issues. In this section we mention a few of these commitments. In the longer term CORI Justice intends to publish an annual update and commentary on these, and any other commitments, so that progress towards their delivery is continually being assessed.

To date, commitments include:
- Raising the lowest social welfare rates (and appropriate child equivalence levels) to 30 per cent of Gross Average Industrial Earnings (GAIE) as set out in the revised NAPS by 2007.
- Keeping tax expenditures under review and amending or terminating them if necessary in the light of changing economic and social priorities.
- Using the potential of the existing tax credit system to more effectively target changes and to pursue further improvements in the tax regime.
- Eliminating long-term unemployment as soon as circumstances permit but in any event not later than 2007.
- Meeting Ireland's obligations under the Kyoto Protocol to reduce greenhouse gas emissions
- Integrating competition and social inclusion polices in recognition of the reciprocal relationship between competitiveness and social inclusion, whereby competitiveness helps to generate the resources to enhance social inclusion, while increased social inclusion enhances competitiveness.
- Meeting the UN target of 0.7 per cent of GNP expended on overseas development assistance by 2012.

2.4 Establishing Priorities

In any country the list of potential reforms is extensive. Consequently, it is always necessary to rationally decide on a set of worthwhile priorities which should be pursued. Making these choices is difficult; no country can do all it wishes to do. However, at present CORI Justice believes that the following should be adopted as national priorities.

- Addressing the social provision deficit
- Minimising social exclusion
- Paying a fairer level of taxation
- Adopting standard fiscal management policies
- Developing long term planning
- Developing a rights-based approach

Each of these priorities is outlined below.

Addressing the Social Provision Deficit
Ireland continues to display serious deficits in its infrastructure and social provision. In a European context our roads, railways, IT broadband and transport systems compare badly. Similarly, our poverty rates, unequal income distribution, growing rich/poor gap and under-equipped health and education systems represent the most visible signs of the extensive gaps in our social provision. In the context of continued economic growth and per capita income well above the European average, the opportunity to address these deficits remains available.

Establishing Priorities

Table 2.1: National Social Protection Expenditure as a % of GDP, for all 25 EU Countries in 2003

Country	% of GDP	Country	% of GDP
Sweden	33.5	Luxembourg	23.8
Denmark	30.9	Poland	21.6
France	30.9	Hungary	21.4
Germany	30.2	Czech Rep	20.1
Belgium	29.7	Spain	19.7
Austria	29.5	**IRELAND GNP**	**19.7**
Netherlands	28.1	Malta	18.5
Finland	26.9	Slovakia	18.4
United Kingdom	26.7	**IRELAND GDP**	**16.5**
Italy	26.4	Cyprus	16.4
Greece	26.3	Lithuania	13.6
Slovenia	24.6	Estonia	13.4
Portugal	24.3	Latvia	13.4

Source: Eurostat (2006:14) and CSO (2005:3)
Note: EU-25 arithmetic average of 23.4% of GDP. Data for Cyprus from 2002.

An analysis of Ireland's spending on social protection against that of other EU countries is telling. Social protection expenditure is defined by Eurostat to include spending on: sickness/health care, disability, old age, survivors, family/children, unemployment, housing and social exclusion initiatives not elsewhere classified (2003: 7). Table 2.1 uses the most recent figures, published by Eurostat, to show the size of this expenditure as a percentage of GDP for 2003 (the latest year for which figures are available). A comparison is also made with Ireland's GNP.

Using either GDP or GNP, Ireland's spending on social expenditure stands out as being well below the EU average (of 23.4 per cent). Only poorer new member states record lower proportions of social expenditure. Chart 2.1 develops this analysis further and examines the difference between the proportion of GDP allocated to social protection expenditure by each of the EU-25 countries and the EU average. Visibly, Ireland has fallen behind.

When social expenditure is assessed on a per capita basis Ireland's position marginally improves. However, when these figures are compared to other countries the Eurostat figures show that the UK government spends 31 per cent more per person on social expenditure than Ireland does. Other comparisons against spending per Irish person include: Belgium 34 per cent more, Germany 38 per cent more, Austria 43 per cent more and Denmark 88 per cent more (Eurostat, 2006:15).

Chart 2.1:   Percentage Divergence in National Social Protection Expenditure levels from the EU average

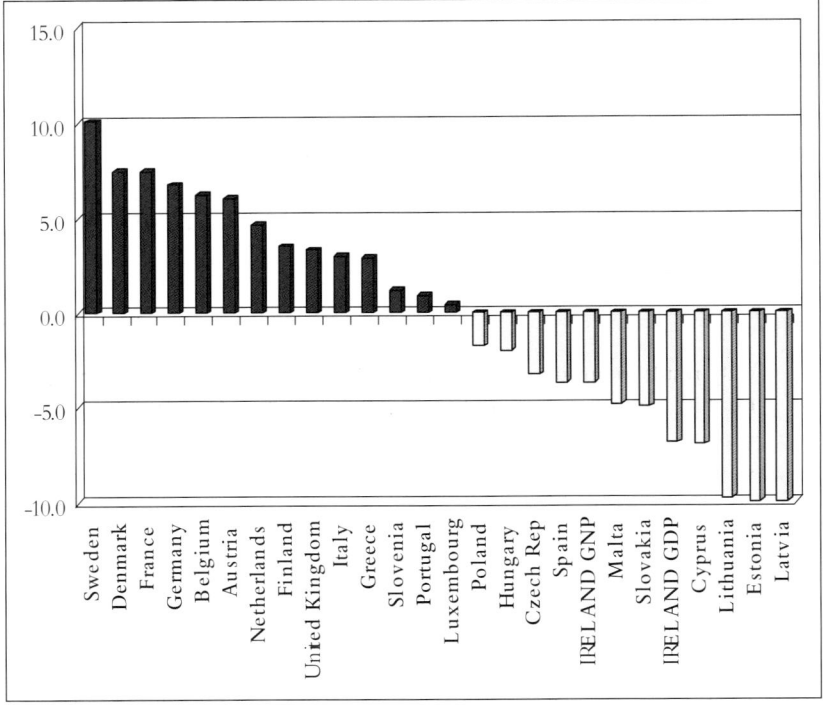

Source: Eurostat (2006:14) and CSO (2005:3)
Note: EU-25 arithmetic average of 23.4% of GDP. Data for Cyprus from 2002.

Given the low levels of unemployment and the low numbers of elderly people in Ireland, relative to the rest of Europe, we would expect Ireland to be below the European average. However these factors are likely to account for only about 10-15 per cent of the gap between Ireland's figure and the European average.

In the context of these figures, it is of no surprise that all the reports mentioned earlier highlight the high levels of poverty and exclusion in Ireland. It is clearly necessary that we address these gaps in our social provision. Given the current strength of the Irish economy there now exists a window of opportunity where these gaps can be appropriately addressed. Section three of this review sets out the policies CORI Justice believes are necessary to achieve this.

Minimising social exclusion

Social exclusion results from a combination of deprivations. In particular, people experience exclusion when they live in poverty, cannot access employment, and do not have a say in the decisions that affect their lives. The agreement *Partnership 2000* described social exclusion as 'cumulative marginalisation: from production (unemployment), from consumption (income poverty), from social networks (community, family and neighbours), from decision-making and from an adequate quality of life' (1996: 4.3). That agreement also stated that:

> Social exclusion is one of the major challenges currently facing Irish society. To minimise or ignore this challenge would not only result in an increase in social polarisation, which is in itself unacceptable, but also an increase in all the attendant problems such as poor health, crime, drug abuse and alienation, which impose huge social and economic costs on our society.

Poor people are excluded from decision-making even when the decisions concern their level of income or their right to work. They are seen by many as a commodity, or are viewed as surplus to the requirements of society, and are dismissed accordingly. Society is now structured in such a way that people in these groups have no future prospects. Social and cultural life today requires money, and very often is organised around the place of employment. People who are poor and unemployed are excluded from the main life of the community.

Exclusion is experienced in many ways and can be multifarious. What does it mean if you are excluded? It means that your opinion is not sought and it doesn't count. In fact, you are not expected to have an opinion; rather you are encouraged to trust the opinion of the shapers and movers of the society. Ultimately exclusion is not only the feeling but also the reality of powerlessness.

When you are one of the excluded, politicians and policy-makers can ignore you without fear of censure or loss of position. When your rights are compromised, the avenues of redress open are very few and haphazard. Since society fears excluded groups, you are always suspect and live under a cloud of being guilty until you prove your innocence.

Observing the conspicuous consumption of the better-off in the society while watching one's own children grow up without proper nourishment or access to appropriate education is demoralising. When these children begin to read reality for themselves, become disillusioned, and drop out of school, the cycle is complete. Another generation is added to the group of alienated and excluded.

People with a disability are, for the most part, among the excluded in our society. They and their families are expected to be grateful for whatever the rest of society decides to do for them. They have an inadequate voice in shaping the decisions that affect them. This needs to change.

The largest excluded group in Irish society is women. Since their exclusion is historically deep-seated and too complex for this publication, we can only acknowledge that it is experienced in various social, political, economic, cultural and religious areas. Exclusion is also experienced by ethnic groups, especially Travellers, and others because of their race, sexual orientation or religious beliefs.

A new excluded group in Irish society comprises migrants, refugees and asylum-seekers. In recent years, people of various ethnic origins have sought refuge here. Others have come here to work and have made a huge contribution to Ireland's booming economy. For many of them, their experience of 'Irish hospitality' has not been good. It is ironic that a country which encouraged emigration as a way of solving its economic problems a few short years ago (when an average of 35,000 people were leaving our shores annually) is now making life difficult for migrants as well as for a substantially lower number of refugees and asylum-seekers who have come here in recent years.

Exclusion is a concern not just of the excluded. When some of its members are not allowed to contribute or participate, all of society is poorer because it is deprived of the creativity, insights, skills and talents of the excluded members.

In the context of Ireland's dramatic economic success over the past few years, it seems to be that the group which has benefited least is the excluded. It remains the case that government has the resources to redress this imbalance and minimise social exclusion.

Paying a fairer level of taxation

Addressing the deficiencies in Ireland's social provision will require the government to allocate further resources to the implementation of policies in this area. Currently, one argument levelled against this move is that funding is unavailable. However, CORI Justice has shown that this argument is false and that sufficient resources are available if the government raised Ireland's tax take to a fairer level. Our 2004 social policy conference specifically focused on this issue.

An analysis in section 3.2 of this review compares Ireland's tax take with that of our fellow European countries. It shows that in 2004 (the latest year for which comparable figures are available) Ireland's tax take was the second lowest in the EU-25. Ireland's tax take stands at just 28.8 per cent of GDP and 36.1 per cent of GNP. These figures imply that Ireland's taxation rate is at least 1.8 percentage points below the EU average (of 37.9 per cent).

Commenting on the future prospects for Ireland Jim Power, the chief economist at Friends First, stated: "we will have to accept that, if we as a nation expect top quality public services, we will have to pay for them. Ireland has one of the lowest levels of taxation as a percentage of GDP in the European Union. Consequently, it is not terribly surprising that it also has one of the poorest levels of public services amongst the more developed EU nations. If we want to change the quality of services, the tax burden will have to rise…the balance between the level of taxation and the quality of public services is a choice we as a nation will have to make over the coming years" (2003:43).

It is an obvious reality that Ireland can never hope to address its deficits in infrastructure and social provision if we continue to collect substantially less tax income than that required by other European countries. Small increases in taxation are certainly feasible and there is little evidence to suggest that such increases would have any significant negative impact on the economy. CORI Justice believes that these increases should not be attained through income taxation, but rather via reforming and broadening the tax base so that Ireland's taxation system becomes fairer.[3]

---

[3] Detailed assessments of these policies are presented in section 3.2.

Adopting standard fiscal management policies

The exchequer comprises two accounts, a current account and a capital account. The former accounts for the day-to-day activities of the state and incorporates inflows of taxation revenue and outflows of state expenditure on wages, social welfare and training programmes among others. The latter primarily accounts for government investment in infrastructure, buildings, roads and so on. Normally it is accepted that a nation's capital account will be in deficit (expenditure greater than revenue), because this generally involves costly investments which generate little immediate revenue. However, in the long run, capital investments are regarded as worthwhile given that their provision facilitates economic activity which in turn produces future flows of taxation revenue.[4]

When managing the current account, the established approach is to plan for a surplus in the account (revenue exceeding expenditure) or to balance the account. In the UK the Chancellor, Gordon Brown, has adopted a "golden rule" for budgetary policy which commits him to balance the current account over a cycle of Budgets while running his capital account in sustained deficit.[5] Producing a budget deficit is not regarded as a problem by economists or by most Finance Ministers. As long as the current account is in surplus or balance, the existence of capital account deficits, equalling small percentages of overall GDP, is accepted; indeed it is expected.

In recent years Ireland has attempted to be an exception to this form of fiscal management. During the boom years of the Celtic Tiger the Irish exchequer was awash with money. In spite of cuts in taxation rates, revenue kept coming in and allowed the exchequer to record sizeable current account surpluses. So large were these surpluses, they exceeded capital account deficits and allowed government to record overall budget surpluses. However, that phenomenon was short-lived, and as the economy slowed down so too did current account revenue. Consequently projections for the overall exchequer balance for the next few years indicate the reappearance of budget deficits. Budget 2006 projections from the Department of Finance indicate that these deficits are being driven by sustained levels of capital account investment amounting to over €7bn a year. This investment represents an important part of Ireland's infrastructural catch-up with the rest of Europe and Eurostat notes that the scale of this investment is such that if it were halved to the EU average Ireland

---

[4] This assumes that value for money is achieved when Governments make capital investments.
[5] This golden rule is often summed up as allowing Britain only to "borrow to invest".

would be recording an overall exchequer surplus (2004:167). However, for the years 2006-2008 the Department has calculated that current account surpluses will average €5.55 billion annually (see table 2.2). The reality of this fiscal outcome is that the Irish Economy has returned to a position that other European countries regard as the 'optimal'. Indeed, if anything the Irish exchequer's position would be regarded as super-healthy given the large current account balances.

It is clear from the Department of Finance projections that there remains significant room for further current account spending over the next few years. As table 2.2 shows, additional spending of up to €1.5 billion a year is feasible. Its effect would only be to reduce the sizeable current account surpluses and to increase marginally the scale of overall budget deficits. Following such a move, the General Government Balance (GGB) as a percentage of GDP (the key indictor used by the European Central Bank to judge fiscal policy control) would be 1.42 per cent in 2006, 1.65 per cent in 2007 and 1.50 per cent in 2008. These outcomes comfortably comply with the 3 per cent limit set in the Stability and Growth Pact. In spite of this additional spending, the average annual current account surplus in the 2006-2008 period would be €4.05 billion.

Table 2.2: Ireland's Current Budget Surplus and General Government Balance, pre and post current spending of €1.5b extra, 2006-2008

	2006	2007	2008
Projected current account surplus	€4,397m	€5,372m	€6,379m
Projected GGB as % of GDP	-0.60%	-0.80%	-0.80%
Current Surplus if €1.5b extra spent	€2,897m	€3,872m	€5,379m
Amended GGB as % of GDP	-1.42%	-1.65%	-1.50%

Source: Calculated from Budget 2006 (2005:D5)

Based on these figures, it is clear that the exchequer can afford to spend significantly more money over the next few years. In the context of the socio-economic problems persisting in Ireland today, problems that are discussed throughout section three of this review, CORI Justice believes that these funds should be used to address them. Major changes could therefore be achieved in the next few years if Ireland is willing to take a more realistic and standard approach to managing its fiscal policy.

Developing long term planning

An essential element of any society is its ability to plan for the future. In that context an important insight into Ireland's future was provided during late 2004 as part of the Central Statistics Office (CSO) report on expected population trends. Entitled *Population and Labour Force Projections, 2006-2036* the report signalled a dramatic demographic transformation due to occur in Ireland over the next three decades. Table 2.3 presents its main findings.

Table 2.3: Projected growth of the Irish population, 2002-2036		
Year	Population Growth	% increase from 2002
2002	3,917,000	–
2006	4,168,000	6.41
2011	4,505,000	15.01
2016	4,854,000	23.92
2021	5,140,000	31.22
2026	5,399,000	37.84
2031	5,613,000	43.30
2036	5,820,000	48.58

Source: CSO (2004:26, 34) using assumption M1F1

As table 2.3 shows the CSO forecast that Ireland's population will climb from approximately 4 million people today to 5.1 million people by 2121 and on to 5.8 million people in 2036. In simple terms, this implies that our population will increase by almost 50 per cent or almost 2 million people in just 34 years (2002-2036).

There are major implications for many public policy areas as a result of this increase. Where will all these extra people be housed? How will they travel around? What additional education and health facilities are required to provide for such additional numbers? How can Ireland ensure that we build a fair and inclusive society which can adequately cater for all these extra people?

CORI Justice believes that these figures necessitate the development of long term planning. Rather than cope with the implications of this population growth once it has happened, we believe it is important to begin to plan now for its arrival. To do this successfully, policies need to be framed within a time frame of at least 10 years. These policies also need to look beyond economic growth as the principal priority driving Government, the policy formation process and society generally.

One welcome development in this area has been to reform the structure of the current model of social partnership such that the new national agreement is based on a ten-year vision. In the 2005 edition of this publication we called for such a development and we welcome its evolution (see CORI, 2005:15). Such agreements allow the Government and social partners to adopt focused long-range strategies as a part of building the Ireland of the future.

Developing a rights-based approach

CORI Justice believes strongly in the importance of developing a rights-based approach to social, economic and cultural issues. The need to develop these rights is becoming ever more urgent for Ireland and the EU.

Social, economic and cultural rights should be acknowledged and recognised just as the civil and political rights have been. Among others, we believe that seven basic rights that are of fundamental concern to people who are socially excluded and/or living in poverty should be acknowledged and recognised. These are the rights to: sufficient income to live life with dignity; meaningful work; appropriate accommodation; relevant education; essential healthcare; cultural respect; and real participation. Until these rights are effectively recognised then Ireland and the EU will continue to have a major credibility problem, as they will be failing to match their commitment to civil and political rights with an equal commitment to social, economic and cultural rights.

To ensure that the recognition of social, economic and cultural rights goes beyond words, however, it is essential to address the question: how can such rights be made justiciable (capable of being vindicated in law)? In particular, how can this be done in a way that respects the political process and does not destroy the balance of power between the judicial and the governmental dimensions of society while also respecting the social, economic and cultural rights of people?

CORI Justice suggests the following as a viable way forward that would respect concerns expressed particularly by politicians while also respecting the need for people's rights to be justiciable. Our proposal has a number of components.

First, these social, economic and cultural rights should be recognised in the Irish Constitution. Following on this recognition there would be a requirement to have legislation ensuring these rights could be vindicated. We suggest the following might achieve this without producing a non-viable situation that would see every individual pursuing, for example, access to appropriate accommodation, all the way up to the Supreme Court.

Second, there would be a legal requirement on each incoming Government to set out concrete targets on each of the range of social, economic and cultural rights recognised in the Constitution. The specific list of rights would already be set out in legislation and should cover the listing outlined above or some similar range of rights.

Finally, the targets set out in such legislation would have to be for specific periods of time e.g. two and four years (these particular time-frames would also be set out in the legislation). Failure to achieve these targets would be justiciable on a class-action or similar basis but not on the basis of every individual bringing their particular case to court.

We believe a mechanism along these lines should be developed and put in place in all EU states. It would mean that social, economic and cultural rights were placed on the same level as civil and political rights. It would also mean that the EU's over-concentration on the economic dimension would be re-balanced in part at least by a growing recognition of the importance of the social dimension to citizens in all EU member states[6].

2.5 NESC Report – The Developmental Welfare State

When considering how Irish society should address these priorities one worthwhile perspective is that offered by NESC in its report entitled *The Developmental Welfare State* (NESC, 2005). Chart 2.2 presents the core structure of the model NESC presented. It comprises three interrelated areas: services, income supports and innovative measures.

---

[6] For a further discussion of this issue see Healy and Reynolds (2003).

Chart 2.2 The Core Structure of the Developmental Welfare State

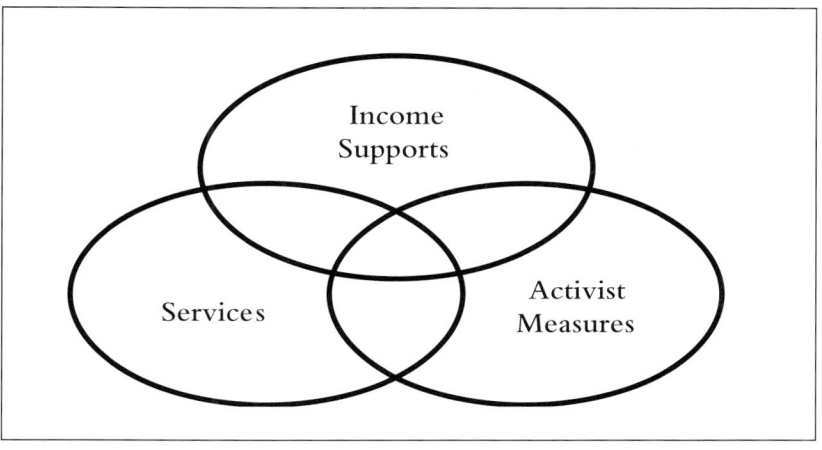

Services
- Childcare
- Education
- Health
- Eldercare
- Housing
- Transport
- Employment services
- Training

Income Supports
- Progressive child income support
- Working age income for participation
- Minimum pension guarantee
- Capped tax expenditures

Activist Measures
- Social inclusion
- Area-based strategies
- Particular community/group projects
- Emerging new needs
- Novel approaches

Source: NESC (2005:144, 156)

In building the developmental welfare state NESC has argued that Irish society should take a 'life-cycle' approach. As table 2.4 shows, such an approach would focus on identifying the needs of children, young adults, people of working age, older people and people challenged in their personal autonomy such as those in care. The council has suggested that for each group we should focus on securing an effective combination of income supports, services and social innovations.

Table 2.4: NESC Life-cycle approach to delivering the Developmental Welfare State

Who?	What? Integration of services, income support and activist measures	How?	
		Governance and leadership	Standards and rights
0-17yrs			
18-29yrs			
30-64yrs			
65+ yrs			
People challenged in their personal autonomy			

Source: NESC (2005:147)

CORI Justice welcomes this approach. We also welcome its incorporation into the new national social partnership agreement. Successfully implementing this approach would underscore each of these groups ability to play a real and sustained role in Irish society and thereby play an important role in tacking social exclusion. This approach provides each sector involved with key challenges if the best options are to be taken and if the approach is to be successfully developed as a template for policy. We look forward to being part of this process.

2.6 Developing a Fairer Ireland

In 2006, it is clearer than ever that Ireland is a country of growing socio-economic divides. Any society is measured by how it treats its most vulnerable people. By this measurement Ireland is failing dismally. Despite the substantial resources which have been available, Ireland's poorest people have been effectively excluded from what is required to live life with dignity. As this review shows, the rich/poor gap continues to increase. Simultaneously, pay increases, special savings schemes and the sustained low-tax environment ensure that many of those who earn most continue to pay less than a fair level of taxation. Consequently our already unequal society grows more unequal. A reversal of this trend will only occur if we as a society focus on developing a fairer Ireland.

To achieve this it is necessary that society as a whole, and leadership in particular, respond by adopting an agenda focused on achieving that goal. In the following pages, we outline what this agenda should entail and how through choices Ireland can become fairer. Throughout the review we address a range of issues including:

- Income
- Taxation
- Work
- Public Services
- Housing and Accommodation
- Healthcare
- Education
- Migration and Interculturalism
- Participation
- Sustainability
- Rural Development
- The Developing World

On each of these issues, we propose a core policy objective. We also provide an analysis of the present situation, review relevant initiatives and outline policy proposals aimed at developing fairness. In doing this, we clearly indicate the choices CORI Justice believes should be made when the available resources are divided in the years immediately ahead.

3. DEVELOPING A FAIRER IRELAND
Objectives, Analysis and Policy Proposals

3.1 Income

> **CORE POLICY OBJECTIVE: INCOME**
> To provide all with sufficient income to live life with dignity. This would involve enough income to provide a minimum floor of social and economic resources in such a way as to ensure that no person in Ireland falls below the threshold of social provision necessary to enable him or her to participate in activities that are considered the norm for society generally.

The sustained high rates of poverty and income inequality in Ireland require greater attention. Tackling these problems effectively is a multifaceted task. It requires action on many fronts ranging from healthcare to education, from accommodation to employment. However, the most important requirement in tackling poverty is the provision of sufficient income to people to enable them to live life with dignity. No anti-poverty strategy can possibly achieve any success without an effective approach to addressing low incomes.

This section addresses the issue of income in four parts. The first examines the extent and nature of poverty in Ireland today while the second profiles our income distribution. The final two sections address potential remedies to these problems by outlining the issues and arguments surrounding the achievement of an adequate social welfare income and the introduction of a basic income.

(a) Poverty
Despite the advances in employment and economic growth achieved over the last few years, the phenomenon of poverty remains large. Its sustained existence remains as one of this country's major failures.

Data on Ireland's income and poverty levels is now provided by an annual survey entitled *EU-SILC (Survey on Income and Living Conditions)*. This survey replaced the *European Household Panel Survey* and the *Living in Ireland Survey* which had run across the 1990s. Since 2003 the *EU-SILC* survey has collected detailed information on income and living conditions from up to 130 households in Ireland each week; giving a total sample of between 5,000 and 6,000 households each year.

CORI Justice has welcomed this new survey and in particular welcomes the speed and accessibility of the data produced. As this survey is conducted simultaneously across all of the EU states its results will possess significant potential to inform the ongoing debate of relative income and poverty levels across the EU member states. It will also allow informed analysis of the relative position of the citizens of member states. In particular, this analysis will be informed by a set of 18 agreed indicators of social exclusion which the EU Heads of Government adopted at Laeken in 2001. These indicators (known as the Laeken indicators) will be calculated from the survey results and cover four dimensions of social exclusion: financial poverty, employment, health and education.

Finally, the change to this new survey has resulted in some minor changes in the way poverty and income levels are measured and reported. These changes are outlined below before we review the results from the recent report which deals with data from 2004.

What is poverty?
The National Anti-Poverty Strategy (NAPS) published by government in 1997 adopted the following definition of poverty:

> *People are living in poverty if their income and resources (material, cultural and social) are so inadequate as to preclude them from having a standard of living that is regarded as acceptable by Irish society generally. As a result of inadequate income and resources people may be excluded and marginalised from participating in activities that are considered the norm for other people in society.*

Where is the poverty line?
How many people are poor? On what basis are they classified as poor? These and related questions are constantly asked when poverty is discussed or analysed.

In trying to measure the extent of poverty, the most common approach has been to identify a poverty line (or lines) based on people's incomes. In recent years the European Commission and the UN among others have begun to use a poverty line located at 60 per cent of median income. The median income is the income of the middle person in society's income distribution, in other words it is the middle income in society. This poverty line is the one adopted in the new EU-SILC survey and differs from the previous Irish poverty line (prior to 2003) which was set at 50 per cent of mean (average) income. This switch to using median income is to be welcomed as it removes many of the theoretical and technical criticisms that have been levelled against using relative income measures to assess poverty.[7] In cash terms there is very little difference between the poverty line drawn at either 60 per cent of median income or 50 per cent of mean income.[8]

While the 60 per cent median income line has been adopted as the primary poverty line; alternatives set at 50 per cent and 70 per cent of median income are also used fairly often to clarify and lend robustness to assessments of poverty.

Using information gathered in the *EU-SILC* survey for 2004, the CSO established that the median income per adult in Ireland was €309.18 (2005:15) Consequently, the income poverty lines for a single adult derived from this average were:

50 per cent line - €154.59 a week
60 per cent line - €185.51 a week
70 per cent line - €216.43 a week

Updating the 60 per cent median income poverty line to 2006 levels, using predicted increases in average industrial earnings (ESRI Medium-Term Review 2005:66), produces a relative income poverty line of €203.55 for a single person. In 2006, any adult below this weekly income level will be counted as being in poverty.

---

[7] In particular the use of median income ensures that it is possible to eliminate poverty (a rate of 0 per cent), a feature that was theoretically impossible when poverty lines were calculated using mean income.

[8] For example in 2003 the CSO reported that the 60 per cent median income line was €14 higher than the 50 per cent mean income line. In some other European countries the opposite situation was found.

Table 3.1 applies this poverty line to a number of household types to show what income corresponds to each household's poverty line. The figure of €203.55 is an income per adult equivalent figure. This means that it is the minimum weekly disposable income (after taxes and including all benefits) that one adult needs to receive to be outside of poverty. For each additional adult in the household this minimum income figure is increased by €134.34 (66 per cent of the poverty line figure) and for each child in the household the minimum income figure is increased by €67.17 (33 per cent of the poverty line).[9] These adjustments are made in recognition of the fact that as households increase in size they require more income to keep themselves out of poverty. In all cases a household below the corresponding weekly disposable income figure is classified as living in poverty. For clarity, corresponding annual figures are also included.

Table 3.1: The Minimum Weekly Disposable Income Required to Avoid Poverty in 2006, by Household Types

Household containing:	Weekly poverty line	Annual poverty line
1 adult	€203.55	€10,621.24
1 adult + 1 child	€270.72	€14,126.25
1 adult + 2 children	€337.89	€17,631.26
1 adult + 3 children	€405.06	€21,136.27
2 adults	€337.89	€17,631.26
2 adults + 1 child	€405.06	€21,136.27
2 adults + 2 children	€472.24	€24,641.27
2 adults + 3 children	€539.41	€28,146.28
3 adults	€472.24	€24,641.27

One immediate implication of this analysis is that most weekly social assistance rates paid to single people are €37.75 below the poverty line.

---

[9] For example the poverty line for a household with 2 adults and 1 child would be calculated as €203.55 + €134.34 + €67.17 = €405.06.

How many have incomes below the poverty line?

The most up-to-date data available on poverty in Ireland comes from the 2004 *EU-SILC* survey, conducted by the CSO. Table 3.2 presents their key findings showing poverty levels among the Irish population. Using the EU poverty line set at 60 per cent of median income, the findings reveal that in 2004 almost one in every five of those living in Ireland was living in poverty. The table also indicates that there has been an overall growth in the proportion of the population living below these lines over the last decade. Data for 1994, 1998, 2001, 2003 and 2004 show that the proportion of the population in poverty has risen from 15.6 per cent in 1994 to 19.4 per cent in 2004.

Table 3.2: Percentage of population below relative income poverty lines, 1994-2004					
	1994	1998	2001	2003	2004
50% median income line	6.0	9.9	12.9	11.6	11.1
60% median income line	**15.6**	**19.8**	**21.9**	**19.7**	**19.4**
70% median income line	26.7	26.9	29.3	27.7	28.7

Source: CSO (2005:5) and Whelan et al (2003:12), using national equivalence scale

As it is sometimes easy to overlook the sheer scale of Ireland's poverty problem it is useful to translate the poverty percentages into numbers of people. Using the percentages for the 60 per cent poverty line above and population statistics from the CSO (2004:48, 2005:52) we can calculate the numbers of people in Ireland who have been in poverty for the years 1994, 1998, 2001, 2003 and 2004. These calculations are presented in table 3.3 below. The results give a better insight into how large the phenomenon of poverty is.

Table 3.3: The numbers of people below relative income poverty lines in Ireland, 1994-2004			
	% of persons in poverty	Population of Ireland	Numbers in poverty
1994	15.6	3,585,900	559,400
1998	19.8	3,703,000	733,194
2001	21.9	3,847,200	842,537
2003	19.7	3,978,900	783,843
2004	19.4	4,043,800	784,497

Source: Calculated using CSO (2005:5) and Whelan et al (2003:12), using national equivalence scale and CSO (2004:48, 2005:52)

The fact that there are now almost 785,000 people in Ireland living life on a level of income that is this low must be a major concern. As we have shown earlier (see table 3.1) these levels of income are low and those below them clearly face difficulty in achieving what the NAPS described as "*a standard of living that is regarded as acceptable by Irish society generally*". A further question arising from these figures was posed by at the conclusion of an editorial in *The Irish Times* when it commented following the publication of the 2000 poverty figures (these figures reported a poverty rate of 20.9%). Given the scale and growth of Ireland's poverty it asked: "how viable is such a society in the long run?" (5 September 2002).

Who are the poor?
In recent years two interchangeable phrases have been used to describe those who are living on incomes below the poverty line, namely those *'living in poverty'* and those *'at risk of poverty'*. The latter of these terms is the most recent, introduced following a European Council meeting in Laeken in 2001. There it was proposed that those with incomes below the poverty line should be termed as being at risk of poverty.

The results of the EU-SULC survey provided a breakdown of those below the poverty line. This section reviews those findings, starting with a broad overview in table 3.4 and then proceeding to a detailed assessment of the different groups in poverty.

Table 3.4 presents figures for the risk of poverty facing people when they are classified by their principal economic status (the main thing that they do). These risk figures represent the proportion of each group that are found to be in receipt of a disposable income that is less than the 60 per cent median income poverty line. Apart from a small group classified as 'others' (those who cannot be described under the six principal status headings), the group of the Irish population that are at highest risk of poverty are the ill and disabled. Almost one in every two people who are classified as ill/disabled live in poverty. The next biggest group at risk of poverty are the unemployed. 37 per cent of this group live in poverty and when broken down by gender the table shows that the risk levels are much greater for unemployed males. Almost one in three of those on home duties (primarily women) live with incomes below the poverty line while 26 per cent of the retired are in poverty. A closer assessment of the risk levels of poverty among the retired reveals that their risk of poverty rate has climbed to its current level from a rate of 8.2 per cent in

1994 (see Whelan et al, 2003:24). Students, whether living in poor families while completing their secondary education or while attending post-secondary education also have a high poverty rate at 23.6 per cent. The lowest poverty risk figure is recorded for those at work (employees, self-employed, farmers) with 7 per cent of this group living below the poverty line.

Table 3.4: Risk of poverty among all persons aged 16yrs + by principal economic status, 2004

	Male	Female	Total
At work	7.5	6.4	7.0
Unemployed	41.0	25.9	37.2
Students and school attendees	19.7	27.8	23.6
On home duties	*	31.8	32.1
Retired	27.9	20.1	26.1
Ill/disabled	52.9	38.2	47.3
Other	*	53.5	52.3
Total	**18.0**	**20.8**	**19.4**

Source: CSO (2005:11), using national equivalence scale
Note: * no recorded figure as sample occurrences were too small for estimation

One obvious conclusion to draw from table 3.4 is that the highest risk of poverty is concentrated among those dependent on the social welfare system. As CORI Justice has pointed out for some time, it is essential that adequate welfare payments are provided for these groups so that their poverty is addressed and reduced.

The working poor

The growth in jobs over recent years has been dramatic and many have benefited from the rapid rise in the number of jobs available. However, it is important to realise that having a job is not, of itself, a guarantee that one lives in a poverty-free household. As table 3.4 indicates 7 per cent of those at work are living at risk of poverty. Translating this into numbers of people suggests that among the 1.89 million workers in Ireland in 2004, just over 132,000 were at risk of poverty.[10]

---

[10] Figures calculated using the risk of poverty figures in table 3.4 and results from the Quarterly National Household Survey (CSO, February 2006: 7).

This is a remarkable statistic. Action is urgently required to address this problem. Developments in both Budgets 2005 and 2006, to take those on the minimum wage out of the tax net are a welcome move in this direction. Similarly, attempts to increase awareness among low income working families of their entitlement to the Family Income Supplement (FIS) are also welcome. However, the most effective mechanism available within the present system to address the problem of the working poor would be to make tax credits refundable. We will address this proposal later.

Child poverty
One of the most vulnerable groups in any society is children and consequently the issue of child poverty is one that deserves particular attention. Child poverty is measured as the proportion of all children aged less than 16 years who live in households that have an income below the 60 per cent of median income poverty line. The age category of 0-15 years is chosen to measure child poverty as it corresponds to the international definition of children used by the International Labour Office (ILO).

In 2004 there were approximately 865,000 children aged between 0 and 15 years living in Ireland.[11] Of these, table 3.5 indicates that 21.9 per cent were at risk of poverty. This amounts to 189,530 children. The scale of this statistic is shocking. Given that our children are our future, this finding is not acceptable. Furthermore, the fact that such a large proportion of our children are living below the poverty line has obvious implications for the education system and the success of these children within it.

Table 3.5: Percentage of children at risk of poverty, 2004			
	Male	Female	Total
Children (under 16 years)	20.6	23.2	21.9

Source: CSO (2005:11), using national equivalence scale.

---

[11] This figure is calculated from a combination of data from the CSO (2005:52) and results from Census 2002 (2003, volume 2:27).

There is widespread support for increasing child benefit if child poverty is to be eliminated. Child benefit is also a very effective component in any strategy to improve equality. This remains a key route to tackling child poverty and is of particular benefit to those families on the lowest incomes. The strength of this approach was recently underscored by the findings of research outlined by Professor Greg Duncan of the Northwestern University of Chicago when he delivered the annual Geary lecture at the ESRI in December 2005.

CORI Justice believes that child benefit should be substantially increased. We oppose the inclusion of child benefit as part of the parents' tax assessment. However, we do support the introduction of a refundable tax credit to all families with children.

Older people
The CSO have indicated that 11.2 per cent of the Irish population are aged over 65 years – some 452,960 people (CSO, 2005:52). Results from Census 2002 also indicated that almost 3 in ten of this group live alone. When poverty is analysed across the age groups dramatic differences between the young, middle aged and old are visible. The 2004 figures show that 17.6 per cent of all those aged between 15-64 live in relative income poverty while 27.1 per cent of those aged 65 and over are in this situation (see tables 3.6 and 3.7 below).

Over time the risk of being in poverty has increased sharply for the elderly. Table 3.6 shows how the proportion of older people who are in poverty changed between 1994 and 2004. In 1994 this stood at 5.9 per cent, by 1998 it had risen to 32.9 per cent and in 2001 it peaked at 44.1 per cent. The most recent set of figures for 2004 suggests that this has decreased slightly to a position where over one in four of Ireland's elderly are at risk of poverty. While this recent decrease is to be welcomed, it remains a concern that so many of this countries senior citizens are living on so little.

Table 3.6: Percentage of older people (65yrs+) below the 60 per cent median income poverty line.					
	1994	1998	2001	2003	2004
Aged 65 +	5.9	32.9	44.1	29.8	27.1

Source: Whelan et al (2003: 28) and CSO (2005:10).

The Ill /Disabled

As table 3.4 showed the ill and disabled are the group with the highest risk of poverty with 47.3 per cent of this group at risk of poverty. Over time the situation of this group has visibly deteriorated with previous poverty studies by the ESRI showing that this group's risk of poverty has increased rapidly over the last decade, climbing from 29.5 per cent in 1994 (Whelan et al, 2003:24). This dramatic increase in the risk of poverty is an issue of concern. It implies that in 1994 approximately three out of every ten persons who are ill or disabled were at risk of poverty and that by 2003 this had increased to almost five out of every ten. Consequently, although the ill and disabled only account for a small proportion of those in poverty, among themselves their experience of poverty is worryingly high. CORI Justice believes there is a clear need to initiate targeted policies to assist this group. These include job creation, retraining (see section on work) and further increases in social welfare supports. There is also a very strong case to be made for introducing a non-means tested cost of disability allowance. This proposal, which has been researched and costed in detail by the National Disability Authority, would provide an extra weekly payment of between €10 and €40 to somebody living with a disability (calculated on the basis of the severity of their disability).

Poverty and gender

Consistently, the results of income surveys indicate that among all adults, women in Ireland experience a greater risk of poverty than men. Table 3.7 presents the picture for 2004.

Table 3.7: Risk of poverty by gender and age in 2004			
	Males	Females	Total
Age 0-14	19.5	23.1	21.2
Age 15-64	16.4	18.8	17.6
Age 65+	25.8	28.2	27.1
Total	**18.0**	**20.8**	**19.4**

Source: CSO (2005:11), using national equivalence scale.

Across all age groups, females are at a higher risk of poverty than males. Among those over 65 years it is likely that the greater dependency of elderly women on social welfare payments and pensions, whose growth has lagged behind average income growth, is a central part of the reason behind this trend

As noted earlier in table 3.4, the 2004 data record that 32 per cent of those working full time in the home were at risk of poverty. Since 1994 this figure has climbed from 20.9 per cent (see Whelan et al, 2003:24). The 2004 EU-SILC results also indicate that 35.7 per cent of all single-adult households and 48.3 per cent of single-parent households are at risk of poverty (CSO, 2005:11). All these classifications are households primarily headed by women and help to further explain the growth and scale of female poverty risk.

Poverty by area
The 2004 EU-SILC results show that poverty is more likely to occur in rural areas than urban areas. The risk of poverty in rural Ireland was 7.5 per cent higher than in urban Ireland with at risk rates of 24.1 per cent and 16.6 per cent respectively. Poverty levels were also greater in the BMW (Border, Midland and Western) region than in the Southern and Eastern region with at risk rates of 26.0 per cent and 17.2 per cent respectively (CSO, 2005:11).

Another study into the distribution of poverty across Ireland has been published by the Combat Poverty Agency and ESRI during 2005. Entitled *Mapping Poverty* (Watson et al, 2005) the study used data from 2000 to assess what differences there were between counties. Overall the study suggested that the structural issues driving poverty were unemployment, non-participation in the labour market due to illness/disability or old age, lone parenthood, low levels of education and social class background. While the differences were small the study did point out that the highest levels of poverty are found in Donegal, Leitrim, Longford and Mayo with the lowest in counties around Dublin.

The poverty gap
As part of the 2001 Laeken indicators the European Union requested that all member countries begin to measure the relative at-risk-of poverty gap. This indicator assesses how far below the poverty line is the income of the median (middle) person in poverty. The size of that difference is calculated as a percentage of the poverty line and therefore represents the gap between the income of the middle person in poverty and the poverty line. The higher the percentage figure gets the greater the poverty gap and the further people are falling beneath the poverty line. As there is a considerable difference between being 2 per cent and 20 per cent below the poverty line this approach is significant.

The 2003 and 2004 EU-SILC results provided figures for this indicator for the first time. It calculated that the poverty gap was 21.5 per cent in 2003 and that it decreased to a figure of 19.8 per cent in 2004. For that year this figure implies that 50 per cent of those in poverty had an equivalised income below 80.2 per cent of the poverty line. The reduction in the poverty-gap size between 2003 and 2004 is important and welcome. Over time we look forward to monitoring the movement of this indicator. It is crucial that as part of Ireland's approach to addressing poverty that we see this figure continue to decline.

The incidence and persistence of poverty

Regrettably, the latest EU-SILC figures do not provide a breakdown of the incidence of poverty. These are figures which reveal the proportion of all those in poverty who belong to particular groups in Irish society. However, there are figures available from the ESRI surveys between 1994 and 2001. Table 3.8(a) provides this data on those below the 60 per cent of median income poverty line classifying them by the labour force status of the head of household. It shows that:

- In 2001, the majority of households in poverty were headed by a person outside the labour force. When figures for households headed by a retired person, a person who is ill/disabled and a person on 'home duties' are combined they account for 59.7 per cent of all the households in poverty.
- Households headed by a person working full time in the home are the largest single group living in poverty (29 per cent).
- Households headed by a retired person make up the next largest group of households living in poverty (18.8 per cent).
- Households headed by an unemployed person and living in relative income poverty have decreased since 1994 from 41.1 per cent to 7.3 per cent in 2001.

Another of the Laeken indicators is an indicator of persistent poverty. This indicator measures the proportion of those being below the 60 per cent of median income poverty line in the current year and for two of the three previous years. Persistent poverty therefore identifies those who have experienced sustained levels of poverty which is seen to seriously harm their quality of life and increase their levels of deprivation.

Table 3.8(a): Incidence of persons below 60% of median income by labour force status, 1994-2001

	1994	1997	1998	2000	2001
Employee	8.3	11.5	6.0	15.4	18.8
Self-employed	10.1	7.8	8.3	8.2	6.6
Farmer	10.6	8.0	10.4	8.9	7.6
Unemployed	41.1	29.6	22.9	12.2	7.3
Ill / Disabled	6.2	10.4	9.1	10.7	11.9
Retired	6.0	9.1	12.0	16.3	18.8
Home Duties	17.8	23.6	31.4	28.4	29.0
Total All	100.00	100.00	100.00	100.00	100.00

Source: Whelan et al (2003: 24), equivalence scale A.

Table 3.8 (b): Percentage of persons in persistent poverty, 1997/1998/2000/2001

	1997	1998	2000	2001
60% of median income	10.1	10.3	12.7	15.6

Source: Whelan et al (2003: 46).

The 2003 and 2004 EU-SILC survey did not produce any results for this measure – the survey needs to run for three years before it is possible to provide this insight. However, the ESRI did examine this issue using data from the Living in Ireland Surveys for 1997, 1998, 2000 and 2001. They found that in 2001 15.6 per cent of persons in Ireland were persistently poor. That is, they had an income below the poverty line in 2001 and for two of the previous three years. The table also notes that the rate of persistent poverty has increased across the period from 10.1 per cent in 1997 to 15.6 per cent in 2001. It therefore implies that as the rate of poverty continued to increase many of those living below the poverty line are remaining there for longer.

CORI Justice believes that this is an important indicator of the experience of poverty in Ireland. We look forward to the results of the 2005 and 2006 EU-SILC which will provide us with more up-to-date data on this issue.

Poverty and social welfare recipients

CORI Justice has always pointed out the very important role that social welfare plays in addressing poverty. Our continued campaign to increase the rates of social welfare reflects this belief [see section 3.1(c) below]. As part of the EU-SILC results the CSO have provided an interesting insight into the role that social welfare payments play in tackling Ireland's poverty levels. They have calculated what the levels of poverty are before and after the payment of social welfare benefits.

Table 3.9 presents these results and shows that without the social welfare system Ireland's poverty rate in 2004 would have been 39.8 per cent. The actual poverty figure of 19.4 per cent reflects the fact that social welfare payments reduced poverty by 20.4 per cent. The small increases in social welfare in 2000 and 2001 are reflected in the smaller effects achieved in those years. If the government commits more money to social welfare payments, as agreed under the *NAPS* and *Sustaining Progress*, these figures measuring the role of social welfare in reducing poverty will increase.

Table 3.9: The role of social welfare payments in addressing poverty				
	2000	2001	2003	2004
Poverty levels before social welfare	35.3	35.6	37.2	39.8
Poverty levels after social welfare	20.9	21.9	19.7	19.4
The role of social welfare	**-14.4**	**-13.7**	**-15.7**	**-20.4**

Source: CSO (2005:5), using national equivalence scale.

As social welfare payments do not flow to everybody in the population it is interesting to examine the impact they have on alleviating poverty among certain groups such as the elderly. Without any social welfare payments 87.4 per cent of all those aged over 65 years in Ireland would be living in poverty. Benefit entitlements reduce the poverty level among this group to 27.1 per cent (CSO, 2005:10). While this poverty rate is still very high, the fact that almost nine out of every ten of the elderly would be in poverty without benefits underscores the importance of these payments to the elderly.

Table 3.4 and the subsequent analysis have shown that many of the groups in Irish society who experienced increases in their poverty levels over the last decade have been dependent on social welfare payments. These include pensioners, the unemployed, lone parents and those who are ill or disabled. Table 3.10 presents the results of an analysis of five key welfare recipient groups performed by the ESRI using poverty data for five of the years between 1994 and 2001. These are the years that the Irish economy grew fastest and the core years of the famed 'Celtic Tiger' boom. Between 1994 and 2001 all categories experienced large growth in their poverty risk. For example, in 1994 only 5 in every 100 old age pension recipients were in poverty; in 2001 this had increased ten-fold to almost 50 in every 100. The experience of widow's pension recipients is similar.

Table 3.10: **Percentage of persons in receipt of welfare benefits/assistance who are below the 60 per cent median income poverty line, 1994/1997/1998/2000/2001**

	1994	1997	1998	2000	2001
Old age pension	5.3	19.2	30.7	42.9	49.0
Unemployment benefit/assistance	23.9	30.6	44.8	40.5	43.1
Illness/disability	10.4	25.4	38.5	48.4	49.4
Lone Parents allowance	25.8	38.4	36.9	42.7	39.7
Widow's pension	5.5	38.0	49.4	42.4	42.1

Source: Whelan et al (2003: 31).

The lesson to be learnt from table 3.10 centres on the inadequacy of social welfare payments. Throughout the last decade CORI Justice has repeatedly pointed out how these have failed to rise in proportion to earnings elsewhere in society. The primary consequence of this is that recipients have slipped further and further back and as a consequence more and more have fallen into poverty. It is clear that adequate levels of social welfare need to be delivered and we outline our proposals for this below.

Poverty and deprivation

Income, alone, does not tell the whole story concerning living standards and command over resources. As we have seen in the NAPS definition of poverty it is necessary to look more broadly at exclusion from society because of a lack of resources. This would involve looking at other areas where "as a result of inadequate income and resources people may be excluded and marginalised from participating in activities that are considered the norm for other people in society" (NAPS, 1997). Although income is the principal indicator used to assess the well-being and ability to participate in society there are other measures used. In particular these measures assess the standards of living people achieve by assessing deprivation through use of different indicators. To date assessments of deprivation in Ireland have been limited and confined to a small number of items. While this is regrettable, the information gathered is worth considering.

Deprivation in the EU-SILC survey

CORI Justice, among others, has continued to express its discomfort with the latest range of deprivation measures provided by the CSO in the EU-SILC survey. There are clear problems with the phrasing and location of the questions within the questionnaire used to collect the information. The end effect of this has been to incorrectly overstate the scale of deprivation among some of the eight indicators collected. Unfortunately, limited progress has been made on addressing these crucial methodological and measurement issues over the first two years of the survey. Looking forward we believe that a whole new approach to measuring deprivation needs to be taken. Continuing to collect information on a limited number of static indicators is problematic and not a true representation of the dynamic nature of Irish society and the ever changing set of items needed to participate in Irish society.

In the context of the above reservation, the details presented in table 3.11 should be interpreted. It shows that the rates of deprivation recorded across a set of eight items varied between 2.7 and 8.7 per cent of the Irish population. Overall 81.7 per cent of the population were not deprived of any item while 9.9 per cent were deprived of one item, 2.9 per cent were without two items and 5.4 per cent were without three or more items (CSO, 2005:13).

Table 3.11: Levels of deprivation for eight items among the population in 2004

No substantial meal on at least one day in the past two weeks	5.2%
Without heating at some stage in the past year	5.4%
Experienced debt problems arising from ordinary living expenses	8.7%
Unable to afford two pairs of strong shoes	3.8%
Unable to afford a roast once a week	4.5%
Unable to afford a meal with meat, chicken or fish every second day	3.7%
Unable to afford new (not second-hand) clothes	5.8%
Unable to afford a warm waterproof coat	2.7%

Source: CSO (2005:12).

Deprivation and poverty combined: consistent poverty

'Consistent poverty' combines deprivation and poverty into one indicator. It does so by calculating the percentage of the population who are simultaneously experiencing poverty and are also registering as being deprived of one or more of the items in table 3.11. As such it captures a sub-group of the poor.

Over the last decade consistent poverty rates have fallen from 9 per cent in 1994 to 4.1 per cent in 2001. Due to the new EU-SILC survey and its measurement problems (outlined above) previous figures are not comparable to the 2003 and 2004 results. In 2004 some 6.8 per cent of the Irish population were in consistent poverty this translates to a figure of 274,978 people of whom 82,175 are children (9.5 per cent of Ireland's children live in consistent poverty).[12]

For some time CORI Justice has criticised this consistent poverty measure. It captures a very limited proportion of those in poverty and as such does not reflect the Government's laudable definition of poverty contained in the National Anti-Poverty Strategy (NAPS). Furthermore, a major critique of this method of assessing poverty is that the deprivation indicators it uses have not changed since 1987. This is puzzling given the substantial changes witnessed by Irish society since then. Indeed it is telling that Ireland is the only country in the world to use the consistent poverty measure. Others, such as Breadline Britain and UK Poverty and Social Exclusion Survey, have pursued a more logical path in assessing deprivation. In these surveys current levels of deprivation are measured using up-to-date lists of necessities. Such a methodology presents a more realistic picture of current deprivation and a set of more useful and informative results.

In 2002 the ESRI reviewed the consistent poverty measure and concluded that "on its own this (measurement) does not tell the whole story nor does it represent the best way to frame a poverty target in current circumstances". It further added that "poverty monitoring over the period to 2007 would more usefully take a broader focus than the consistent poverty measure as constructed to date" (Nolan et al, 2002: 52, 63). Overall, CORI Justice believes that a fundamental rethink on this measure is necessary if it is to be taken seriously as a poverty measurement tool. In spite of some work by the ESRI and government committees in this area during the last year, limited progress has been made.

---

[12] The soundness of these consistent poverty figures is still questionable and they should continue to be used with caution.

Deprivation of food: food poverty

In 2004 the Society of St. Vincent de Paul, the Combat Poverty Agency and Crosscare published a report examining those deprived of an adequate diet entitled *Food Poverty and Policy*. Its purpose was to review the nature and extent of income-related constraints on food consumption in Ireland. The report also suggested a number of policy responses to the issue.

The report defined food poverty as: "the inability to access a nutritionally adequate diet and the related impacts on health, culture and social participation". It found that among those living in poverty three main constraints were imposed on their food consumption. These were: (i) it affects food affordability through the choice and quantity of food that can be bought and the share of the household budget that is allocated to food; (ii) it impacts on access to food through the retail options available and the capacity to shop in terms of transport and physical ability; (iii) issues such as personal skills and knowledge, social pressure and cultural norms interact with structural and economic constraints to produce a complex set of factors contributing to food poverty. Consequently, the experience of food poverty among poor people was that they: eat less well compared to better off groups; have difficulties accessing a variety of nutritionally balanced good quality and affordable foodstuffs; spend a greater proportion of their weekly income on food; and know what is healthy but are restricted by a lack of financial resources to purchase and consume it.

The report found that those most at risk of food poverty were low-income households as well as the unemployed, the elderly, the homeless, Travellers and refugees/asylum-seekers. To address the problem of food poverty the report advocates a targeted food and nutrition policy initiative as part of the NAPS. It suggests that this policy would address financial constraints, affordability and accessibility of food, knowledge gaps, community initiatives, direct provision and food banking.

Deprivation of heat in the home: fuel poverty

Another area of deprivation that has received attention in recent times is deprivation of heat in the home often labelled as fuel poverty. A study by Healy (2004) for the Policy Institute at Trinity College Dublin found that 227,000 homes in Ireland experience fuel poverty. This equates to approximately 17.5 per cent of the total housing stock. The risk of being in fuel poverty was found to be highest among social welfare recipients, lone parents, local authority tenants, households with children and among the elderly. The repercussions of not having enough heat in the home can be severe for many and in particular for the elderly. The report suggests that the presence of fuel poverty could be a factor in as many as 2,000 winter deaths each year. Addressing this issue, like all issues associated with poverty and deprivation, requires a multi-faceted approach. Clearly, living on a low income is a major factor and underscores the need to continue to increase the income levels of those dependent on state pensions, unemployment benefit or living on the minimum wage. A further policy is to target households that require assistance in becoming more energy efficient. In particular many older local authority houses need to be upgraded.

Poverty among local authority tenants

The results of the 1999-2000 *Household Budget Survey* revealed that when all the state's households are classified by tenure (ownership/rent status) those households who rented from local authorities had the lowest incomes. These households recorded an average disposable income of €306.85 per week. This income level was 44.4 per cent below the national average of €551.60. In November 2002, Dublin City Council published a report profiling its tenants. The report entitled *Profile of Households Accommodated by Dublin City Council* provided an insight into the socio-demographic, income and spatial patterns of 24,073 households and 67,960 individuals during 2001. The survey's findings are quiet stark.

The report found that 62.5 per cent of all households accommodated by Dublin City Council were in poverty. When income levels were assessed by person, the report concluded that 60.7 per cent of all those living in Dublin City Council accommodation were at risk of poverty. This figure is almost three times the percentage of 21.9 per cent in the national population for 2001. The poverty status of children living in Dublin City Council accommodation is particularly startling. Of the 25,050 children living in the households, 65.9 per cent of them were living in households that were in poverty. This equates to approximately 16,500 children. Again when a comparison is made between this situation and the national picture the extent of the poverty recorded becomes more visible. In 2001 23.4 per cent of Ireland's children lived in households with income below the poverty line. Therefore child poverty among the population housed by Dublin City Council runs at 2.8 times the national level.

Overall the report found that poverty divided evenly between men and women - 59.8 per cent for men and 61.4 per cent for women. However the report noted that poverty rates increased with age. Of those tenants aged over 65 years more women than men were found to have incomes below half the average national income. These poverty rates were 70.3 per cent and 65.5 per cent respectively.

While the poverty levels recorded were high for all types of local authority households, the report highlighted three household types that possessed the greatest risk of experiencing poverty. These are lone parent households (61.7 per cent in poverty), single adult households (74.9 per cent in poverty) and large families with two or more adults and four or more children (78.8 per cent in poverty).

The experience of poverty

For some years there existed a lack of information on the life experiences of those families living on a low income. Fortunately a number of recent publications have addressed this void and provided an insight that further underscores the extent and implications of poverty.

One very interesting report published in 2004 provided a detailed assessment of the amount of money those living in poor households need to spend to achieve an acceptable lifestyle. Entitled *Low Cost But Acceptable Budgets for Three Households* the report was compiled by the Vincentian Partnership for Social Justice (2004). In reaching their conclusion the authors examined the prices of hundreds of goods and services and established the amount of each needed by three different household types each week. As part of the study controversial areas of consumption such as spending on alcohol, tobacco, pets, savings, insurance were ignored. More crucially, spending on contingencies such as the costs associated with unexpected illness, breakages etc were excluded.[13] While this is unrealistic, it underscores the fact that the report established the baseline figures for what a household needs to survive each week.

The report found that when necessary expenditure levels were compared with welfare entitlements there were shortfalls of between €6.29 and €23.62 a week for two household types, namely a lone parent with two children and an unemployed couple with two children. When examining the situation of an elderly couple reliant on income from state pensions the report found that they had a surplus €66.08 per week but that this figure ignored any medical costs alongside the other listed above.

---

[13] A subsequent assessment of the cost of these contingencies by the Vincentian Partnership (2005) in conjunction with the Money Advice and Budgeting Service (MABS) concluded that these contingencies were likely to account for additional expenditure averaging €30 per household per week.

In concluding their study the Vincentian Partnership called for increases in social welfare rates, improvements in the provision of childcare to disadvantaged families and the provision of long-term insurance schemes for the elderly (2004:85-87).

Poverty: a European perspective

Irish people experience one of the highest risks of poverty when compared to all the other EU member states. Table 3.12 presents data recently published by Eurostat reporting the 'at risk of poverty' (proportions of the population living below the poverty line) rates calculated using the 60 per cent of median income poverty line in each country. The risk of poverty which Irish people face is 1.4 per cent higher than that in the UK, almost 5 per cent higher than Germany, and 9.4 per cent higher than in Luxembourg, Hungary and Slovenia. The lowest poverty risk levels are in the Czech Republic (8 per cent) while the only countries recording poverty levels higher than Ireland were Greece and Slovakia.

Table 3.12: The risk of poverty in the European Union

Country	Poverty Risk	Country	Poverty Risk
Greece	21	Cyprus	15
Slovakia	21	Malta	15
IRELAND	**19.4**	Austria	13
Spain	19	Denmark	12
Italy	19	France	12
Portugal	19	Netherlands	12
Estonia	18	Finland	11
United Kingdom	18	Sweden	11
Lithuania	17	Luxembourg	10
Poland	17	Hungary	10
Latvia	16	Slovenia	10
Belgium	15	Czech Rep	8
Germany	15	**EU-25 Average**	**16**

Sources: CSO, 2005:5; Eurostat, Statistics in Focus 13/2005: 4
Note: Data is the most up-to-date available to Eurostat with figures corresponding to the years 2002 or 2003 for most countries. Irish data is for 2004.

Income

The average risk of poverty in the EU-25 is 16 per cent. Chart 3.1 develops the findings in table 3.12 further and calculates the difference between national poverty risk levels and the EU-25 average. It reflects the fact that Ireland's poverty problem is large and exceptional by European standards. It also underscores the need for Ireland to address this issue with greater vigour.

Chart 3.1: Percentage difference in National Poverty risk from EU-25 average

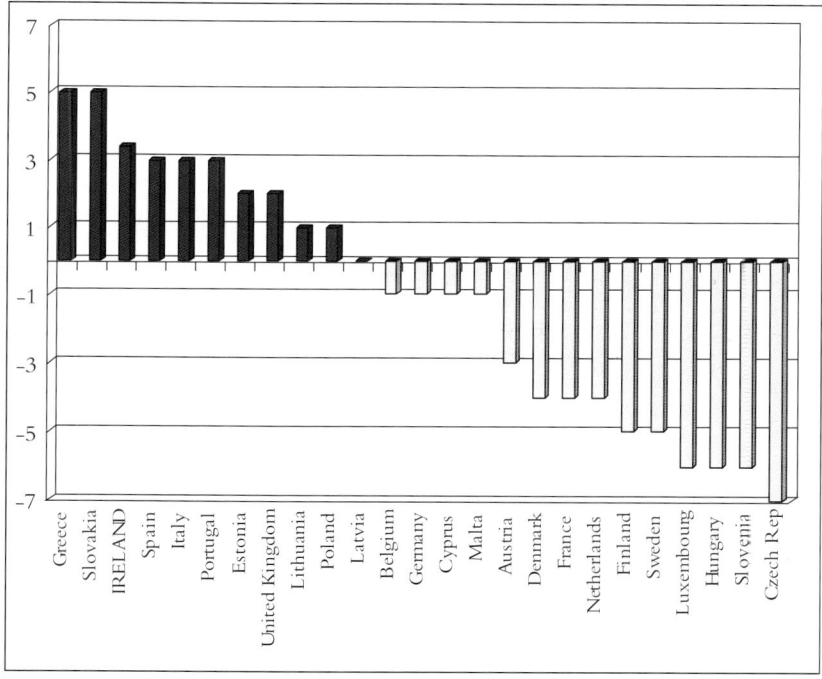

Source: CSO, 2005:5; Eurostat, Statistics in Focus 13/2005: 4
Notes: EU-25 average poverty risk is 16 per cent
See data source notes attached to table 3.12 above

(b) Income Distribution

As we have already outlined, poverty remains a significant problem despite dramatic economic growth. The purpose of economic success should be to improve the living standards of all of the population. A further loss of social cohesion will ensure that large numbers of people continue to experience deprivation, and the gap between them and the better off will widen. This has implications for all of society and not just for those who are poor.

Analysing the annual accounts of income and expenditure provides us with some information on trends in the distribution of national income. However, the limitations of this accounting system need to be acknowledged. Unpaid work is not included. Many environmental factors, such as the depletion of natural resources, are registered as income but not seen as a cost. Pollution is not registered as a cost but cleaning up after pollution is seen as income. Increased spending on prisons and security, which are a response to crime, are seen as increasing national income but not registered as reducing human well-being.

The point is, of course, that national accounts do not include items that cannot easily be assigned a monetary value. Progress cannot be measured by economic growth alone. Many other factors are required as we highlight elsewhere in this review. However, it is still of interest and of value to look at the distribution of national income. As we have acknowledged already Ireland is doing very well when one uses the yardstick of economic growth as the basis of measurement. However, when judging economic performance, and making judgements about how well Ireland is really doing, it is important to look at the distribution of national income as well as its absolute amount.

Trends in Ireland's income distribution: 1987-2004

It is useful in this context to focus on trends in income distribution among households in Ireland since the late 1980s. The results of studies by Collins and Kavanagh (1998) and Collins (2002) combined with the recent CSO (2005) income figures provide a useful insight into the pattern of Ireland's income distribution over 17 years. Table 3.13 combines the results from these three studies and reflects the distribution of income in Ireland as tracked by four surveys in that period.

Over 17 years the share of the bottom 50 per cent of the income distribution has fallen from 25.25 per cent in 1987 to 22.53 per cent in 2004. Comparing the share of the bottom two deciles (the bottom 20 per cent) between 1987 and 2004 shows that those in this group now account for 5.14 per cent of the total income in society versus 6 per cent in 1987.

Table 3.13: The distribution of disposable income, 1987-2004 (%'s)

Decile	1987	1994/95	2000/01	2004
Bottom	2.28	2.23	1.93	2.10
2nd	3.74	3.49	3.16	3.04
3rd	5.11	4.75	4.52	4.27
4th	6.41	6.16	6.02	5.69
5th	7.71	7.63	7.67	7.43
6th	9.24	9.37	9.35	9.18
7th	11.16	11.41	11.20	11.11
8th	13.39	13.64	13.48	13.56
9th	16.48	16.67	16.78	16.47
Top	24.48	24.67	25.90	27.15
Total	100.00	100.00	100.00	100.00

Source: Collins and Kavanagh (1998:173), Collins (2002), CSO (2005:8-9)
Notes: Data for 1987, 1994/95 and 2000/01 are from various Household Budget Surveys. 2004 data from EU-SILC.

The most recent data on income distribution, from the 2004 EU-SILC survey, indicates a further shift in the distribution of Ireland's income. In 2004 the top 10 per cent of the population received their biggest ever share at 27.15 per cent of the total income while the poorest 50 per cent received a smaller share at 22.53 per cent.

Table 3.14 outlines the cash values of these income shares in 2004 as found by the EU-SILC survey. It shows that the top 10 per cent of households receive an average weekly disposable income (after all taxes and having received all benefits) of just over €2,000, a sum that is almost thirteen times greater than the €155 per week received by those households in the bottom decile. In 2004 the average household disposable income was €740.61 a week.

Table 3.14: Amounts of disposable income, by decile in 2004.		
Decile	Weekly disposable income	Annual disposable income
Bottom	€155.45	€8,111.38
2nd	€225.04	€11,742.59
3rd	€316.16	€16,497.23
4th	€421.46	€21,991.78
5th	€550.45	€28,722.48
6th	€679.74	€35,468.83
7th	€822.87	€42,937.36
8th	€1,004.56	€52,417.94
9th	€1,219.84	€63,651.25
Top	€2,010.53	€104,909.46

Source: Calculated from CSO (2005:8-9)

Income distribution: a European perspective

Another of the eighteen indicators adopted by the EU at Laeken assesses the income distribution of member states by comparing the ratio of equivalised disposable income received by bottom quintile (20 per cent) to that of the top quintile. Table 3.15 presents the most up-to-date results of this indicator for all 25 member states. Over time the Irish figure has remained above the European average at 5.0. Overall, the greatest differences in the shares of those at the top and bottom of the income distribution are found in many of the new and poorer member states. However, some EU-15 members including the UK, Italy, Spain and Portugal also record large differences.

Income Distribution and Budget 2006

For some time CORI Justice has monitored the income distribution impact of annual Budgets. In doing this analysis we first look exclusively at the effect on the distribution of income as a result of increases in social welfare and from changes to the tax bands and credits. A more comprehensive analysis of these Budget changes which includes the effects of increases in wages/increments and benefits from the SSIA accounts are explored subsequently

Looking solely at tax and social welfare changes, chart 3.2 (a) shows that a single person who is long term unemployed gained more from Budget 2006 than did a single person who is earning €100,000. A long term unemployed single person received a weekly gain of €17 (€887 a year) compared to a gain of €14.46 a week (€755 a year) for a single person earning €100,000. The other figures in chart 3.2(a) show single people on €25,000 a year were €5.17 a week better off while those on €50,000 became €14.57 a week better off. Couples who are long-term unemployed gained €28.30 a week while those on €25,000 a year were €10.92 a week better off. Couples who are unemployed got €28.30 extra each week compared to €8.78 for couples with 2 earners on an annual income of €50,000.

Table 3.15: Ratio of Disposable Income received by bottom quintile to that of the top quintile in the EU-25.

Country	Ratio	Country	Ratio
Portugal	7.2	France	4.2
Latvia	6.1	Cyprus	4.1
Greece	6.0	Belgium	4.0
Estonia	5.9	Netherlands	4.0
Slovakia	5.8	Austria	3.8
Italy	5.6	Luxembourg	3.7
United Kingdom	5.3	Finland	3.5
Spain	5.1	Czech Rep	3.4
IRELAND	**5.0**	Denmark	3.4
Poland	5.0	Hungary	3.3
Lithuania	4.5	Sweden	3.3
Malta	4.5	Slovenia	3.1
Germany	4.4	**EU-25 Average**	**4.8**

Source: Eurostat on-line database http://epp.eurostat.cec.eu.int
Notes: Data is the most up-to-date available to Eurostat with figures corresponding to the years 2002 or 2003 for most countries. Irish data is for 2004.

Chart 3.2 (a): Income Distribution and Budget 2006 – CORI Analysis

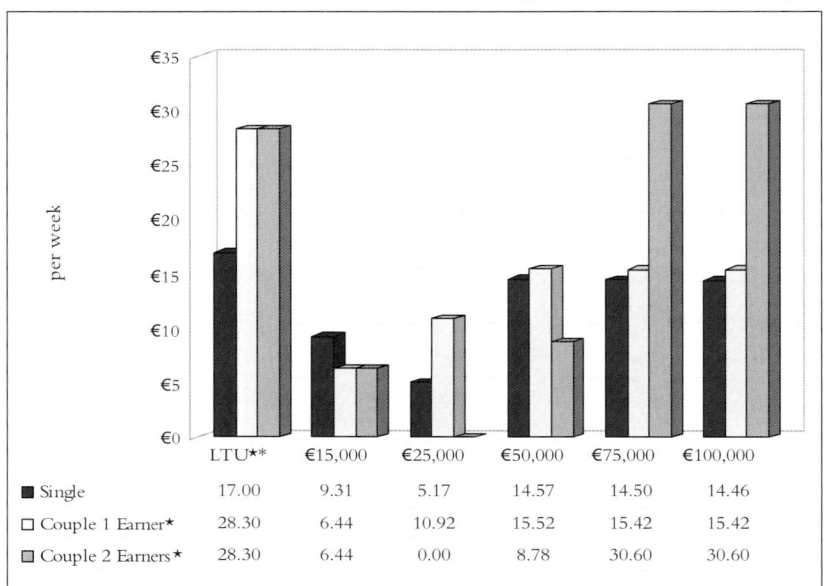

Notes: * Except in LTU case where there is no earner
** LTU: Long Term Unemployed

The tax and welfare decisions taken in Budget 2006 reflected the agenda CORI Justice has been advocating for some time. Consequently we welcomed the Budget and commented at the time on the positive effects it would have on the income distribution and the general fairness agenda. These budgetary changes have also been assessed by the ESRI using their tax-benefit model entitled *SWITCH*. Reporting in the ESRI's *Quarterly Economic Commentary* Callan et al presented the figures graphed in Chart 3.2(b). These show how the gains from the Budget were distributed among the income distribution – analyses in 20% groups (quintiles). Based on that analysis they concluded that "Budget 2006 strongly favoured low-income groups with smaller percentage gains for those on higher income" (2006:61). When reflecting on the effect of these Budget changes on poverty they also noted that "the net impact on the head count of poverty at 60 or 70 per cent of median income has been limited. However, more sophisticated measures taking into account the depth and distribution of poverty indicate a stronger impact" (2006:63).

Chart 3.2 (b): Income Distribution and Budget 2006 – ESRI Quintile Analysis

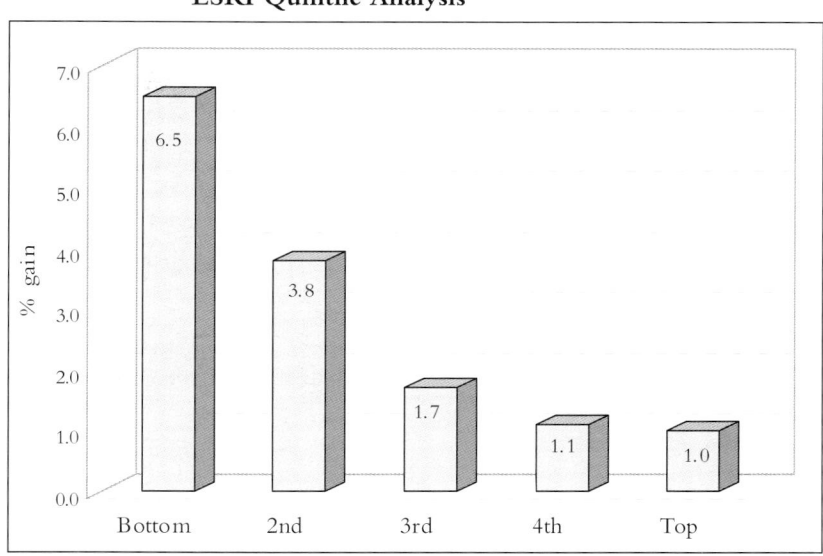

Source: Callan et al (2006:61)

When assessing how much better off people are going to be in 2006 it is important that wage increases and tax changes be included as well as social welfare increases. Unemployed people, for example, gain nothing from wage increases or tax reductions while those with jobs may gain from both. In our calculations we have included the general wage increase in *Sustaining Progress*, a phased increase to reflect inflation in a new arrangement as well as the impact of Budget changes on social welfare and taxation. We have not included the impact of the benchmarking increases for public servants, as they do not apply to everyone. Single people who are long-term unemployed are €17.00 a week (€887 a year) better off in 2006 following the budget. Those on €25,000 a year are €20.46 a week (€1,067 a year) better off while those on €50,000 gained €37.50 a week (€1,957 a year). Couples who are long-term unemployed became €28.30 a week (€1,477 a year) better off. Couples with one income on €25,000 a year benefited by €30.33 a week (€1,583 a year) while those on €50,000 will be €38.46 a week (€2,007 a year) better off in 2006. Couples with two incomes on €25,000 a year will be €19.41 a week (€1,013 a year) better off while those on €50,000 gained €40.80 a week (€2,129 a year).

The impact of Budget 2006 on the distribution of income in Ireland can be further assessed by examining the rich-poor gap. This measures the gap between the disposable income of a single person on long-term unemployment and a single person on €50,000 per annum. Budget 2006 has widened the rich-poor gap by €34.50 per week.

(c) Achieving an Adequate Level of Social Welfare

Over recent years there has been some progress on benchmarking social welfare payments. These have centred on two things, the 2001 *Social Welfare Benchmarking and Indexation Working Group* (SWBIG) and the 2002 *National Anti-Poverty Strategy (NAPS) Review*.

Social welfare benchmarking and indexation working group

In its final report the SWBIG agreed that the lowest social welfare rates should be benchmarked. A majority of the working group, which included CORI Justice, also agreed that this benchmark should be index-linked to society's standard of living as it grows, and that the benchmark should be reached by a definite date. The working group chose Gross Average Industrial Earnings (GAIE) to be the index to which payments should be fixed. The group further urged that regular and formal review and monitoring of the range of issues covered in its report should be provided for. The group expressed the opinion that this could best be accommodated within the structures in place under the National Anti-Poverty Strategy and the National Action Plan for Social Inclusion. The SWBIG report envisaged that such a mechanism could involve

- the review of any benchmarks/targets and indexation methodologies adopted by government to ensure that the underlying objectives remain valid and are being met
- the assessment of such benchmarks/targets and indexation methodologies against the various criteria set out in the group's terms of reference to ensure their continued relevance
- the assessment of emerging trends in the key areas of concern - e.g. poverty levels, labour market performance, demographic changes, economic performance, competitiveness, etc.
- identification of gaps in the area of research and assessment of any additional research undertaken in the interim.

CORI Justice strongly endorses this position and urges Government to ensure

Income

that such a mechanism is established forthwith and that it keeps these issues under constant review.

National Anti-Poverty Strategy (NAPS) review 2002
In 2002, the NAPS review set the following as key targets:

> *To achieve a rate of €150 per week in 2002 terms for the lowest rates of social welfare to be met by 2007 and the appropriate equivalence level of basic child income support (i.e. child Benefit and Child Dependent Allowances combined) to be set at 33 per cent - 35 per cent of the minimum adult social welfare payment rate.*

CORI Justice welcomed this target. It was a major breakthrough in social, economic and philosophical terms. We also welcome the reaffirmation of this target in *Towards 2016*. That agreement stated that "achieving the NAPS target of €150 per week in 2002 terms for lowest social welfare rates by 2007" (2006:52). The target of €150 a week was equivalent to 30 per cent of Gross Average Industrial Earnings (GAIE) in 2002.[14] This means that social welfare rates will be benchmarked to increases in average industrial wages from now on. If this commitment is delivered upon it will mean that the gap between the present level of the lowest social welfare payments and 30 per cent of GAIE will be bridged by 2007.

CORI Justice has calculated the projected growth in €150 between 2002 and 2007 when it is indexed to the estimated growth in GAIE. Table 3.16 presents the expected growth rates and calculates that the lowest social welfare rates for single people should reach €185.80 by 2007.

Table 3.16: Estimating growth in €150 a week (30% GAIE) for 2002-2007

	2002	2003	2004	2005	2006	2007
% Growth of GAIE	–	+6.00	+3.00	+4.50	+3.60	+4.80
30% GAIE	150	159.00	163.77	171.14	177.30	185.80

Source: GAIE growth rates from CSO Industrial Earnings and Hours Worked (September 2004:2) and ESRI Medium Term Review (Bergin et al, 2003:49).

---

[14] GAIE is calculated by the CSO on the earnings of all individuals (male and female) working in all industries. The GAIE figure in 2002 was €501.51 and 30 per cent of this figure equals €150.45 (CSO, 2006: 2).

Progress towards achieving this target had been slow up until Budget 2005. At its first opportunity to live up to the NAPS commitment the government granted a mere €6 a week increase in social welfare rates in Budget 2003. This increase was below that which CORI Justice requested in our *Pre-Budget Briefing for Budget 2003* and also below that recommended by the government's own tax strategy group. In Budget 2004 the increase in the minimum social welfare payment was €10. This increase was again below the €12 a week CORI Justice sought in our *Pre-Budget Briefing for Budget 2004*. Following Budget 2004 CORI Justice argued for an increase of €14 in Budget 2005. The Governments decision to deliver an increase equal to that amount in that Budget marked a significant step towards honouring this commitment and is a step we warmly welcome. Budget 2006 followed suit, delivering an increase of €17 per week to those in receipt of the minimum social welfare rate.

Following Budget 2006 the current minimum level of social welfare is €165.80 a week. To fulfil the NAPS commitment Budget 2007 will need to increase the minimum level of unemployment assistance by €20 a week. Table 3.17 outlines the updated scale of increase for social welfare for 2005 to 2007.

Table 3.17: Proposed approach to addressing the gap, 2005-2007			
	2005	**2006**	**2007**
Min. SW. payment in €'s	148.80	165.80	185.80
€ amount increase each year	14.00	17.00	20.00
Delivered	√	√	?

CORI Justice strongly urges government to honour its commitment in this area and to provide this increase in December 2006. The earlier poverty figures underscore the inadequacy of social welfare payments throughout the last few years (see table 3.10) and make clear the need for increasing social welfare payments to an adequate level. Similarly the failure of social welfare payments to seriously address poverty throughout recent years was pointed out by the CSO in their report entitled *Measuring Ireland's Progress*. Using European data they concluded that "social transfers and pensions reduced the 'at risk of poverty' rate in Ireland in 2000 from 37 per cent to 20 per cent. This was one of the lowest risk reductions in the EU" (2003:38).

The NAPS commitment was very welcome and is one of the few areas of the anti-poverty strategy that is adequate to tackle the scale of the poverty,

Income

inequality and social exclusion being experienced by so many people in Ireland today. It remains crucial that this commitment is delivered upon.

Social welfare payments after 2007

An important element of the NAPS commitment to increasing social welfare rates is the acknowledgement that the years from 2002-2007 marks a period of 'catch-up' for those in receipt of welfare payments. Once the existing gap has been bridged the increases necessary to keep social welfare payments at a level equivalent to 30 per cent of GAIE become much smaller. In that context, we welcome the commitment of the new national agreement to "achieving the NAPS target of €150 per week in 2002 terms for lowest social welfare rates by 2007" and that "the value of the rates to be maintained at this level over the course of the agreement" (2006:52).

To make this point, CORI Justice has calculated the increases necessary from Budget 2008 (delivered in December 2007) onwards to 2010 needed to maintain the link with 30 per cent of GAIE. Table 3.18 shows the increases required over these periods to ensure the lowest social welfare rate is at 30% of GAIE each year. Using projections from the ESRI these suggest an average increase of approximately €10.10 from 2008.

Table 3.18: Increases in minimum social welfare payments, 2008-2010

	2007	2008	2009	2010
30% GAIE updates	185.80	199.00	206.50	216.00
€ amount increase each year	–	+13.20	+7.50	+9.50

Source: Calculated using GAIE growth rates from ESRI Medium Term Review (FitzGerald et al, 2005:66).

Whether or not 30 per cent of GAIE is adequate to eliminate the risk of poverty is an issue to be monitored through the EU-SILC studies and in particular to be addressed when data on persistent poverty emerges.

Individualising social welfare payments

The issue of individualising payments so that all recipients receive their own social welfare payments has been on the policy agenda in Ireland and across the EU for several years. CORI Justice welcomed the report of the Working Group, *Examining the Treatment of Married, Cohabiting and One-Parent Families under the Tax and Social Welfare Codes*, which addressed some of the individualisation issues. More work needs to be done to progress this issue. It should be given greater priority in the policy development process and all payments for adults should be individualised without delay.

(d) Basic Income

Over the past number of years major advances have been achieved in the case for introducing a basic income in Ireland. These include the publication of a *Green Paper on Basic Income* by the government in September 2002 and the publication of a book by Charles M.A. Clark entitled *The Basic Income Guarantee* (2002). The European Commission decision to "decouple" agricultural payments and pay Irish farmers an annual payment also enhances the basic income argument. Both publications and the EU decision are discussed below.

The case for a basic income

CORI Justice has argued for a long time that the present tax and social welfare systems should be integrated and reformed to make them more appropriate to the changing world of the twenty-first century. To this end CORI has argued for the introduction of a basic income system.

A basic income is an income that is unconditionally granted to every person on an individual basis, without any means test or work requirement. In a basic-income system every person receives a weekly tax-free payment from the Exchequer, and all other personal income is taxed, usually at a single rate. For a person who is unemployed, the basic-income payment would replace income from social welfare. For a person who is employed the basic-income payment would replace tax credits in the income-tax system.

Basic income is a form of minimum income guarantee that avoids many of the negative side effects inherent in social welfare payments. A basic income differs from other forms of income support in that

- it is paid to individuals rather than households
- it is paid irrespective of any income from other sources
- it is paid without conditions. It does not require the performance of any work or the willingness to accept a job if offered one
- it is always tax free.

There is real danger that the plight of large numbers of people excluded from the benefits of the modern economy will be ignored. Images of rising tides lifting all boats are often offered as government's policy makers and commentators assure society that prosperity for all is just around the corner. Likewise, the claim is often made that a job is the best poverty fighter and consequently all priority must be given to getting everyone a paid job. These images and claims are no substitute for concrete policies to ensure that all are included. Twenty-first-century society needs a radical approach to ensure the inclusion of all people in the benefits of present economic growth and development. Basic income is such an approach.

As CORI Justice has designed it, a basic income system would replace social welfare. It would guarantee an income above the poverty line for everyone. It would not be means tested. There would be no "signing on" and no restrictions or conditions. In practice a basic income recognises the right of every person to a share of the resources of society.

The Basic Income system ensures that looking for a paid job and earning an income, or increasing one's income while in employment, is always worth pursuing, because for every euro earned the person will retain a large part. It thus removes the many poverty traps and unemployment traps that may be in the present system. Furthermore, women and men get equal payments in a basic income system. Consequently the basic income system promotes gender equality because it treats every person equally.

It is a system that is altogether more guaranteed, rewarding, simple and transparent than the present tax and welfare systems. It is far more employment friendly than the present system. It also respects other forms of work besides paid employment. This is crucial in a world where other forms of work need to be recognised and respected. It is also very important in a world where paid employment cannot be permanently guaranteed for everyone seeking it. There is growing pressure and need in Irish society to ensure recognition and monetary reward for such work. Basic income is a transparent, efficient and affordable mechanism for ensuring such recognition and reward.

Basic income also lifts people out of poverty and the dreadful dependency mode of survival. In doing this it also restores their self-esteem and broadens their horizons. Poor people however are not the only ones who should welcome a basic income system. Employers for example should welcome it because its introduction would mean they would not be in competition with the social welfare system. Since employees would not lose their basic income when taking a job, there would always be an incentive to take up employment.

A basic income system would create a platform for meaningful work. It would benefit paid employment as well as other forms of work. It would also have a substantial impact on reducing income poverty. The present tax and welfare systems were designed for a different era. They have done well in addressing major problems of the second half of the twentieth century. The world however is changing radically. A new system is required for the twenty-first century. Basic income is such a system.

Ten reasons to introduce basic income
i   It is work and employment friendly.
ii It eliminates poverty traps and unemployment traps.
iii It promotes equity and ensures that everyone receives at least the poverty level of income.
iv It spreads the burden of taxation more equitably.
v   It treats men and women equally.
vi It is simple and transparent.
vii It is efficient in labour-market terms.
viii It rewards types of work in the social economy that the market economy often ignores, e.g. home duties, caring, etc.
ix It facilitates further education and training in the labour force.
x   It faces up to the changes in the global economy.

Green Paper on basic income
CORI Justice welcomed the publication of the government's *Green Paper on Basic Income* (2002). In particular it welcomed the fact that the Green Paper vindicates our previous claims that a basic income system would have a far more positive impact on reducing poverty than the present tax and welfare systems.

The Green Paper shows that a basic income system would have a substantial impact on the distribution of income in Ireland. As a result of its introduction it would improve the incomes of 70 per cent of households in the bottom four deciles (i.e. the four tenths of the population with lowest incomes) and raise half of the individuals that would be below the 40 per cent poverty line under "conventional" options above this poverty line. According to the Green Paper these impacts would be achieved without any resources additional to those available to "conventional" options.

The critical test of any tax and welfare system is its impact on people with lower incomes. In that context the Green Paper shows that a basic income system is far more effective at tackling poverty than the present tax/welfare system. Therefore it should form part of a comprehensive strategy to totally eliminate income poverty in the years immediately ahead.

When one looks at the "losers" identified in the Green Paper, two key issues need to be borne in mind. The first of these is that over a three-year implementation period of a basic income system all the "losers" would be better off than they are at present. They would simply not gain as much under Basic Income as they would under the present system. The second issue is that the 'losers' in the bottom four deciles can be easily targeted and compensated through the Social Solidarity Fund that forms part of the basic income structure. In addition the analysis concluded that a basic income system could encourage some people to move from the unofficial economy into regular employment.

On the macro-economic aspects the Green Paper itself acknowledges that the findings of previous studies were very tentative, speculative and hard to quantify. The Green Paper uses the tax rate (including PRSI replacement) of 47.7 per cent which previous studies showed was required to fund basic income, based on January 1999 estimates. Since then the economy has grown significantly and the revised rate, based on the Revenue Commissioner's estimates of the tax base, is likely to be below 43 per cent (compared to the present situation with a marginal tax rate of 42% plus additional social insurance payments).

The choice between a basic income system and the "conventional" tax/welfare options is a trade-off between greater equity and a possible risk of slightly lower economic growth versus less equity and less risk to higher economic growth. At a time when so much concern is expressed about the country's failure to use its recent economic growth to build a fairer society, the argument in favour of introducing a basic income system is further strengthened.

The resources of recent years were more than adequate to introduce a full basic income system in Ireland. It is regrettable that the resources were not used to introduce such a system. Its introduction would have produced a much fairer tax and welfare system. It would have moved beyond models that were appropriate to the twentieth century but are not capable of effectively addressing the new economic realities of the twenty-first century. Also, basic income would be far more effective than the present tax/welfare system at addressing the income inequality, increased insecurity and social exclusion that accompany the "new economy".

The basic income guarantee

The publication of *The Basic Income Guarantee: ensuring progress and prosperity in the 21st century* by Charles M.A. Clark adds another influential voice to the debate on basic income.

Initially Clark states that "the great challenge of the twenty-first century economy is to promote real efficiency and equity not only to ensure future progress, but also to ensure that all get to benefit from this progress"(2002:22). To achieve this he identifies and outlines a basic income guarantee proposal.

The system he proposes is based on the fiscal year 2001/2002. In it Clark proposes that the universal basic income payments should be: €142.21 for adults aged 80+, €135.86 for adults aged 65-79, €109.20 for adults aged 18-64 and €43.17 for those aged up to 17. The total cost of these payments in 2001/2002 would be €18.68bn.

The proposal also incorporates a social solidarity fund designed to compensate low-income households that might be adversely affected by the introduction of a basic income. This fund is estimated to cost €804.9m for the year. Aside from basic income expenditure, additional government spending is estimated at €5.379bn while administrative costs attached to the introduction of the basic income scheme are calculated to cost €141m. The introduction of this proposal would also produce a series of exchequer savings.[15] These would evolve from the need not to fund the living costs associated with various employment programmes, education grants and from administrative savings in the Department of Social and Family Affairs. These savings combine to a total of €1.137bn. Table 3.19 presents these costs and savings figures. It also shows that Clark identified that the net costs of this proposal would be €23.875bn in 2001/2002.

---

[15] These savings are discussed in more detail in Clark (2002:45) and Ward (1994:84-88).

Table 3.19: Net Costs of Basic Income System, 2001 (€m's)	
Basic Income Costs	18,686.77
Social Solidarity Fund	804.90
Other Govt. Expenditure	5,379.88
Administration	141.08
Total Costs	**25,012.63**
- Savings	- 1,137.08
Net Costs	**23,875.55**

Source: Adapted from Clark (2002: 46)

To fund the proposal a flat tax rate of 47.14 per cent was established as necessary. Clark notes that this tax rate would result in Ireland retaining its position as a low-tax economy as measured by the OECD tax to GDP ratio. Following the introduction of this scheme Ireland would have a tax level equal to 34.9 per cent of GDP, a figure which would be lower than the corresponding figures for 2001 in all other EU economies (2002: 64)[16].

A further significant contribution of this research is that it proceeds to calculate the impact of the basic income proposal on poverty and income inequality. These calculations indicate that a basic income system that incorporated a social solidarity fund would result in the complete elimination of poverty as measured using the 50 per cent of mean income. Furthermore the system would also reduce child income poverty from a 1995 level of 23.2 per cent to 0 per cent. Finally the impact of the basic income proposal on the distribution of disposable income is to enhance equality by increasing the share of the total income received by the poorest sixty percent of society (2002: 122 and 124).

Basic income and decoupling
The Irish Government's decision to accept the European Commission's proposals to 'decouple' agriculture payments meant that all Irish farmers now receive a payment unconnected to what they produce. In effect this sees the introduction of a Basic Income payment for all Irish farmers.

---

[16] For details on a pathway to introduce a basic income see: Clark and Healy (1997) and Ward (1994).

Over the past fifteen years CORI Justice, has advocated the introduction of such an approach as the only sensible way of ensuring a viable future for people living in rural Ireland. Most recently, we urged Government to decouple these payments in our response to a request from the Minister for Agriculture and Food to submit our views on 'decoupling'.

This decision by Government also means that the sectors in receipt of a 'basic income type' payment in Ireland now include all farmers, children and older people (entitled to some form of old age pension). While we have always advocated the introduction of a basic income system through provision of payments to all, we are happy with its development sector by sector.

Among the commitments on income adequacy contained in the new social partnership agreement *Towards 2016* are the following:

On minimum social welfare rates
- The lowest social welfare rate for a single person will be benchmarked at 30% of gross average industrial income (GIAE) in 2007.[17] The value of the rates will be maintained at this level over the course of the agreement.

On children
- Progress towards the existing NAPS target for those relying on social welfare payments, which the parties agree remains valid and appropriate – i.e. that the combined value of child income support measures be set at 33-35% of the minimum adult social welfare payment rate.
- Progressing, as a priority, further work aimed at assisting children in families on low incomes. This could include enhancing existing provisions or the introduction of new or reformed mechanisms. Child income supports which avoid employment disincentives will be reviewed by the Department of Social and Family Affairs as a priority and this work, which will be informed by the NESC study on a second tier child income support, will be completed within one year.

---

[17] GAIE is calculated by the CSO on the earnings of all individuals (male and female) working in all industries. The GAIE figure in 2002 was €501.51 and 30 per cent of this figure equals €150.45 (CSO, 2006: 2).

On pensions/income supports for older people
- Future policy in this area will be considered in the context of the National Pensions Review, the outcome of the further work requested in relation to mandatory pensions, the publication of a Green Paper by the Government on pension policy and the views expressed by stakeholders including social partners.
- Enhancement of social welfare pensions over the period, having regards to available resources, building on the existing Government commitment for a rate of €200 per week for social welfare pensions to be achieved by 2007.
- To increase the level of qualified adult allowance for pensioner spouses to the level of the state non-contributory pension.
- To provide an adequate income in retirement which, as far as possible, is related to pre-retirement income. The target income level suggested in the National Pensions Policy Initiative (1998) was 50% of pre-retirement earnings from all sources, including social welfare supports, private and occupational pensions and savings and investments.

On people with disabilities
- Issues around cost of disability will be considered following the development of a needs assessment system provided for under Part 2 of the Disability Act, 2005.

On poverty indicators
- The approach to effective poverty measurement will be reviewed in the light of the timing difficulties in relation to EU-SILC and as part of the wider examination of data availability in the lifecycle framework. The Office for Social Inclusion (OSI) will carry this work forward as part of their responsibility for data and technical supports necessary for developing monitoring and evaluating the NAPinclusion and social inclusion measures in other national strategies. ;This will include a specific focus on developing the type of data required to underpin the lifecycle approach. The Technical Advisory Group for OSI will be expanded to include technical experts from the social partner pillars.

Policy Proposals on Income

A series of short-term and medium-term initiatives is required if the reality of poverty and income inequality is to be addressed once and for all in Ireland. These measures, which are necessary to bring about greater societal fairness, are outlined below.

- Acknowledge that Ireland has a serious poverty problem that to date has not been adequately addressed by government.

- Adopt a National Fairness Strategy to address Ireland's growing poverty problem. The strategy should contain specified goals and targets and be structured similar to the UN Millennium Development Goals (see section 3.12).

- Honour the NAPS and *Towards 2016* commitment that the lowest social welfare payment for a single person will be benchmarked to 30 per cent of GAIE by 2007. To achieve this CORI Justice proposes a social welfare increase of €20 for this group in Budget 2007.

- Pursue budgetary policies that will continue to address the imbalances of previous years where the major beneficiaries were the better off.

- Poverty-proof all public policy initiatives and provision.

- Equality-proof all public policy initiatives and provision.

- Address the problems of child poverty through measures such as increasing child benefit substantially and not taxing it and/or through substantially increasing the early childcare supplement.

- Introduce a refundable tax credit for all children irrespective of the labour status of their parents. This would address both child poverty and childcare costs (see section 3.2).

- Move towards the individualisation of social welfare payments.

- Raise the 'qualifying adult' social welfare payments until they reach the single-adult payment rate.

- Introduce a cost of disability allowance as a means of addressing the poverty and social exclusion experienced by people with a disability.

- Move to publish a Green Paper on pension's policy and in particular address income adequacy among those dependent on state pensions.

- Adopt a new approach to measuring deprivation - one that uses regularly updated indicators reflective of society as it currently is.

- Address the high and sustained levels of persistent poverty being experienced by many Irish households.

- Continue to resource the production of up-to-date data in the area of poverty and social exclusion and ensure the publication of such data as soon as they become available.

- Move towards introducing a basic income system. This should be achieved by ensuring that all initiatives in the area of income and work constitute a positive move towards the introduction of a full basic income guarantee system.

- Government should support a public debate on the Green Paper on Basic Income. Further research on basic income should also be supported.

3.2 Taxation

> **CORE POLICY OBJECTIVE: TAXATION**
> To collect sufficient taxes to ensure full participation in society for all, through a fair tax system in which those who have more, pay more, while those who have less, pay less

The issue of taxation is central to budget deliberations and to policy development at both macro and micro level. Consequently it is crucial that clarity exist with regard to both the objectives and instruments aimed at achieving these goals. To ensure the creation of a fairer and more equitable tax system, policy development in this area should adhere to our core policy objective outlined above. Over the years CORI Justice has worked to increase the level of analysis and debate addressing this area. This has included publishing a book entitled *A Fairer Tax System for a Fairer Ireland* (Reynolds and Healy, 2004) to accompany our 2004 social policy conference, submitting a detailed document on the need to reform tax expenditures (tax breaks and reliefs) to the Department of Finance in March 2005 and releasing a *Policy Briefing* on Taxation in November 2005.[18]

A review of the current state of Ireland's fiscal position reveals a set of government accounts which are the healthiest in Europe. Indeed, throughout the history of the Irish State there have been few periods when the exchequer has been in such good shape. Budget 2006 projected overall budget deficits averaging €3.3 billion per year from 2006-2008. However, these deficits are only occurring due to the scale of capital expenditure necessary to allow Ireland to catch up with the rest of Europe. The exchequer's current account remains healthily in surplus, averaging €5.5 billion over each of the next three years (Department of Finance, 2005:D5). However, Ireland continues to be an economy with a limited taxation base; one that is skewed towards consumption and income. CORI Justice believes that now is an opportune time for the government to completely reassess the taxation system. It should widen the tax base significantly and thereby introduce greater equity to the system.

---

[18] This section draws on much of the analysis presented in these documents.

The remainder of this section outlines Ireland's relative taxation position, the anticipated future taxation needs, further approaches to reforming and broadening the tax base and proposals for building a fairer tax system.

Ireland's total tax take

The most recent data on the size of the Irish tax burden has been produced by the OECD (2005) and Eurostat (2004) and is detailed alongside that of the 24 other EU states in table 3.20. The definition of taxation employed by both organisations incorporates all compulsory payments to central government (direct and indirect) alongside social security contributions (employee and employer) and the tax receipts of local authorities.[19] The tax burden of each country is established by calculating the ratio of total taxation revenue to national income as measured by gross domestic product (GDP). Table 3.20 also compares the tax burdens of all EU member states against the average tax burden of 37.9 per cent.

Of the 25 member states, the highest tax ratios can be found in Sweden, Denmark, Belgium and Finland while the lowest appear in Lithuania, Ireland, Slovakia, Latvia and Malta. Overall, Ireland possesses the second lowest tax burden at 30.2 per cent, some 7.7 per cent below the EU average.

GDP is accepted as the benchmark against which tax levels are measured in international publications. However, in Ireland some suggestions have been made to the effect that gross national product (GNP) should be the used. This argument is based on the fact that Ireland's large multinational sector is responsible for significant profit outflows which if counted (as they are in GDP but not in GNP) exaggerate the scale of Irish economic activity.[20] Commenting on this Collins stated that "while it is clear that multinational profit flows create a considerable gap between GNP and GDP, it remains questionable as to why a large chunk of economic activity occurring within the state should be overlooked when assessing its tax burden" and that "as GDP captures all of the economic activity happening domestically, it only seems logical, if not obvious, that a nations' taxation should be based on that activity" (2004:6).[21] He also noted that using

---

[19] See Eurostat (2004:32-34) for a more comprehensive explanation of this classification

[20] Collins (2004:6) notes that this is a uniquely Irish debate and not one that features in other OECD states such as New Zealand where noticeable differences between GDP and GNP also occur.

[21] See also Bristow (2004:2) who makes a similar argument.

GNP will overstate the scale of the tax base in Ireland because it excludes the value of multinational activities in the economy but does include the tax contribution of these companies. As such, the size of the tax burden carried by Irish people and firms is exaggerated. This also suggests to international observers and internal policy makers that the Irish economy is not as tax-competitive as it truly is.

Table 3.20: Total tax revenue as a % of GDP, for EU-25 Countries in 2004

Country	% of GDP	+/- from average	Country	% of GDP	+/- from average
Sweden	50.7	+12.8	United Kingdom	36.1	-1.8
Denmark	49.6	+11.7	**Ireland GNP**	**36.1**	**-1.8**
Belgium	45.6	+7.7	Greece	35.7	-2.2
Finland	44.3	+6.4	Estonia	35.2	-2.7
France	43.7	+5.8	Spain	35.1	-2.8
Austria	42.9	+5.0	Germany	34.6	-3.3
Italy	42.2	+4.3	Poland	34.2	-3.7
Luxembourg	40.6	+2.7	Cyprus	32.5	-5.4
Slovenia	39.8	+1.9	Malta	31.3	-6.6
Netherlands	39.3	+1.4	Latvia	31.3	-6.6
Hungary	37.7	-0.2	Slovakia	30.8	-7.1
Czech Rep	37.6	-0.3	**Ireland GDP**	**30.2**	**-7.7**
Portugal	37.1	-0.8	Lithuania	28.8	-9.1

Source: OECD (2005:2), Eurostat (2004:239) and CSO National Income and Expenditure Accounts (2005:1)
Notes: Data for all non OECD countries from Eurostat (2004)
EU average (unweighted) is 37.9 per cent

CORI Justice believes that it would be more appropriate to calculate the tax burden by comparing GNP and an adjusted tax-take figure which excludes the tax paid by multi-national companies. As figures for their tax contribution are currently unavailable, we have simply used the unadjusted GNP figures and presented the results in table 3.20. In 2004 this stood at 36.1 per cent.

In the context of these figures, the question needs to be asked: if we expect our economic and social infrastructure to catch up to that in the rest of Europe, how can we do this while simultaneously gathering less taxation income than it takes to run the infrastructure already in place in most of those other European countries? Simply, we will never bridge the social and economic infrastructure gaps unless we gather a larger share of our national income and invest it in building a fairer and more successful Ireland.

Small increases in taxation are certainly feasible and are unlikely to have any significant negative impact on the economy. An increase of just one per cent in the GDP to tax ratio (from 30.2 to 31.2) would produce an extra €1.48bn each year in taxation income for the government. Were Ireland to increase its total taxation levels to that of the UK (from 30.2 to 36.1), a country hardly regarded as being high tax, the exchequer would have an additional income each year of €8.76bn.[22]

For some time, CORI Justice has been to the fore in calling for Ireland to increase its tax take towards that of other European countries. In recent years, the Irish tax take has begun to increase. It has climbed from 28% in 2002 to 30.2% in 2004. We welcome this move and note that it has occurred, as we suggested it would, with virtually no macroeconomic or competitiveness implications. Ireland should remain a low-tax economy, but not one incapable of adequately supporting the economic, social and infrastructural requirements necessary to complete our convergence with the rest of Europe.

Effective tax rates

Central to the ongoing debate on taxation in Ireland are effective tax rates. These rates are calculated by comparing the total amount of income tax a person pays with their pre-tax income. For example, a person earning €50,000 who pays €10,000 in taxation will have an effective tax rate of 20 per cent. Calculating the scale of income taxation in this way provides a more accurate reflection of the burden of income taxation faced by earners.

Following Budget 2006 we have calculated effective tax rates for a single person, a single income couple and a couple both earners. Table 3.21 presents the results of this analysis. For a single person with an income of €15,000 the effective tax rate will be 0%, rising to 12.5% of an income of €25,000 and 37.0% of an income of €120,000. A single income couple will have an effective tax rate of 0% at an income of €15,000, rising to 4.9% at an income of €25,000, 5.1% at an income of €30,000 and 34.0% at an income of €120,000. In the case

---

[22] An increase of this nature is not currently necessary given the strength of the Irish economy.

of a couple where both are earning and where their combined income is €15,000 their effective tax rate is 0.00%, rising to 2.0% for combined earnings of €25,000, 3.1% when their combined earnings are €30,000 and 28.5% for combined earnings of €120,000.

| Table 3.21: Effective Tax Rates following Budget 2006 ||||
Income Levels	Single Person	Couple 1 earner	Couple 2 Earners
€15,000	0.0%	0.0%	0.0%
€25,000	12.5%	4.9%	2.0%
€30,000	14.7%	5.1%	3.1%
€50,000	26.9%	19.7%	12.8%
€70,000	31.9%	26.7%	17.4%
€90,000	34.6%	30.6%	23.3%
€100,000	35.6%	32.0%	25.4%
€120,000	37.0%	34.0%	28.5%

Source: CORI Justice (2005:4).

In all cases, these effective tax rates are low when compared with the situation internationally and that which prevailed in Ireland over most of the last decade. Chart 3.3 illustrates the downward trend in effective income tax rates for three selected household types since 1997. These are a single earner on €25,000; a couple with 1 earner on €40,000; and a couple with 2 earners on €60,000. Their experiences are similar to those on other income levels and are similar to the effective tax rates of the self-employed over that period (see Budget 2005, annex A).

Reviewing the figures in chart 3.3 and table 3.21 one has to question what potential remains for future reductions in income taxation levels. As the situation stands the burden carried by those on different income levels is small but fair given that those earning more, pay more. Of course, income taxation is not the only form of taxation and, as the review below will suggest, there are many in Ireland not paying their fair share.

Chart 3.3: Effective tax rates in Ireland, 1997-2006

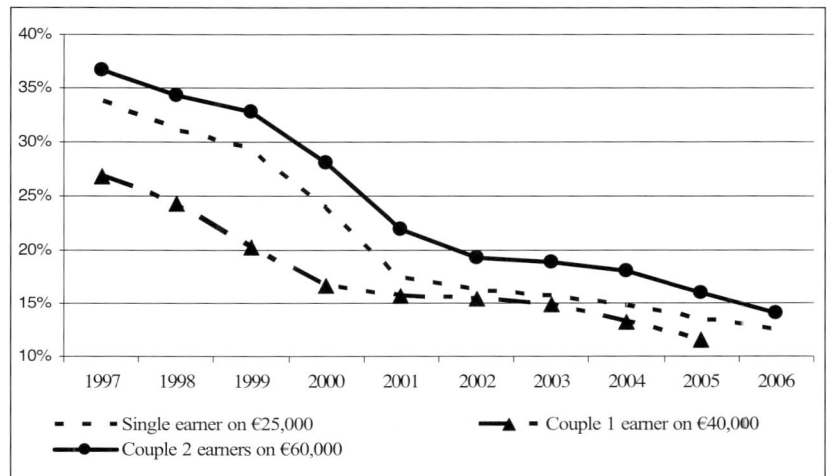

Source: Department of Finance, Budget 2006 (2005;Annex A C19).

Future taxation needs

Government decisions to raise or reduce overall taxation revenue needs to be linked to the demands on its resources. These demands depend on what Government is required to address or decides to pursue. A valuable review of Ireland's future taxation needs was presented in a paper to our 2004 social policy conference (Collins, 2004:9-14). In that paper Collins points out that in the immediate term tax increases are not essential if the government avails of the funds available to it in the current account surplus (see section 2 earlier). However in the medium-term he indicated that the government faced a series of demands which will necessitate increases in the amount of taxation its collects. These demands include:

- contributions to the European Union from 2007 onwards when Ireland becomes a net contributor
- payments for fines imposed under the Kyoto protocol
- increases in Overseas Development Assistance (ODA) contributions
- increases in social welfare payments in accordance with the NAPS
- increases in spending on education, healthcare and pensions as a result of an increase in the numbers of children and the elderly in the population over the next 20 years.

Developing a Fairer Ireland

A further item that can be added to this list is the additional funding required to finance local government up to and after 2010. An indication of the size of this commitment was provided by a recent report by Indecon Economic Consultants (2005) commissioned by the Department of Environment, Heritage and Local Government. Among its conclusions the report pointed out the likelihood of an annual 'funding gap' of between €415m and €1,500m up to 2010. Thus the report recommended that central government provide 'a significant increase in the level of resources available to local authorities over the period to 2010' (2005:193, 194).

Research by Bennett et al (2003) also provides some insight into future exchequer demands. Table 3.22 presents estimates as a percentage of GDP for the costs of healthcare and pension in Ireland in the years 2025 and 2050. As the population ages these figures will increase substantially, almost doubling between 2002 and 2050 from 8.9 to 16.7 per cent of GDP.

Table 3.22: Projected Costs of Healthcare and Pensions in Ireland, as % GDP			
	2002	2025	2050
Healthcare	6.0	6.3	8.8
Pensions	2.9	4.5	7.9
Healthcare + Pensions	**8.9**	**10.9**	**16.7**

Source: Bennett et al (2003)

The implication of these findings is that in the years to come Ireland will have to raise additional taxation revenue to meet these demands. Collins points out that this is particularly the case for the decade post-2007 when Ireland begins to meet some of these new demands while simultaneously continuing to invest heavily in developing its infrastructure. In the longer term he suggested that spending on capital projects will reduce to average European levels (it is currently twice the average) and that at that stage options will be open to Government to consider reductions in taxation levels once again (Collins, 2004:14).

Is a higher tax-take problematic?
Suggesting that any country's tax take should increase normally produces negative responses. People think first of their incomes and increases in income tax, rather than more broadly of reforms to the tax base. Furthermore, proposals

that taxation should increase are often rejected by suggestions that they would undermine economic growth. However, a review of the performance of the British and US economies over recent years is interesting in light of this issue.

Over the last number of years Britain has achieved low unemployment and higher levels of growth compared to other EU countries (OECD, 2004). These have been achieved simultaneously with increases in its tax/GDP ratio. In 1994 this stood at 33.7 per cent and in 2004 it had increased 2.4 percentage points to 36.1 per cent of GDP. Furthermore, in his March 2004 Budget the British Chancellor Gordon Brown indicated that this ratio would increase again to reach 38.3 per cent of GDP in 2008-09 (2004:262). His announcement of these increases was not met with predictions of economic ruin or doom for Britain and projections of economic growth suggest that it will remain high compared to other EU countries (IMF, 2004).

Taxation and competitiveness

Another argument made against increases in Ireland's overall taxation levels is that it will undermine competitiveness. However, the suggestion that higher levels of taxation would damage our position relative to other countries is not supported by international studies of competitiveness. Annually the World Economic Forum publishes a *Global Competitiveness Report* ranking the most competitive economies across the world. Table 3.23 outlines the top fifteen economies in this index as well as the ranking for Ireland (which comes 26th). It also presents the difference between the size of the tax burden in these, the most competitive, economies in the world and Ireland for 2004.[23]

---

[23] This analysis updates that first produced by Collins (2004:15-18).

Developing a Fairer Ireland

Table 3.23: Differences in taxation levels between the world's 15 most competitive economies and Ireland.

Competitiveness Rank	Country	Taxation level versus Ireland
1	Finland	+14.1
2	United States	-4.8
3	Sweden	+20.5
4	Denmark	+19.4
5	Taiwan	*not available*
6	Singapore	*not available*
7	Iceland	+11.7
8	Switzerland	-0.8
9	Norway	+14.7
10	Australia	+1.4
11	Netherlands	+9.1
12	Japan	-4.9
13	United Kingdom	+5.9
14	Canada	+2.8
15	Germany	+4.4
26	IRELAND	-

Source: World Economic Forum (2005:xvii)
Notes: a) Taxation data from OECD (2005:4).
b) For some countries comparable data is *not available*.
c) Taxation data for Australia and Japan is only available for 2003

Only two countries, the US and Japan, have noticeable lower taxation levels compared with Ireland. Of the other leading competitive economies all collect a greater proportion of national income in taxation. Over time Ireland's position on this index has deteriorated. Between 2002 and 2005 Ireland slipped from 23rd to 26th on the global competitiveness index. The reasons stated for Ireland's loss of competitiveness included decreases in economic growth, poor performances by public institutions and a decline in the technological competitiveness of the economy (WEF, 2003: xv). Interestingly, a major factor in that decline would seem to be related to underinvestment in state funded areas: education; research; infrastructure; and broadband connectivity. Each of these areas is dependent on taxation revenue and they have been highlighted by the report as necessary areas of investment to achieve enhanced competitiveness. As such, lower taxes do not feature as a significant priority; rather it is increased and targeted government spending.

A similar point was expressed by the Nobel Prize winning economist Professor Joseph Stiglitz while visiting Ireland in June 2004. Commenting on Ireland's long-term development prospects he stated that "all the evidence is that the low tax, low service strategy for attracting investment is shortsighted" and that "far more important in terms of attracting good businesses is the quality of education, infrastructure and services." Professor Stiglitz, who chaired President Clinton's Council of Economic Advisors, added that "low tax was not the critical factor in the Republic's economic development and it is now becoming an impediment".[24]

Reforming and broadening the tax base

The methods by which the tax base should be reformed and broadened are an issue worth considering. CORI Justice believes that there is merit in developing a tax package which places less of an emphasis on taxing people and organisations on what they earn by their own useful work and enterprise, or on the value they add or on what they contribute to the common good. Rather, the tax that people and organisations should be required to pay should be based more on the value they subtract by their use of common resources. Whatever changes are made should also be guided by the need to build a fairer taxation system, one which adheres to our core policy principal above.

There are a number of approaches available to Government in reforming the tax base. Our recent book entitled *A Fairer Tax System for a Fairer Ireland* outlined in detail many of these options (Reynolds and Healy, 2004). A shorter review is presented below.

Corporation Tax

Following Budget 2003, the standard rate of corporation tax was reduced from 16 per cent to 12.5 per cent at a full year cost of €305m. This reduction followed another reduction in 2002 which brought the rate down from 20 per cent to 16 per cent. The total cost in lost revenue to the exchequer of these two reductions is estimated at over €650m per annum.

---

[24] In an interview with John McManus, Irish Times, June 2nd 2004.

Serious questions remain concerning the advisability of pursuing this policy approach. Ireland's corporation tax rate is now considerably below the corresponding rates in the rest of Europe. Windfall profits are flowing to a sector that is already extremely profitable. In particular, the Irish Banking sector is now recognised as one of the most profitable in Europe, a factor significantly related to the low levels of taxation these institutions pay.[25]

Across the relevant academic literature no evidence of substance exists to support the contention that corporations would leave if the corporate tax rate were higher – at 17.5 per cent for example. Furthermore, the logic of having a uniform rate of corporation tax for all sectors is questionable. At a recent CORI social policy conference David Begg stated, "there is no advantage in having a uniform rate of 12.5 per cent corporation tax applicable to hotels and banks as well as to manufacturing industry" (2003:12). This Irish position contrasts to that adopted in the UK, where for example industries earning profits from the North Sea oil reserves pay a corporation tax rate of 50 per cent (40 per cent up to 2006), a rate considerably higher than that applied to other industries[26].

As the European Union expands corporation tax competition is likely to intensify. Already Estonia and the Isle of Man have put in place a zero per cent corporation tax rate, Cyprus has set its rate at 10 per cent and Hungary continues to reduce its rate; others are likely to follow.[27] Over the next few years Ireland will be forced to either ignore tax rates as a significant attraction/retention policy for foreign investors (this would be a major change in industrial policy) or to follow suit and compete by further cutting corporation tax. Consequently, there is a serious danger that Irish corporation taxes will be forced down to zero per cent during the next few years. Sweeney has warned of a dangerous situation where Ireland ends up "leading the race to the bottom" (2004:59). The costs of such a move, in lost exchequer income, would be enormous and CORI Justice believes that the government must now make a decision on whether this is the path they wish to follow.

---

[25] The annual reports of the major banking institutions also highlight, and at times boast about, further reductions in their tax liabilities via write-offs, investments etc. which result in the banks paying an effective tax rate considerably less than 12.5 per cent.

[26] Ironically, recent agreements by the Irish government with offshore exploration companies will result in any such companies paying a corporation tax rate of 0 per cent.

[27] Interestingly, the Isle of Man has retained a 10 per cent rate on the profits of banking institutions.

An alternative direction for corporation tax is to set a minimum rate for all EU countries. Given the international nature of company investment these taxes are fundamentally different from internal taxes, and the benefit of a European agreement which sets a minimum rate is clear. These would include protecting Ireland's already low rate from being driven down even lower, protecting the jobs in industries which might move to lower taxing countries and protecting the revenue generated for the exchequer by corporate taxes. Commenting on these impending developments Professor John Bradley of the ESRI stated that "any strategic planner worth her salt should now look to a future where Irish international competitive advantage will rest on the quality of our infrastructure, the excellence of our education system, our ability to innovate, and the wider benefits of living and working in Ireland, rather than simply on a low corporate tax rate. Such advantages are less easily eroded by tax-cutting copy-cat competitors" (Irish Times, April 10th 2003). The comments of Paul McGowan, a tax partner with KPMG, are also of interest. Speaking at the Finance Dublin conference in March 2004 he suggested that Ireland should negotiate a Europe wide corporate tax deal setting a minimum rate which Ireland would then adopt and hold without question for the next 25 years.

CORI Justice believes that an EU wide agreement on a minimum rate of corporation tax should be negotiated. We believe that the minimum rate should be set well below the 2004 EU average rate of 31.32 per cent but above the existing low Irish level. A rate of 17.5 per cent seems appropriate.

Tax Expenditures/ Tax Reliefs

One of the most welcome public policy developments over the past few years has been the action taken by Government to address the provision of the sizeable number of tax expenditures, primarily in the form of tax reliefs. In November 2004 the Revenue Commissioners estimated that the annual cost of tax reliefs was €8.4 billion, a value that is equal to 22 per cent of the total taxation collected each year in Ireland.[28] Over the years these schemes allowed many to avoid contributing their fair share in taxes and consequently CORI Justice has called for some time for their reform.

---

[28] The Revenue Commissioners Statistical Report (2004:8) indicates that the total taxation collected in 2003 equalled €37.7b.

As part of that process the Department of Finance commissioned a number of reports on the scale, extent, merit and distribution of these schemes. The findings of these reports span some 1,000 pages and are of some interest (see Department of Finance 2006 Vols I, II, III). While it is impossible to summarise these findings over a few paragraphs, three examples give a good indication of what the reports found.

In 2000 the government introduced a tax relief scheme for capital investments in Hotels and Holiday Camps. An assessment by Indecon Consultants for the Department of Finance found that up to 2006 these schemes resulted in a net loss in tax revenue (revenue forgone) of €120.5m (Department of Finance, 2006 Vol. I:73). The report recommended that the scheme now be abolished; a decision that Budget 2006 has since taken. As part of this review Indecon also considered the distribution of these tax reliefs. Table 3.24 presents the results of a confidential survey of Ireland's Accountancy and Tax professionals carried out by the consultants. In the survey these professionals were asked to indicate where in the income distribution were the recipients of this schemes located. The figures therefore represent indicative views based on the judgement and expertise of these professionals.[29] They indicate that all these benefits flowed to investors with a gross income of over €100,000 per annum and that two-thirds of those who benefited had annual gross incomes in excess of €200,000. Table 3.24 also reports a similar distribution analysis of those investors who availed of tax reliefs for multi-storey car parks. It presents an even more skewed allocation to those with incomes in excess of €200,000. In terms of tax revenue forgone this scheme cost the exchequer €15.9m.

An assessment of the tax reliefs associated with the Urban renewal scheme by Goodbody Economic Consultants identified that between 1999 and mid-2006 the total cost of this scheme in terms of tax revenue forgone was €1,423m. When considering the equity implication of this scheme they concluded that "the tax benefits of the scheme have accrued to relatively few high income individuals" and that "it is difficult to escape the conclusion that the scheme has had very negative equity impacts" (Department of Finance, 2006 Vol. II p84-86). Budget 2006 also abolished this scheme.

---

[29] Accurate income distribution figures are unavailable as the Revenue Commissioners did not collect detailed information on these schemes.

Table 3.24: The % distribution of investors utilising two tax relief schemes according to the views of Accountancy and Tax Professionals – by annual gross income

Gross Annual Income of Investors	Hotels and Holiday Camps	Multi-storey Car Parks
Likely to be earning in excess of €200,000	66.7%	83.3%
Likely to be earning between €100,000 and €200,000	33.3%	16.7%
Likely to be earning between €50,000 and €100,000	0.0%	0.0%
Likely to be earning less than €50,000	0.0%	0.0%
Total	**100.0%**	**100.0%**
Net tax forgone up to 2006	**€120.5m**	**€15.9m**

Source: Department of Finance (2006, Vol I: 73-76, 297-298).

In seriously addressing these tax expenditures CORI Justice believes that Budget 2006 took an important step towards achieving a fairer taxation system in Ireland. In responding to the budget we welcomed the Minister's moves to address the problems arising from the provision of various tax reliefs and in particular addressing the way in which these schemes were being exploited to minimise the tax bills of very high earners. Consequently, we welcomed the Minister's Budget statement that "my basic aim is to see that everybody pays an appropriate amount of income tax relative to their ability to do so. This is the cornerstone of tax equity". There is something profoundly unfair about a system where millionaires pay no tax and those on very low incomes do pay tax.

Many of our proposals have been implemented as part of the Budget 2006 reforms. In particular we welcome reforms to tax reliefs in the pension system which cap the size of these reliefs and minimise the opportunities for using pensions to avoid paying a fair share of tax. Similarly, we welcome the cap on the maximum value of the pension (though the pension fund limit of €5m still seems excessively generous and is twice that available in the UK) and the limits placed on the size of contributions. We called for the removal of many other schemes including those for urban renewal, multi-storey car parks and stallion and greyhound fees among others. The decision to abolish these reliefs is very welcome.

The suggestion in table 3.24 that it is the better-off who principally gain from the provision of tax exemption schemes is underscored by reports published by the Revenue Commissioners entitled *Effective Tax Rates for High Earning Individuals* (2002 and 2005). These reports provide details of the Revenue's assessment of the top 400 earners in Ireland and the rates of effective taxation they faced.[30] Table 3.25 presents their findings and shows that many of Ireland's highest earning individuals successfully use tax planning, schemes and loopholes to reduce their tax liability. These studies found that property tax reliefs, such as those provided for hotels and car parks, were the most effective in reducing the tax rates of the highest earners. Comparing the figures from 1999/00 and 2001 shows that over time the number of top earners benefiting from very low tax levels has reduced slightly from 18.25 per cent to 14.50 per cent. Figures from the Revenue Commissioners further indicate that in 2001 41 people earning over €500,000 used various tax relief schemes to reduce their income tax liability to zero. These included 11 individuals who earned more than €1 million in 2001. An additional 242 individuals earning more than €100,000 also paid no tax.

Table 3.25: The Distribution of Effective Tax Rates of the Top 400 Earners, 1999/00 and 2001		
Effective Tax Rate	1999/00 % of Total	2001 % of Total
Less than 15%	18.25	14.50
15%-29%	11.00	14.25
30%-44%	57.75	71.25
45% +	13.00	0.00
Total	100.00	100.00

Source: Revenue Commissioners (2002 and 2005).

Looking to the future, we welcome the Budget announcement by the Minister that the Revenue Commissioners will now collect full information on the costs of all tax reliefs. Given the vast scale of these schemes, it is important that the full costs of their implementation are known so that these can be compared to the benefits. CORI Justice believes that the costs and benefits of all tax relief schemes must be assessed to justify their establishment and retention. Only where these benefits surpass the costs should the reliefs be introduced/retained.

---

[30] The effective taxation rate is calculated as the percentage of an individual's total pre-tax income that they pay in taxation.

Land value taxes

Taxes on wealth are minimal in Ireland. We are the exception to the rule among developed countries in having no residential property tax. Revenue is negligible from capital acquisitions tax because it has a very high threshold where bequests and gifts within families are concerned and it treats family farms and firms very generously.

Within this area the issue of land rent taxation is one that has received added attention in the recent past. Two papers at our 2004 Social Policy Conference directly addressed this issue (see O'Siochru, 2004:23-57; and Dunne, 2004:93-122) and the Chambers of Commerce of Ireland published a report entitled *Local Authority Funding – Government in Denial* (2004) which called for an annual site tax. Where residential property tax is concerned CORI Justice believes the introduction of an annual land rent tax would have a very positive impact on Ireland's tax situation. It would lead to a substantial broadening of the base at a single stroke and would also lead to a reduction of the tax-take required from other sources, thus providing an opportunity for Government to produce a just and fair tax system.

A 'land value' or 'land rent' tax is based on the annual rental value of land. The annual rental site value is the rental value that a particular piece of land would have if there were no buildings or improvements on it. It is the value of a site, as provided by nature and as affected for better or worse by the activities of the community at large. The tax falls on the annual value of land at the point where it enters into economic activity, before the application of capital and labour to it.

The arguments for a land-rent tax are to do with fairness and economic efficiency. Most of the reward of rising land values goes to those who own land, while most of the cost of the activities that create rising land values does not. This is because rising land values – for example, in prosperous city centres or prime agricultural areas – are largely created by the activities of the community as a whole and by government regulations and subsidies, while the higher value of each particular site is enjoyed by its owner.

This means that it often pays land owners to keep sites unused in order to sell them later when (they hope) land values will have risen. Speculation on rising land values distorts land prices, generally making them significantly higher than they would otherwise be. NESC (2002:96) points out that the introduction of a tax on development land would have minimal economic effects given the immobility of land.

A land value tax is positive on both efficiency and equity grounds. From an efficiency perspective a site value tax would be a major step toward securing the tax base as it could not move to any location providing greater tax reductions. In doing this it would move the tax away from a transaction (such as stamp duty) which can make the tax base vulnerable as it is dependent on maintaining and increasing the scale of the transactions and move it instead to an immovable physical asset which is a much securer base. It would have other efficiency impacts such as ensuring that derelict sites were developed and that land would not be held over, as appears to be the situation at present, in an attempt to increase its value by creating artificial scarcity of land for development.

A land value tax is also positive on equity grounds. High land values in urban areas of Ireland are mainly a product of the economic and social activity in those areas. Consequently, it can be argued that a substantial portion of the benefits of these land values should be enjoyed by all the members of the community and not just the site owners. As well as this the increasing site values are closely linked to the level of investment in infrastructure those areas have received. Much of that investment has been paid for by taxpayers. It can be argued that a substantial portion of the benefits of the increasing site value should go to the whole community through the taxation system and not just remain with the site owner who may well have made no contribution to the investment that produced the increased value.

In short, land-rent taxation would lead to more efficient land use within the structure of social, environmental and economic goals embodied in planning and other legislation.

Sustainability/eco/carbon taxes

Sustainable development is now a major issue. As the world has come to recognise that the supply of land, clean water and air is not infinite, new questions emerge concerning sustainability. For example, as pressure mounts on the availability, not to mention the quality, of water on our planet, it is not simply environmentalists who warn us of impending disasters. Even institutions such as the World Bank are changing their approach to policy development to reflect this concern.

Taxation

The finite nature of our environment demands that we take account of environmental costs along with other factor costs. Measures to protect the environment have necessarily involved intervention in the market, because market forces do not themselves provide for environmental protection. Up to now this "intervention" has been by legislated regulatory measures.

In the long run, however, a more comprehensive approach is required. In recent years the sheer increase in the volume of economic activities has often negated regulatory gains. A key step would be to include in prices – and thereby internalise – the environmental costs occasioned by economic activity. It is difficult to devise any methodology capable of tracing and attributing with any accuracy all the costs/damage wrought upon the environment by a particular activity. Thus in many cases the internalisation can be achieved only in an arbitrary way, i.e. by taxes/charges based on broad national assessment.

The success of the plastic bag tax in reducing consumption of bags by 95 per cent in its first year, while simultaneously raising €11m for environmental projects, highlights the benefits of these types of taxes. CORI Justice welcomed the Budget 2003 commitment by government to impose carbon taxes. Given the support for this measure from leading government ministers, the all-party Oireachtas Committee on the Environment and the 2004 Enterprise Strategy Report we were disappointed that the Government chose to renege on its promise to introduce this scheme. The excuse used by the Department of Finance against the scheme's introduction was that the revenue collected would be small and not worthwhile collecting. This conclusion is ironic given the advise by the Department itself, the ESRI and the Enterprise Strategy group among others that the appropriate approach was to introduce this tax at a small level initially and to increase it over time.

Given Ireland's pollution record (see section 3.10b) there can be little doubt that over the next few years more environmental taxes will be necessary. This may involve reversing the 2004 carbon tax decision or it may involve adopting an alternative strategy.

One such alternative was outlined by Douthwaite at our 2004 Social Policy Conference (2004: 125-137). He suggested that a tradable quota system could be introduced by the Government. To achieve this, Ireland would divide the total tonnage of carbon dioxide it is allowed to emit under the agreement it reached with its EU partners under the Kyoto arrangements – its 1990 emissions plus 13 per cent – by its current population and issue permits for that amount – roughly 15.5 tonnes of CO2 per head – to the population, perhaps at the rate of 1.3 tonnes each month. Citizens could then sell on these permits, through the financial institutions, and polluters such as large firms and oil distribution companies would have to purchase them. The price received for these permits would vary according to the demand for fossil energy and just how well Ireland and the rest of the EU was doing in getting emission levels down. If the EU economy was booming and a lot of energy was being used, the price of the permits would be high but, equally, so would be the price of petrol, electricity and home-heating oil. If the economy was depressed, these prices, and the amount we got for our permits, would fall. This builds an automatic cushion against higher energy prices into the system, which protects, in particular, the least well-off who, although they spend a greater proportion of their incomes on energy, spend less on it in absolute terms. The provision of this cushion is very important since, as energy is used in the production of everything we use and consume, all prices will go up as a result of any restrictions on energy use. The proceeds from the permit sales would also provide the average person with enough extra purchasing power to cover the higher costs of the fuels and (because of the higher energy prices) the other goods and services they buy, provided that their purchases are not excessively energy-intensive. However, if some individuals were able to cut their direct and indirect fuel use below their entitlement, they would make themselves better off. On the other hand, if they continued to drive around in their SUVs, they would have to pay more frugal people for the privilege. The fact that fossil fuels themselves and goods made with significant amounts of fossil energy would cost more would encourage people to find lower-fossil-energy alternatives and enable the transition to renewable energy sources to gather pace. In short, a quota system would give people the price signals to move in the right direction.[31]

Two other potential environmental taxes are also worth considering. First, it is worth considering a reformatting of the current system of vehicle taxes such that those cars that pollute most pay most. The Kyoto protocol and the associated system of carbon trading have highlighted the costs of these emissions and a fairer allocation of vehicle taxation where the largest polluters pay most seems sensible. A second measure would be to levy a small tax on

---

[31] A more comprehensive outline of this proposal is presented in Douthwaite (2004) and in Feasta/NEF (2006).

Kerosene, the high-powered fuel used by airplanes. This fuel is currently untaxed and the idea of such a tax has been gaining increasing support at a European level. In particular this tax is seen as offering potential to collectively raise a large amount of money across all EU countries; money that would be ring-fenced for use in anti-poverty projects in the developing world. CORI Justice believes that such a tax would have limited, if any, effect on the aviation industry and offers a way for EU countries to raise badly needed funds for addressing development issues.[32]

Taxes on financial speculation: the Tobin tax

Global currency trading has been increasing dramatically throughout the last few decades. It is estimated that a very high proportion of all financial transactions traded are speculative currency transactions. During the early 1990s this speculation resulted in a series of currency crises which had major implications for many developing countries where there was a decline in economic activity and a consequent increase in the levels of poverty. These speculative transactions are completely free of taxation.

There is growing support worldwide for the introduction of a tax on such speculative exchange transactions. The Tobin tax, proposed by the Nobel Prize winner James Tobin, provides a potential solution. It is a progressive tax, designed to target only those profiting from currency speculation. Therefore, it is neither a tax on citizens, nor on business.

The majority of foreign exchange dealings are done by one hundred of the world's largest commercial and investment banks. The scale of their dealings is estimated at US$1.5 trillion worth of currency every day; all this in essentially unregulated financial markets. In 1998 the financial institution with the largest share of this market, Citibank, engaged in foreign exchange transactions worth US$8.5 trillion, a value in excess of the corresponding US GDP for that same year.[33]

---

[32] Development issues are discussed in more detail in section 3.12.

[33] The top 10 control 52 per cent of the market and include Citibank/Salomon Smith Barney (US), Deutsche Bank (Germany), Chase Manhattan Bank (US), Warburg Dillon Read (US), Goldman Sachs (US), Bank of America (US), JP Morgan (US), HSBC (UK), ABN Amro (Netherlands) and Merill Lynch (US).

The scope of the Tobin tax varies. Initially, James Tobin suggested a tax on all purchases of financial instruments denominated in another currency. More recently, Canadian economist Rodney Schmidt has broadened the tax to include all foreign exchange transactions. These would include simple exchanges of one currency for another (spot transactions) as well as complex derivative financial instruments including forwards, swaps, futures and options if they involve two currencies.

The rate would be determined by each country enacting the tax, but the tax range recommended to produce moderate market calming and revenue-raising outcomes is between 0.1 and 0.25 per cent. While this may seem very small to consumers, relative to VAT rates and income taxes, the impact on the margins of currency speculators would be enough to curb their activities.

The revenue from the tax would be considerable – somewhere in the region of €50 -100 billion per year. Though the effect of the tax over time would be to reduce the volume of currency speculation and thus the potential revenue from the tax, nevertheless the intake will remain high. It is proposed that the revenue generated by this tax be used for national social development and international development co-operation purposes. According to the United Nations, the amount of annual income raised from the tax would be enough to guarantee to every citizen of the world basic access to water, food, shelter, health and education. Therefore, this tax has the potential to wipe out the worst forms of material poverty throughout the world.

When James Tobin first put forward his idea he envisaged the tax being adopted by every country in the world simultaneously. Otherwise, he argued, speculators would "flock" to those countries without Tobin tax laws. Since such international agreement seemed improbable, the tax was seen by many as a worthy but impracticable proposal. However, over recent years the work of economists and financial experts has demonstrated that universal simultaneous adoption is not vital for a successful implementation. Essentially, foreign currency markets are concentrated on a global scale and if the principal countries implement the tax, this would suffice to cover the planet as a whole. Eight major countries account for more than 80 per cent of world exchange transactions, the foremost four for 65 per cent. In the City of London, the largest financial centre with 33 per cent of the world total, the 10 biggest banks account for 50 per cent of transactions. What is needed is for one major region of the world to implement the tax. Consequently, CORI Justice believes the

EU region should adopt policies towards the introduction of this financial speculation/trading tax.

Windfall taxes on rezoned land

The vast profits being made by property speculators on the rezoning of land by local authorities raises questions. In response CORI Justice has suggested two approaches. In the short-term we believe that a substantial tax should be imposed on the profits earned from such decisions. As rezonings are made by elected representatives in the interest of society generally, it seems appropriate that a sizeable proportion of the windfall gains they generate should be made available to local authorities and used to address the ongoing housing problems they face (see section 3.5).

In the longer term, CORI Justice believes that a number of changes should be made to the way in which zoning decisions occur. The principal change we propose is the introduction of a law confining the rezoning of land to those lands in the ownership of local authorities. Operationally, this legislative change would require local authorities to first purchase land (either voluntarily or compulsorily) before then proceeding to rezone it. Taking the example of land being rezoned from agricultural use to development/housing use the process would involve a local authority purchasing the land at agricultural prices plus a small margin for the owner. The rezoning would then occur while the land was in local authority ownership and so the windfall gain on the land's value would be internalised to the local authority. The land would then be sold on to the developing agent. Simply, this change would eliminate speculation and ensure that all windfall gains resulting from rezoning would be retained by the local authority. CORI Justice believes that the profit from this process should then be targeted on addressing the ongoing social housing problems being experienced in Ireland.

Building a fairer taxation system

The need for fairness in the tax system was clearly recognised in the first report of the Commission on Taxation more than twenty years ago. In that volume it stated:

> "...in our recommendations the spirit of equity is the first and most important consideration. Departures from equity must be clearly justified by reference to the needs of economic development or to avoid imposing unreasonable compliance costs on individuals or high administrative costs on the Revenue Commissioners."
> (1982:29)

The need for fairness is very obvious today. All the issues raised above have a fairness dimension. Here we address some further issues that arise particularly in the present income tax system.[34]

Standard rating discretionary tax expenditures

One crucial step towards achieving a fairer tax system is to standard rate all discretionary tax reliefs/expenditures, making them available at the 20% rate only. If there is a legitimate case for making a tax relief/expenditure available then it should be made available in the same way to all. It is unfair that some people can claim certain tax reliefs at a rate of 20% (the standard tax rate) and others with higher incomes can claim it at a higher rate. That unfairness is further exacerbated by the fact that it is those who are better off who can claim these reliefs at the upper rate.

As part of preparing our November 2005 *Policy Briefing* on Taxation, CORI Justice engaged in an examination of the available data for these schemes. Based on this we estimated that the exchequer could collect an additional €2 billion in revenue if all tax relief schemes were made available only at the standard rate. While the available data is less than desirable, a feature which the Revenue Commissioners acknowledge, we suspect that this estimate understates the additional revenue which the exchequer would collect were all discretionary tax expenditures standard rated. Standard rating tax expenditures offers the potential to simultaneously make the tax system fairer and fund these necessary developments without any significant macroeconomic implications.

Keeping the minimum wage out of the tax net

A major achievement of Budget 2005 was the decision by the Minister of Finance to remove those on the minimum wage from the tax net. This decision which was updated in Budget 2006 has an important impact on the growing numbers of working-poor and addresses an issue CORI Justice has highlighted for some time. In delivering this policy the government's decision to increase tax credits is also welcome. As we show below, the system of tax credits offers greater potential for making the tax system fairer. As the minimum wage increases it is important that the tax credits are adjusted to retain this welcome situation.

---

[34] A more detailed discussion of the issues contained in this section can be found in Healy and Reynolds (2004:151-188).

Increasing tax credits rather than widening tax bands

During 2005, both the Taoiseach and the Minster for Finance indicated that there would be no more cuts in income tax rates. CORI Justice welcomes this commitment. Any future income tax changes will now be concerned with changes to either tax credits or tax bands. In the context of achieving fairness in the taxation system, changes to tax credits rather than tax bands are more desirable. To illustrate the impact of these options we can take an example. If €700 million were available for distribution in a Budget it could be used to either (i) increase the 20 per cent tax band by €5,500 or (ii) increase tax credits by €512 a year. The impact of these two approaches would be:

(i) Increasing the tax band by €5,500 would be of no benefit to anyone with incomes at or below the top of the current band (i.e. €29,400 for a single person) but would provide a benefit of €1,210 a year to a single person earning more than €34,900. Single people with incomes in the €29,400-34,900 range would benefit by a proportion of the €1,210. (The thresholds for married people with one or two incomes are different but the impacts are along the same trajectory as identified for single people here.)

(ii) Increasing the tax credit by €512 a year would mean that every earner with a tax bill in excess of €512 a year would benefit by that amount.

In terms of fairness, increasing tax credits is a fairer option than widening the standard rate tax band. Government should always take this option when it has money available to reduce income taxes. It has the additional advantage of addressing the 'working poor' issue which is emerging as a growing problem that requires a policy response.

Introducing refundable tax credits

The move from tax allowances to tax credits was completed in Budget 2001. This was a very welcome change because it put in place a system that had been advocated for a long time by a range of groups including the CORI Justice. One problem persists however, a problem that the old system of tax allowances also had. If a person does not earn enough to use up his or her full tax credit then he or she will not benefit from any tax reductions introduced by government in its annual budget. In effect this means that, under the present system, those with the lowest pay will not benefit in any way at budget time.

Developing a Fairer Ireland

A simple solution exists to rectify this problem: make tax credits refundable. This would mean that the part of the tax credit that an employee did not benefit from would be "refunded" to him/her by the state. A Working Group established under the *Programme for Prosperity and Fairness* examined the feasibility of making this happen but did not complete its report.

The major advantage of making tax credits refundable would lie in addressing the disincentives currently associated with low-paid employment. The main beneficiaries of refundable tax credits would be low-paid employees (full-time and part-time). Chart 3.4 displays the impacts of the introduction of this policy across the various gross income levels. It clearly shows that all of the benefits from introducing this policy would go directly to those on the lowest incomes.

Chart 3.4: How much better off would people be if tax credits were made refundable?

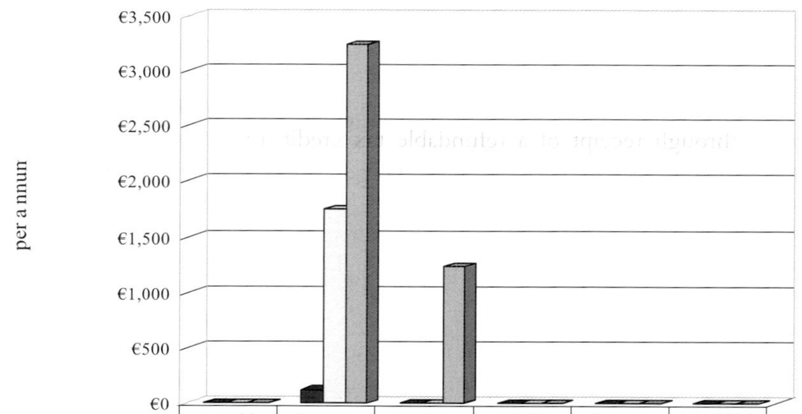

	LTU**	€15,000	€25,000	€50,000	€75,000	€100,000
■ Single	0	120	0	0	0	0
□ Couple 1 Earner*	0	1750	0	0	0	0
▨ Couple 2 Earners*	0	3240	1240	0	0	0

Notes: * Except in LTU case where there is no earner
  ** LTU: Long Term Unemployed

Following the introduction of refundable tax credits, all subsequent increases in the level of the tax credit would be of equal value to all employees.

As regards administering this reform the central idea recognises that most people with regular incomes and jobs would not receive a cash refund of their tax credit because their incomes are too high; they would simply benefit from the tax credit as a reduction in their tax bill. Therefore, as chart 3.4 shows no change is proposed for these people and they would continue to pay tax via their employers, based on their net tax liability after their employers have deducted tax credits on behalf of Revenue Commissioners. For other people on low or irregular incomes, the refundable tax credit could be paid in either of two ways:

- The person entitled to the credit could apply for it to the Revenue Commissioners at the end of the year

or

- They could be given the option of requesting that their tax credit be paid directly e.g. into their bank account, by the Department of Social and Family Affairs (DSFA); in these cases employers would not subtract the tax credit from the gross tax liability of these people. Instead, the DSFA would supply them with a book of payments (as is done with Child Benefit payments at present). [In this situation it is important to point out that nobody on social welfare would see their income increase through receipt of a refundable tax credit. In a situation where they were receiving such a credit their social welfare payment would be reduced by the value of the tax credit.]

In order to qualify for a refundable tax credit a person would have to satisfy the following criteria:

- They must be 21-64 years of age. (The refundable tax credit could also be made available for people over 65+ depending on what funding Government made available)

and

- They must be currently working for at least 12 months, for the equivalent of at least 8 hours per week, as evidenced by tax/PRSI returns

Employees and self-employed, including farmers, are encompassed within the proposal. Spouses could opt to receive the 'married' part of the personal tax credit and the Home Working Spouse tax credit directly from DSFA.

Developing a Fairer Ireland

Following the introduction of refundable tax credits, all subsequent increases in the level of the tax credit would be of equal value to all employees. Chart 3.5 shows how the benefits of a €100 a year increase in tax credits would be distributed under a system of refundable tax credits. This simulation displays the equity attached to using the tax-credit instrument to distribute budgetary taxation changes. The benefit to all categories of income earners (single/couple, one-earner/couple, two-earners) is the same. Consequently, in relative terms, those earners at the bottom of the distribution do best.

Chart 3.5: How much better off would people be if tax credits were increased by €100 per person and this was refundable?

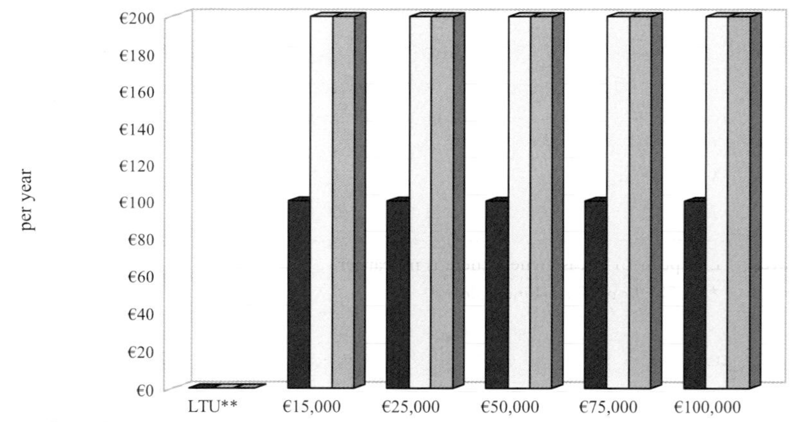

	LTU**	€15,000	€25,000	€50,000	€75,000	€100,000
Single	0	100	100	100	100	100
Couple 1 Earner*	0	200	200	200	200	200
Couple 2 Earners*	0	200	200	200	200	200

Notes: * Except in LTU case where there is no earner
** LTU: Long Term Unemployed

The benefits of adopting a refundable tax credits system is further underscored by a comparison between chart 3.5 and chart 3.6. Chart 3.6 shows the allocation of gains across all categories of earners. It shows that the gains are allocated equally to all categories of earners above €25,000. However, there is no benefit for these workers whose earnings are not in the tax net.

Chart 3.6: How much better off would people be if tax credits were increased by €100 per person?

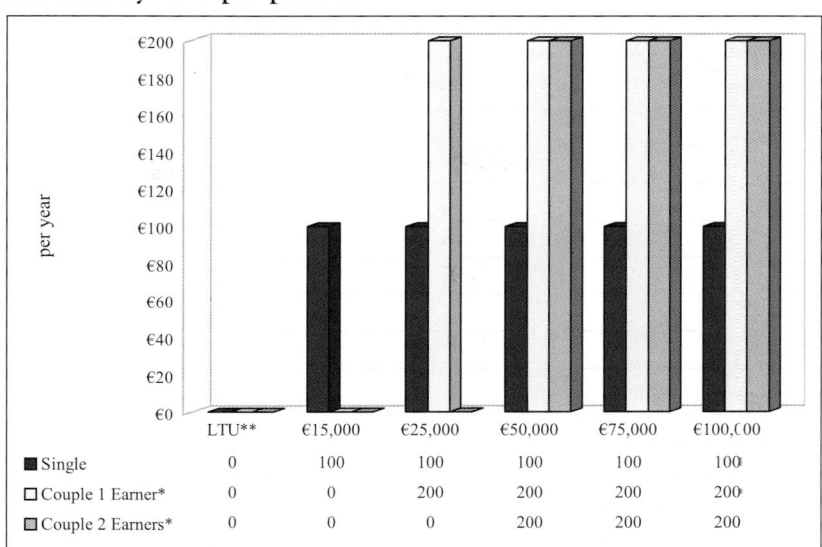

Notes: * Except in LTU case where there is no earner
** LTU: Long Term Unemployed

Overall the merits of adopting this approach are: that every beneficiary of tax credits could receive the full value of the tax credit; that the system would improve the net income of the workers whose incomes are lowest, at modest cost; and that there would be no additional administrative burden placed on employers. In reviewing this issue Rapple stated that "the change is long overdue" (2004:140). If the tax system is to be fair then tax credits should be made refundable.[35]

---

[35] We have also proposed the introduction of a refundable tax credit for children. This policy proposal has been outlined in our *Policy Briefing* on Taxation (November 2005:5) and is available from our website.

Reforming individualisation

CORI Justice has long supported the individualisation of the tax system. However, the process of individualisation followed by government is deeply flawed and unfair. The cost to the exchequer of this transition has been in excess of €0.75 billion, and almost all of this money has gone to the richest 30 per cent of the population. A significantly fairer process would have been to introduce a basic income system that would have treated all people fairly and ensured that a windfall of this nature did not accrue to the best off in this society.

All the predictions currently indicate that there will be a future increase in the level of unemployment. Given the current form of individualisation, couples who see one partner lose his/her job will end up even worse off than they would have been had the current form of individualisation not been introduced.

Before individualisation was introduced, the standard-rate income-tax band was €35,553 for all couples. After that they would start paying the higher rate of tax. Now, the standard-rate income-tax band for single-income couples is €38,400, while the band for dual-income couples is €58,800. If one spouse (of a couple previously earning two salaries) leaves a job voluntarily or through redundancy, the couple loses the value of the second tax band.

Making the taxation system simpler

Our tax system is not simple. In a recent book reviewing Ireland's taxation system Bristow (2004) argues that "some features of it, notably VAT, are among the most complex in the world". The reasons given to support this complexity vary but they are focused principally around the need to reward particular kinds of behaviour which is seen as desirable by legislators. This, in effect, is discrimination in favour of one kind of activity or against another. There are many arguments against the present complexity and in favour of a simpler system.

Discriminatory tax concessions in favour of particular positions are often very inequitable. They often contribute far less to equity than might appear to be the case. On many occasions they fail to produce the economic or social outcomes which were being sought. Sometimes they generate very undesirable effects. At other times they may be a complete waste of money since the outcomes they seek would have occurred without the introduction of a tax incentive. Having a complex system also has other down-sides. It can, for example, have high compliance costs both for tax-payers and for the Revenue Commissioners who are responsible for collecting tax.

For the most part society at large gains little or nothing from the discrimination contained in the tax system. In some cases this discrimination causes very negative effects. Mortgage interest relief, for example, and the absence of any residential or land-rent tax have contributed to the rise in house prices. Complexity makes taxes easier to evade, invites consultants to devise avoidance schemes and greatly increases the cost of collection. It is also inequitable because those who can afford professional advice are in a far better position to take advantage of that complexity than those who cannot afford to do this. A simpler taxation system would serve Irish society and all individuals within it, irrespective of their means, better.

In conclusion, we outline our key policy proposals with regard to taxation.

Policy Proposals on Taxation

- **Commit to increasing Ireland's total tax take towards the EU average.**

- **Integrate the tax and welfare systems**

- **Make tax credits refundable.**

- **Continue to adjust tax credits so that the minimum wage remains out of the tax net.**

- **Integrate Family Income Supplement (FIS) with the tax system.**

- **Proceed with individualisation in the income tax system in a fair and equitable manner.**

- **Ensure that changes in the income-tax system benefit those on low to middle incomes as much as they benefit the better off in cash terms.**

- Poverty-proof all budget tax packages to ensure that tax changes do not further widen the gap between those with low income and the better off.

- Move to negotiate an EU wide agreement on minimum corporate taxation rates (a rate of 17.5% would seem fair in this situation).

- Put in place procedures within the Department of Finance and the Revenue Commissioners to monitor on an ongoing basis the cost and benefits of all current and new tax expenditures.

- Ensure that the distribution of all changes in indirect taxes discriminate positively in favour of those with lower incomes.

- Move decisively to shift the burden of taxation from income tax to eco-taxes on the consumption of fuel and fertilisers, as well as on the disposal of waste. In doing this, government should ensure that the impact of this on people with low incomes should not be negative.

- Introduce carbon and environmental taxes.

- Develop policies which allow taxation on wealth to be increased.

- Investigate the possibility of introducing a tax on currency transactions such as the Tobin Tax.

- Investigate the possibility of introducing a site value tax. This, and the preceding proposal, could lead to substantial reductions in income tax.

- Standard rate all discretionary tax expenditures.

- Increase the rate of capital gains tax from 20 to 25 per cent.

- Introduce a windfall tax on the profits generated from all land rezonings.

3.3 Work

> **CORE POLICY OBJECTIVE: WORK**
> To ensure that all people have access to meaningful work

One of the major achievements of recent years has been the increase in employment and the reduction in unemployment, especially long-term unemployment. In 1991 there were 1,155,900 people employed in Ireland. That figure has increased by more than eight hundred thousand to 1,980,600; during 2006 the employment figure is expected to exceed two million. Overall, the size of the Irish labour force has expanded significantly and today equals over two million people (2,071,900), almost seven hundred thousand more than in 1991 (see chart 3.7). Over the same period, the number of people unemployed [measured on an International Labour Office (ILO) basis] has gone from 198,500 to 91,300. In the intervening years, the number unemployed had exceeded 220,000 (in 1993). This transformation is remarkable and has marked a major, and very welcome, shift in Irish society. It has also provided new challenges as well as raising new questions.

Chart 3.7: The Numbers of People in the Labour Force and Employed in Ireland, 1991-2005.

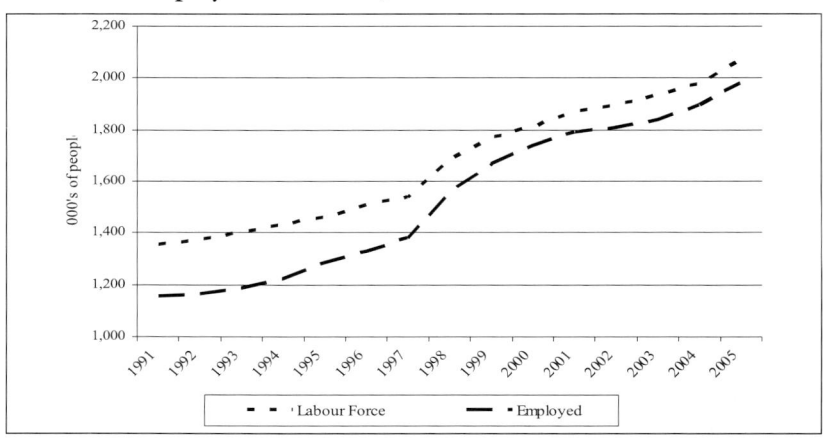

Source: CSO, QNHS (March 2005:17; February 2006:7)

The numbers unemployed

At the outset it is important to outline what the term 'unemployment' means. The *Quarterly National Household Survey* (QNHS) unemployment data uses the definition of 'unemployment' supplied by the International Labour Office (ILO). It lists as unemployed only those people who, in the week before the survey, were unemployed *and* available to take up a job *and* had taken specific steps in the preceding four weeks to find employment. Any person who was employed for at least *one hour* is classed as employed. By contrast, the live register includes part-time employees (those who work up to three days a week), seasonal and casual employees entitled to Unemployment Assistance or Benefit.

As chart 3.8 shows, the period from 1993 was one of decline in unemployment. During mid-2001 Irish unemployment reached its lowest level at 3.6 per cent of the labour force. Since then the slowdown in the international and domestic economy has brought about some increases in the rates. By August 2001 unemployment, as measured by the QNHS (ILO basis), stood at a rate of 4.2 per cent (78,500 people). A year later, in August 2002, it had increased by 7,700 people, giving an unemployment rate of 4.6 per cent. The corresponding figure for Sep-Nov 2003 showed a small decrease in those unemployed of 300, bringing the unemployment rate to 4.5 per cent or 85,900 people. Figures record 91,300 (4.4 per cent of the labour force) as unemployed for the quarter Sep-Nov 2005 (see table 3.26).

During the past year Ireland has been dramatically successful from the perspective of job creation and controlling unemployment. As table 3.26 shows, there was a substantial increase in the labour force of 92,200 during 2005. This occurred due to increased labour force participation by various groups, demographic factors and the arrival of immigrant workers (CSO, 2006:1). Accompanying that increase was a large increase in employment (of 86,500).

Of the 91,300 people classified as unemployed in 2005, 54,300 were men and 37,000 were women. The corresponding unemployment rates for men and women are 4.5 per cent and 4.2 per cent respectively. Overall some 74,200 of the unemployed are recorded as searching for full-time work, while 17,000 are seeking part-time employment. The latter group is primarily comprised of unemployed females (13,500 women).

Work

Table 3.26: Labour Force changes 2004–2005			
	Sep-Nov 2004	**Sep-Nov 2005**	**Change**
Labour Force	1,979,700	2,071,900	+92,200
In Employment	1,894,100	1,980,600	+86,500
Unemployed	85,600	91,300	+5,700
of whom LT Unemployed	28,900	27,600	-1,300
Unemployment Rate	4.3%	4.4%	+0.1%
LT Unemployment Rate	1.5%	1.3%	-0.2%

Source: CSO, QNHS February 2006:18
Note: LT = Long Term

Youth unemployment

An examination of the age structure of the unemployed indicates a sustained problem of youth unemployment. As table 3.27 shows, this is particularly of concern among those aged 15-19. Over the last year their unemployment rates have decreased to 2003 levels, from 13.4 per cent to 12.2 per cent. For these aged 20-24 their unemployment rate has climbed higher to 7.6 per cent in 2005. In the context of an overall unemployment rate of 4.4 per cent these figures are of concern. Furthermore, the rate of increase in unemployment among this group remains a major issue. Given the projections for further increases in unemployment in the years ahead, the fate of any low-skilled individuals who have become unemployed is a concern; a point also made by NESF in their recent document entitled *Creating a More Inclusive Labour Market* (NESF, 2006). Depending on the extent of the economic slowdown, the potential for these individuals to become long-term unemployed must be monitored.

Table 3.27: Unemployment rates across the age groups, Sep-Nov 2004 and 2005			
Age Group	Sep-Nov 2004	Sep-Nov 2005	Change
15-19	13.4	12.2	-1.2%
20-24	7.1	7.6	+0.5%
25-34	4.0	4.3	+0.3%
35-44	3.4	3.2	-0.2%
45-54	3.4	3.5	+0.1%
55-59	2.8	3.1	+0.3
60-64	1.9	1.8	-0.1
65+	0.3	0.9	+0.6
Overall	**4.3**	**4.4**	**+0.1**

Source: CSO, QNHS February 2006:17

Another factor relevant to any assessment of youth unemployment is its association with other societal problems and in particular suicide. The results of an eight-year study of suicides in County Kildare (1995-2002) was recently published in the *Journal of Clinical Forensic Medicine* by McGovern and Cusack (2004). One of their key findings was that unemployed males under the age of 30 were the most likely group to commit suicide.[36]

Long-term unemployment

Alongside the decline in the overall unemployment numbers chart 3.8 shows that since 1994 the numbers classified as long-term unemployed (unemployed for more than one year) have decreased. However, since 2002 this trend has begun to change and the overall number of people in this category has increased.

Of the 91,300 people unemployed in November 2005, 56,700 were unemployed for less than one year, while 27,600 were long-term unemployed. This figure marked a small but welcome decrease since 2004. However, both the 2005 and 2004 long-term unemployment rates are considerably smaller than the 10.4 per cent recorded in 1988 and they mark a major decrease in the level of structural unemployment. It also illustrates the extent to which Irish unemployment levels are now dominated by frictional factors. However, the return of cyclical unemployment in late 2001, and throughout both 2002 and 2003, underscores the necessity to maintain a focus on ensuring that the long-term unemployment problem is not allowed to return.

---

[36] The issue of suicide is also assessed in section 3.6.

Chart 3.8: The Numbers of Unemployed and Long-Term Unemployed in Ireland, 1991-2005.

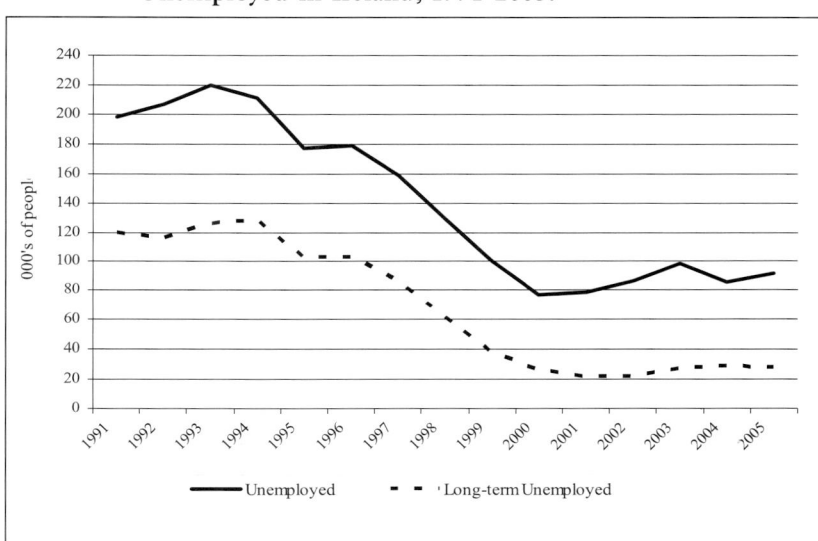

Source: CSO, QNHS February 2006:18

Of the 91,300 people unemployed in November 2005, 56,700 were unemployed for less than one year, while 27,600 were long-term unemployed. This figure marked a small but welcome decrease since 2004. However, both the 2005 and 2004 long-term unemployment rates are considerably smaller than the 10.4 per cent recorded in 1988 and they mark a major decrease in the level of structural unemployment. It also illustrates the extent to which Irish unemployment levels are now dominated by frictional factors. However, the return of cyclical unemployment in late 2001, and throughout both 2002 and 2003, underscores the necessity to maintain a focus on ensuring that the long-term unemployment problem is not allowed to return.

Work and the National Anti-Poverty Strategy Review 2002

The NAPS Review 2002 set the following as key targets:

- to eliminate long-term unemployment as soon as circumstances permit but in any event not later than 2007
- to reduce the level of unemployment experienced by vulnerable groups towards the national average by 2007
- to achieve the objectives set out in the National Employment Action Plan to increase employment rates.

CORI Justice welcomed the target to eliminate long-term unemployment and we urge government to make every effort to ensure that this target is achieved no later than 2007. Consequently it is of concern that the numbers classified as long-term unemployed have remained fairly static since 2004 – between 27,500 and 28,100. To date, little progress has being made towards achieving this target and therefore the question arises whether the government has abandoned it?

We also welcomed the NAPS commitment to reduce the level of unemployment experienced by vulnerable groups towards the national average. Recent moves focused on lone parents are to be welcomed. However, specific targets and indicators are required to ensure that the NAPS target is met. To date progress on establishing these has been limited.

The need to recognise all work

A major question being raised by the current labour-market situation concerns assumptions underpinning culture and policy making in this area. One such assumption concerns the priority given to paid employment over other forms of work. Most people recognise that a person can work very hard even though he or she does not have a conventional job. Much of the work done in the community and in the voluntary sector fits under this heading. So too does much of the work done in the home. CORI Justice's support for the introduction of a basic income system comes, in part, from a belief that all work should be recognised and supported.

The need to recognise voluntary work has been acknowledged in the government's White Paper, *Supporting Voluntary Activity* and by the Taoiseach who has stated that: "voluntary activity forms the very core of all vibrant and inclusive societies". A recent report presented to the Joint Oireachtas

Committee on Arts, Sport, Tourism, Community, Rural and Gaeltacht Affairs provided one small insight into this issue. It established that the cost to the state of replacing the 475,000 volunteers working for charitable organisations would be a minimum of €205m and could cost up to €485m per year. Another study by Professor Gabriel Kiely of UCD estimated that the average value of full-time caring work within the home was €23,540.40 per annum.

The report of the National Committee on Volunteering entitled *Tipping the Balance* (October 2002) stands as a welcome acknowledgement of this role. The report was prepared to mark the UN International Year of the Volunteer 2001 by Government and representatives of numerous voluntary organisations in Ireland, including CORI Justice. The report suggested a series of recommendations to assist in the future development and recognition of voluntary activity throughout Ireland. In the light of the commitment to 'promote social capital' in the *Programme for Government* (2002), CORI Justice urges that the recommendations of this report be implemented by government.

Labour market and local service provision programmes

Community Employment (CE) started off in a period of high unemployment and was essentially designed to progress unemployed people to the open labour market. It has also been used to provide valuable human resources to providers of essential social services, especially in disadvantaged areas. In recent years there has been a significant reduction in CE places.

The Job Initiative (JI) programme was designed as a supported employment programme for people who were the most vulnerable among the long-term unemployed. In recent months the number of JI places has also been reduced and there has been a major effort by Government and FAS to change it into an active labour market programme.

The Social Economy (SE) programme was designed, primarily, to deliver services in the social economy. In recent years it was transformed into another active labour market programme and there has also been a failure to expand the number of places on the programme to the level committed when it was put in place.

These developments have had a negative knock-on effect on the social services provided by community and voluntary organisations using these programmes. CORI Justice argued that reform would best be undertaken by separating out what was being provided by CE and associated initiatives into three strands, as follows:

- An active labour market programme (ALMP) providing experience and training for people seeking employment in the labour market.
- A Local Services Support Programme to finance the services being provided to local communities by the community and voluntary sector. These services should not be forced to depend on financing being made available solely through the employment of long-term unemployed people.
- A programme that provides 'supported' employment for a number of people who would not benefit from places on an ALMP.

Some progress has been made on moving towards developing these strands. In particular we welcome the introduction of the new Community Services Programme aimed at supporting services delivered by the community and voluntary sector.

CORI Justice welcomes the moving of the SE programme to the Department of Community, Rural and Gaeltacht Affairs(D/CRGA) where it now forms a part of the Community Services Programme. It should maintain its three strands i.e. economically viable, state contracts and demand deficient enterprises. We are very concerned however at the fact that it may be in danger of again becoming primarily an active labour market programme rather than a programme primarily focused on delivering social services through community and voluntary organisations.

CORI Justice believes:

- The JI programme should be maintained and it should continue to provide a form of 'supported employment' as it does at present. It would be better to have the JI programme migrate to D/CRGA and become part of the wider 'social provision' dimension being developed under that department. If this is not going to happen and if persists in its intention to eliminate the JI programme then a replacement programme for the very long-term unemployed must be put in place immediately
- CE should be constantly reviewed and adjusted to ensure it is a focussed and vibrant active measure to progress unemployed people in greater numbers to the open labour market.

Women returning to employment

The growth in employment over the last few years has particularly impacted on women. Rates of female labour-force participation continue to rise. Noticeably, many of these female entrants are women returning after having had a family. A report published in September 2002 entitled *Getting out of the House: Women Returning to Employment, Education and Training* presented some important findings concerning the situation of these women.

The report, by Russell et al of the ESRI, found that almost two-thirds of these women returning tended to have low levels of education, some 38 per cent had no qualifications at all. It also showed that 71 per cent of returnees chose to work part time and that overall the level of payment received by these women was below that which they had received before they left the labour force. These women tend to be "downgrading" their expectations of employment with almost 50 per cent of women stating that they possessed the qualifications and skill to perform a more demanding job than that which they had returned to do.

The report suggests that this phenomenon is due to a series of obstacles which returning women face. These include a lack of childcare facilities, in particular after-school childcare, and a lack of flexibility among employers towards the lifestyle demands of these women. A further problem is the lack of information detailing the availability of re-training programmes and entitlements for these women.

While there should always be adequate support for women choosing to stay in the home, there should also be adequate support for women choosing to return to the labour force. Policy innovations are required if this situation is to change. It is clear that opportunities exist for these women and that with some changes these can be made available. To achieve this CORI Justice believes that additional support is necessary to expand the projects currently funded by the Equality for Women Measure. Reforms to childcare facilities and information processes are equally necessary. In that regard the OECD *Employment Outlook* (2003) suggested that the country needed to provide, or assist in providing, childcare facilities as an essential element in removing those barriers preventing women from returning to the workplace.

Work and people with disabilities

The results of the 2004 QNHS special module on disability revealed that of all persons aged between 15 and 64, 10.9 per cent indicated that they had a longstanding health problem or disability (CSO, 2004). This equates to 298,300 people in Ireland, of whom 155,800 were male and 142,500 were female. Of those individuals only 37 per cent (110,800) were in employment. This is a figure considerably below the participation rate of the overall population in 2004 which stood at 61 per cent. Furthermore, of those employed approximately one-quarter worked part-time while the remaining three-quarters were in full-time employment.

This low rate of employment among people with a disability is of concern. Apart from restricting their participation in society it also ties them into state dependent low-income situations. Therefore it is not surprising that Ireland's poverty figures reveal that people who are ill or have a disability are the group with the highest risk of poverty (see table 3.4). CORI Justice believes that further effort should be made to reduce the impediments faced by people with a disability in achieving employment. In particular consideration should be given to reforming the current situation where many such people face losing their benefits, in particular their medical card, when they take up employment. This situation ignores the additional costs faced by people with a disability in pursuing their day-to-day lives. For many people with disabilities the opportunity to work is denied to them and they are trapped in unemployment, poverty or both.

We welcomed moves in Budget 2005 to increase supports intended to help people with disabilities access employment. Similarly, we welcome the *Workway* campaign, which is aimed at changing awareness and changing attitudes and practices surrounding the employment of people with disabilities. However, new policies, including that outlined above, need to be adopted if the campaign is to be a success.

Migrant workers
The current work-permit system faced by migrant workers in Ireland is of concern, particularly for those migrants working in low-paid service and manufacturing jobs. This system ties the worker to a specific employer and as a consequence makes them entirely dependent on that employer for their income and right to residency in the state.

We welcome the commitments contained in *Towards 2016* aimed at addressing the problems faced by migrant workers especially the commitment that: "the Government has agreed that the Employment Permits Bill will be enacted at the earliest possible date and that economic migration policy will ensure the following:

- That all workers will be allowed to apply for and reapply for their own permit;
- That there will be appropriate consultation with the social partners in determining included and excluded categories of staff/skills for eligibility for work permits;
- That there are adequate safeguards to protect workers' rights in relation to the application for employment permits by:
    - employers inside and outside of the State;
    - employment agencies; and
    - in respect of intra-corporate transfers;
- that the employment of non-EEA students is subject to an application for employment permits;
- that employment permit applications are not approved for wages below the REA/ERO rate or the National Minimum Wage, whichever is appropriate;
- that employment permit holders may transfer to another employment in cases of unfair treatment; and
- that spouses of employment permit holders who are granted residence in Ireland may be granted an employment permit."

(2006: 104)

Speaking at a conference organised by the Immigration Council of Ireland in December 2003 the former UN High Commissioner for Human Rights Mary Robinson described this work-permit system as one which "frighteningly resembles bonded servitude". At the same conference, the former US Congressman Bruce Morrison branded the temporary work visa system as "a terrible mistake" and "an abusive way to think about immigrants". He called on the government to adopt appropriate policies which recognised Ireland's new role as a "destination country" for immigrants.

A report on migrant workers underscores the difficulty faced by them and the exclusion many of them experience. Entitled *Migrant Workers and their Experiences* the report was conducted by Dr Pauline Conroy and Aoife Brennan and commissioned by the Equality Authority, IBEC, the Congress of Trade Unions, the Construction Industry Federation and Know Racism. It consisted of a survey of 36 male and female migrant workers from countries including the Philippines, Russia, the Ukraine, India, Czech Republic, Poland and Lithuania. They held work permits, work authorisations, working visas or were undocumented. More than half were interviewed in the Greater Dublin area, the remainder in the North-East and Border region and the South East region. The survey was conduced in autumn 2002 and focused on those working in agriculture/horticulture, hospitals and health services, the service industry and the IT sector. The authors concluded that:

- The support infrastructure for migrant workers is perceived by those interviewed to be weak, uneven and haphazard.
- Information provided by some employers or some recruitment agencies at the point of recruitment is too limited.
- Manual migrant workers interviewed who work exclusively with their own nationality in non-unionised environments report few difficulties but appear to be unaware that they are working below minimum standards of pay and conditions.
- Some migrant workers find themselves with an irregular employment status and some stated that their employers proposed irregular, even illegal, working conditions.
- The considerable use of overseas diplomatic and consular missions to resolve workplace disputes and express grievances suggested that migrants are poorly supported.
- Migrant workers reported finding themselves in a difficult situation seeking to leave undesirable employment.

They then proceeded to suggest the following reforms:

- Policies and practices to empower the migrant worker including the need to review the current approaches to granting work permits.
- A programme of investment in migrant community associations to support their capacity to network migrant workers to articulate their interests and to communicate employment and other rights information.
- The development of effective channels of communication with migrant workers at point of recruitment and in the workplace concerning their rights and situations.
- The further development of family reunification policies for migrant workers.

- Specific initiatives to support and address the situation of migrant workers in low skills employment in particular those in the agricultural, horticultural and forestry sectors.
- Workplace initiatives to apply the Equality Authority's Code of Practice on Sexual Harassment and Harassment in the Workplace, to develop policies and procedures to combat discrimination and to promote equality and to develop a capacity to address equality issues in the workplace.

(Conroy and Brennan, 2003: 42-44).

In the light of these findings CORI Justice believes that government must implement a rights-based immigration policy which addresses the unnecessary and undesirable restrictions this system imposes on migrant workers and their families. Furthermore, we believe that the *UN Convention on the Protection of Rights of All Migrant Workers and their Families* should be ratified by the government, setting a precedent for all other European countries to follow.

Asylum seekers and work

CORI Justice remains very disappointed that the government continues to reject the proposal to recognise the right to work of asylum seekers. We along with others advocated that where government fails to meet its own stated objective of processing asylum applications in six months, the right to work should be automatically granted to asylum seekers. Detaining people for an unnecessarily prolonged period in such an excluded state is completely unacceptable. Recognising asylum seekers right to work would alleviate poverty and social exclusion among one of Ireland's most vulnerable groups.

The Work of Carers

The work of Ireland's carers receives minimal recognition in spite of the essential role their work plays in society. According to the Carers Association people caring full-time for the elderly and people with disabilities are saving the state approximately €2 billion a year in costs which it would otherwise have to bear. The Caring for Carers organisation (2003) have stated that 78 per cent of the nations carers were caring for frail older people and that almost half of the nations full-time carers were themselves aged over 60. Furthermore, they reported that 21 per cent of carers had more than one dependent.

Results from the 2002 Census give similar indications (CSO, 2003: 25-26). It found that 4.8 per cent of the population aged over 15 provided some care for sick or disabled family members or friends on an unpaid basis. This figure equates to almost 149,000 people of whom 61 per cent (91,000) are women. The dominant caring role played by women was further highlighted by the fact that one in every ten women in Ireland in their 40s and 50s is a carer. When assessed by length of time, the Census found that some 40,000 people provide unpaid help to ill or disabled family members and friends for 43 hours a week or more, a working week considerably in excess of the standard working week for paid workers.

CORI Justice welcomes the ongoing examination of this area by the Oireachtas Joint Committee on Social and Family Affairs. It is crucial that policy reforms be introduced to reduce the financial and emotional pressures on carers. In particular these should focus on addressing the poverty experienced by many carers and their families alongside increasing the provision of respite care for carers and for those for whom they care. In that context, the twenty-four hour responsibilities of carers contrast with the recent improvements in employment legislation setting limits on working-hours of people in paid employment.

Older workers

As the Irish economy continues to grow, demand for workers will continue to occur. It is expected that by 2011, almost 1.2 million workers in Ireland will be aged between 45 and 69. As a consequence a report by National Economic and Social Forum (NESF) entitled *Labour Market Issues for Older Workers* (2003) highlighted the need to facilitate older people in accessing and retaining employment. Its recommendations include:

- More actively explore avenues to promote the benefits of in-work training and retraining for older workers.
- Enhance the provision of supports to older workers, particularly in relation to flexible working, reduced working hours and retraining.
- Put in place a strategy as a matter of priority to implement the recommendations of the Task Force on Lifelong Learning.
- Broaden the remit of the National Training Advisory Committee (NTAC) to include the design and development of a work-based training package that takes account of the specific needs of older workers.
- Examine how best to undertake a regular company-level survey of the training needs of older workers.

- Give greater consideration to the specific educational needs of older workers, including opportunities for progression and the recognition of prior experiential learning. This should apply to programmes like the Vocational Training Opportunities Scheme (VTOS), which provide education opportunities for the unemployed.
- Develop a series of guidelines for employers in relation to older workers and IT and build on the success of the Fast Track to IT (FIT) scheme.
- Extend the Employment Action Plan re-engagement process to those aged over 55 and to those not on the Live Register but currently out of work, such as older women returning to the labour force.

(NESF, 2003: 14-16).

CORI Justice welcomes these recommendations. It is important that they are implemented and that in the years to come Ireland's older people are given every chance to achieve and retain a productive role in society.

The importance of balance

The new situation created by the huge growth in available jobs raises major questions concerning the focus of policy in this area. Should Ireland continue to expend resources to increase further the number of jobs available? Given the problems being experienced in trying to increase the labour supply (by recruiting women, older people and people from abroad), should more emphasis be placed on improving the quality of jobs available, and the education, training and life-long learning capacity of people in the labour force? The latter approach seems more sensible.

Among the commitments on work contained in the new social partnership agreement *Towards 2016* are the following:

On upskilling
Actions to be prioritised will include:
- Increasing participation in Lifelong Learning in particular among the workforce categorised as low-skilled/low paid by enhancing opportunities to access education and training, the development of new skills, the acquisition of recognised qualifications and progression to higher level qualifications to equip all individuals with the skills, capacity and potential to participate fully in the knowledge-based society and progress to better quality jobs.
- Focusing on helping adults from disadvantaged communities including those in rural areas, to acquire basic literacy, numeracy and IT skills and tackling barriers/disincentives to lifelong learning.
- Providing additional supports for students from disadvantaged backgrounds, students with disabilities and mature students to enhance access to further and higher education.
- Formulating a National Skills Strategy which will put in place a strategic framework for the implementation of skills and training strategy into the medium term.

On access to employment
Actions to be prioritised will include:
- Applying the National Employment Action Plan referral process earlier than the current six months.
- Extending the National Employment Action Plan referral process to other groups such as lone parents and those with disabilities, with due regards to the special needs of those groups.

On voluntary activity
- The Government will continue to develop policies on volunteering arising from the package of measures initiated in February 2005. A key principle underlying the Government's approach is that volunteering finds meaning and expression at a local level and that supports and funding should seek, as far as possible, to recognise this reality. The Government remains committed to further developing policy to support volunteering, drawing on the experience in delivering these measured and informed by the recommendations of the Task Force on active Citizenship.

On people with disabilities
- Developing a strategic integrated approach to rehabilitation services within the context of the Multi-Annual Investment Programme with a view to supporting people back into employment, as appropriate, through early intervention and enhanced service provision.
- The elaboration of a comprehensive employment strategy for People with Disabilities including a range of measures to promote education, vocational training and employment opportunities for people with disabilities.

On migrants
- A new framework will be finalised to address the broader issue of integration policy. The Government will develop a comprehensive strategy for all legally resident immigrants following consultation with relevant stakeholders including the social partners which will build on and be linked with progress already achieved in the areas of social inclusion and anti-racism. Appropriate co-ordinating mechanisms to implement such a strategy will be developed and the scope for a role for civil society organisations will also be explored.
- The Government has agreed that the Employment Permits Bill will be enacted at the earliest possible date and that economic migration policy will ensure the following:
  - that all workers will be allowed to apply for and reapply for their own permit;
  - that there will be appropriate consultation with the social partners in determining included and excluded categories of staff/skills for eligibility for work permits;
    - that there are adequate safeguards to protect workers' rights in relation to the application for employment permits by:
    - employers inside and outside of the State;
    - employment agencies; and
    - in respect of intra-corporate transfers;
- that the employment of non-EEA students is subject to an application for employment permits;
  - that employment permit applications are not approved for wages below the REA/ERO rate or the National Minimum Wage, which ever is appropriate;
- that employment permit holders may transfer to another employment in cases of unfair treatment; and
- that spouses of employment permit holders who are granted residence in Ireland may be granted an employment permit.

In conclusion, we outline key policy proposals with regard to work.

Policy Proposals on Work

- Develop employment-friendly income-tax policies which ensure that no unemployment traps exist. Policies should ease the transition from unemployment to employment.

- Place an ongoing emphasis on preparing and enabling unemployed people to access market-place jobs. Such an emphasis would involve
  - increased numbers of places providing quality education and training, re-training and up-skilling
  - expanded opportunities for unemployed people to gain work-place experience
  - constant review and updating of programmes such as Community Employment to ensure they are effective.

- Maintain a sufficient number of active labour-market programme (ALMP) places available to those who are long-term unemployed.

- When ALMPs are mainstreamed, particularly in disadvantaged areas, ensure that sufficient resources are made available to maintain the services that were provided.

- The new Community Support Programme located in the Department of Community, Rural and Gaeltacht Affairs should be expanded and resourced beyond what is committed in the new national social partnership agreement *Towards 2016*.

- If the Job Initiative (JI) programme, is going to be eliminated a new programme must be put in place targeting those who are very long-term unemployed (i.e. 5+ years).

- Increase the education/training grants for participants on Community Employment, Job Initiative and Rate for the Job programmes, and seek accreditation for all education/training and all work done by participants in these programmes.

- Seek at all times to ensure that new jobs have reasonable pay rates.

- Adopt policies to address the worrying trend of youth unemployment. In particular, these should include education initiatives and retraining schemes.

- Adopt policies to address the obstacles facing women when they return to the labour force. These should focus on care initiatives, employment flexibility and the provision of information and training.

- Reduce the impediments faced by people with a disability in achieving employment. In particular address the current situation where many face losing their benefits when they take up employment.

- Implement a rights-based immigration policy which addresses the unnecessary and undesirable restrictions the current work permit system imposes on migrant workers and their families.

- Ratify the *UN Convention on the Protection of Rights of All Migrant Workers and their Families* and as a consequence set a precedent for all other European countries to follow.

- Recognise the right to work of all asylum seekers whose application for asylum is at least six months old (and who are not entitled to take up employment).

- Recognise work that is not paid employment. Everybody has a right to work, i.e. to contribute to his or her own development and that of the community and the wider society. This, however, should not be confined to job creation. *Work* and a *job* are not the same thing.

- Give greater recognition to the work carried out by Carers in Ireland and introduce policy reforms to reduce the financial and emotional pressures on carers. In particular these should focus on addressing the poverty experienced by many carers and their families alongside increasing the provision of respite care for carers and for those for whom they care.

- Request the CSO to conduct an annual survey to discover the value of all unpaid work in the country (including community and voluntary work and work in the home). Publish the results of this survey as soon as they become available.

- Accept and implement the recommendations contained in the report of the National Committee on Volunteering, *Tipping the Balance*.

3.4 Public Services

> **CORE POLICY OBJECTIVE: PUBLIC SERVICES**
> To ensure the provision of, and access to, a level of public services regarded as acceptable by Irish society generally

Increasingly Ireland is being identified as a country whose public services are underdeveloped. Given the wealth of the economy, this is a situation that is far from acceptable. Because poorer people rely on public services more than those who are better off, it is they who are most acutely affected by this shortage.

We address public services over this section and the next three sections on housing and accommodation, healthcare and education. This section assesses public transport, library services, information and communications technology, telecommunications, sports facilities and regulation.

Public transport

Transport remains a most problematic area. Bottlenecks throughout the country are adding to the difficulty and cost experienced by everybody in conducting their lives. The sustained increase in the number of cars is also adding to problems of environmental destruction.[37]

A new transport policy would seek to combine easy access, affordable and high-quality public transport with the high costs of ownership and use of private vehicles. The ongoing failure to give adequate resources to some of the national rail services raises serious questions about government commitment to the environment and to rural and peripheral areas. Furthermore, enhanced support is required for the development of public transport schemes in rural Ireland. For such a policy to be credible it must be comprehensive, adequately resourced and enhance the current provision. These schemes significantly increase the quality of life of those living in remote rural areas, particularly older people.

---

[37] The environmental impact of cars are discussed in 3.10(b).

Library services

Libraries play an important role in Irish society. According to the Library Association of Ireland there are now 850,000 people who are members of public libraries. This is equivalent to 21 per cent of the population. As part of our commitment to providing a continuum of education provision from early childhood to third level. Ireland needs to recognise the potential that the library service offers.

Central to such developments is information and easy access to this information. Coupled with information is the need for easy access to modern means of communication. Libraries are obvious centres with potential to support these objectives. To play this potential role, expansion of the library service is essential. Consequently the modest increase in funding provided in Budget 2006 is a concern. In the long-term a failure to resource this service properly is shortsighted.

Information and communications technology

Increasingly the ability to use information and communications technology (ICT) is becoming a central requirement in modern society. The phenomenon of a technological divide is becoming evident. In particular it is of concern that a number of young people, including early school-leavers, have little or no skill in ICT. Consequently initiatives are necessary to improve information technology provision in schools, as well as to increase its availability in areas such as public libraries and community centres. Government needs to show greater commitment to this area.

It also needs to address the issue of including everybody in the information society. In addressing this issue it is crucial that priority is given to ensuring access is available to those who currently cannot afford the market costs. Ignoring this will ensure that the "digital divide" will widen social exclusion. More, targeted, resources are needed.

Telecommunications

Two issues arise within the topic of telecommunications. First, CORI Justice was concerned by the request in March 2003 by Eircom, Ireland's principal telecommunications company, that they be relieved of their universal public service obligation to provide a telephone for every house in the country. Instead they proposed sharing the €40m per annum cost of this obligation with other telecommunications companies and with consumers. The impact of such a change would be sizeable on the poor and on those living in rural areas. Both would experience an increase in the proportions of their incomes needed to be spent to ensure they had access at home to a telephone land line. We welcome the fact that this change was not introduced; however the fact that it was requested raises concerns that an attempt to revisit this issue may occur in the years ahead. Any such change which would impose additional costs on people who are already isolated from society, physically and financially, should be resisted. In considering any future decisions of this nature the Communications Regulator (ComReg) should take these societal points into account.

A second issue in the telecommunications area concerns one of the consequences of the growth in mobile phone usage over the last few years. This has seen a decline in usage of public payphones. In response to this a large number of these payphones have been decommissioned. Overall, Eircom has reduced the number of payphones across Ireland from about 8,000 in late 2000 to 6,050 in mid-2005. Since then the trend has continued. While it is understandable that some payphones would be removed, it is of concern that some people in society are being left without this vital means of communication. In particular those who are poor and unable to afford the costs involved in running a mobile phone are suffering. Furthermore the impact on small rural areas of the removal of a payphone can be considerable.

We urge care in any further decision to remove more payphones. It must be remembered that the usefulness of a payphone cannot be measured by its revenue alone. The very fact that a payphone is available if needed is a contribution that should not be overlooked. Consequently CORI Justice believes it is necessary that ComReg regulate this situation more closely.

Sports facilities
An insight into the role played by sport in Irish society was provided in a recent ESRI report entitled the *Social and Economic Value of Sport in Ireland* (Delaney and Fahy, 2005). Its findings indicated that: approximately 400,000 adults (15 per cent of the adult population) volunteer for sport in some way each year; 20 per cent of the adult population play sport; 30 per cent of adults are members of sports clubs; and the economic value of sport is between 1-2 per cent of GNP. In reaching its conclusions the report notes that current government policy commitments to promote social capital need to take account of the social aspects of sport and their potential contribution to the further development of social capital and volunteering in Ireland. Similarly it finds that

there should be greater dialogue between those concerned with sports policy and those concerned with policy on social capital and volunteering; their common interest in sport should be recognised and explored; and their efforts to support social capital and volunteering should be co-ordinated.

However, recent studies have also indicated a declining level of participation by Irish people, and in particular young people, in sports activities. Long term this may have significant health consequences. There is a special case to be made for poor areas, most of which have limited, if any, sports facilities. The National Sports Council has developed a creative initiative of local sports partnerships. Some of these are working effectively already and attempting to address this problem. Further funding for local sports partnerships should be made available. Given their huge potential such funding would be most worthwhile.

Regulation
As a result of privatisation, market reform and the European Union there has been a major growth in regulation in Ireland over recent years. The role of this regulation is as a public service to oversee the operation of markets and firms within the economy. During 2002 the government published a consultation document entitled *Towards Better Regulation* and invited comments on its contents and suggestions. CORI Justice welcomed this process and responded by making a number of points and we welcome the fact that many of these points were incorporated into the *White Paper on Better Regulation* (2004).

Central to our opinion on regulation is the view that all regulators, be they currently in existence or established in the future, should be required to consider the societal impact of any reforms they propose before they are implemented. Consequently we suggested that the proposed White Paper on regulation should adopt as its central ideology the view that it is the societal outcome of regulation that is of most importance. Regulation should be judged on how its outcome impacts on social, cultural and sustainability issues within society. Implementing regulation with this as its central aim would certainly achieve better regulation for all. It would also ensure consistently better outcomes for consumers.

We also believe that there should be solid and justifiable reasons for introducing regulation. It should not be introduced just to create choice/competition within the market. For example, to achieve competition in the electricity market the electricity regulator recently increased the price of electricity. While this may achieve competition we question the benefit to people. Furthermore assessment mechanisms should be established to allow an analysis of regulation pre and post its implementation. Central to such an assessment procedure should be an examination of its societal impacts. To achieve this we believe that the NESC progress indicators should be used. We also believe that, as part of the assessment procedure, inputs should be sought from interested parties including the community and voluntary pillar of the social partnership process.

A further important aspect is the need to consider the impact of regulation within the context of regional policy. Cross-subsidisation issues, in postal or electrical services, are important to retain equity between rural and urban dwellers. A further challenge for regulatory authorities must be to retain this inter-regional equity.

Regulation and regulatory law should be framed in such a way as to ensure that it is accessible and interpretable. Currently regulatory law is complex and in many cases requires those being regulated to divert a considerable quantity of resources to keep up with it. Complex regulation will also make it difficult for interested parties to actively participate in the pre and post regulation assessment mechanisms. CORI Justice believes it is important that where regulation has been judged to be a failure, government should alter or reverse it.

Among the commitments on public services contained in the new social partnership agreement *Towards 2016* are the following:

On transport
- There will be a doubling of the cash funding available to the Rural Transport Initiative (RTE) by 2007. Thereafter, a steady increase in funding will be provided for rural transport services, ultimately to a cash level about four times the 2005 allocation. The community and voluntary sector has a vital contribution to make and role to play in local and rural transport services and has been actively involve din the development of RTI.
- The Public Transport Partnership Forum will continue to provide a means for consultation with the Social Partners on matters relating to public transport.

On telecommunications
- Continue to explore technical options to address the requirements of people living in underserved areas, and remote rural areas.

On sport and culture
- Commitments on sport include:
- Increasing support for sports infrastructure and sporting organisations recognising that sport has the potential to be a driver for social change and that targeting specific groups can address issues of exclusion and inequality.
- Promoting sport in education settings.
- Achieving the Irish Sport Council target for 2006 to 2008 to increase by 3% the numbers of children taking part in sport. This will involve the implementation of the complete national roll-out of the Local Sports Partnership (LSP) network and the associated roll-out of the Buntús programme for primary schools and pre-schools through the LSP network.

Commitments on culture include:
- Continue to endeavour to make arts more accessible to all including the support of programmes in socially deprived.

On Regulation
- Government will publish a consultation document in 2006 seeking views of the Social Partners, representative groups and other interested stakeholders on the most appropriate appeals mechanisms for the key economic regulators, reflecting best international practice, as well as the specific regulatory arrangements and market structures operating in individual sectors.

Policy Proposals on Public Services

- Target funding strategies to ensure that far greater priority is given to providing an easy-access, affordable and high-quality public transport system.

- Allocate additional resources to the Rural Transport Initiative, which increases significantly the quality of life of those living in remote rural areas, particularly older people.

- Provide substantial additional resources for the development of library services throughout the country.

- Increase the provision of open-access information technology in public libraries.

- Take the necessary steps to include everybody in the information society.

- Introduce a system (e.g. a swipe card) that ensures people on low incomes can access information communications technology on an ongoing basis.

- Adopt further information-technology programmes to increase the skills of schoolchildren, early school-leavers and the unemployed.

- Regulate the removal of public payphone services. This is particularly necessary for poor areas and rural areas where the revenue generated by a payphone can give a misleading interpretation of its significance to the community.

- Provide additional funding to the Sports Partnership initiative.

- Adopt policies which ensure that all types of regulation are judged against how they impact on social, cultural and sustainability issues within society. Implementing regulation with this as its central aim would achieve better regulation for all.

- Ensure equality of access across all public services.

3.5 Housing and Accommodation

> **CORE POLICY OBJECTIVE:**
> **HOUSING & ACCOMMODATION**
> To ensure that adequate accommodation is available for all people and to develop an equitable system for allocating resources within the housing sector

Housing and accommodation policy

Issues concerning housing and accommodation have had a major profile in recent years. Most of that profile, however, was concerned with the provision and cost of privately owned accommodation. A comparison of European housing tenures illustrates the existence of three main models of housing provision: an owner-occupier sector, a rental sector and a social housing sector. Table 3.28 gives details of a European study which showed that in 2000 Ireland possessed one of the highest rates of owner occupation in the EU. Results from Census 2002 also found that 18.5 per cent of Ireland's population lived in rented accommodation. Compared to other countries Irish housing policy supports owner occupation to the detriment of all other forms of housing tenure; a feature which reflects the policy choices of government.

Ireland's level of home ownership reflects the high value Irish people put on owning their own homes. It also reflects public policy which provided a variety of tax incentives to those who have the resources to invest in housing. Since the 1970s it has been the policy of successive Irish governments to subsidise owner occupation heavily. This has been achieved by the abolition of local rates on residential property and the subsequent failure to implement a system of residential property tax. More recently investment policies have been introduced that favour investment in residential development, for example investors in urban renewal schemes stood to gain over 419 per cent on their investment (Bacon, 1998). These policy developments, combined with policies of mortgage-interest tax relief and very favourable tenant purchase schemes have resulted in an extremely high level of home ownership. Owner-occupiers make up 82.3 per cent of the Irish population – this is considerably higher than the EU average of 63.4 per cent. Government housing policy has resulted in a housing system that is not tenure neutral and which has led to the residualisation of the rental sector, both public and private.

Housing and Accommodation

Table 3.28: EU Owner Occupation Rates, 1995-2000.

Country	% in 1995	% in 2000
Spain	80.3	85.4
Greece	80.7	83.6
IRELAND	**80.9**	**82.3**
Italy	71.3	75.4
Belgium	67.2	72.9
Luxembourg	67.6	70.8
United Kingdom	68.7	70.5
Finland	64.3	68.1
Denmark	57.6	65.2
Portugal	60.0	65.2
France	56.5	62.5
Sweden	58.5	59.9
Austria	49.1	53.9
Netherlands	48.1	53.0
Germany	41.7	43.3
EU-15	59.7	63.4

Source: CSO (2003: 55) and Eurostat, ECHP.

Ireland's level of home ownership reflects the high value Irish people put on owning their own homes. It also reflects public policy which provided a variety of tax incentives to those who have the resources to invest in housing. Since the 1970s it has been the policy of successive Irish governments to subsidise owner occupation heavily. This has been achieved by the abolition of local rates on residential property and the subsequent failure to implement a system of residential property tax. More recently investment policies have been introduced that favour investment in residential development, for example investors in urban renewal schemes stood to gain over 419 per cent on their investment (Bacon, 1998). These policy developments, combined with policies of mortgage-interest tax relief and very favourable tenant purchase schemes have resulted in an extremely high level of home ownership. Owner-occupiers make up 82.3 per cent of the Irish population – this is considerably higher than the EU average of 63.4 per cent. Government housing policy has resulted in a housing system that is not tenure neutral and which has led to the residualisation of the rental sector, both public and private.

The down-the-line effect of this policy is the lack of adequate accommodation for larger and larger numbers of households. The value of home ownership should be discussed in the light of present realities. These include: the increasing prices paid for houses and for land rezoned for housing; the burden of mortgage repayments especially on young families; the ghettoisation of local authority housing because private owners object to developments which may seem to devalue their properties; difficulties in providing suitable accommodation for special groups including Travellers, homeless people, asylum-seekers, young offenders and drug abusers.

The housing crisis

During the last decade improved levels of economic growth combined with low interest rates resulted in high levels of housing inflation. This in turn resulted in a crisis in housing provision in both the public and the private sectors. In the private sector this crisis is evident from the rapid increase in house prices and from the severe difficulties experienced by first-time buyers seeking affordable houses. In the public sector the demand (waiting lists) for social housing has increased substantially in the past five years at a time when house building in the public sector has been at a very low level.

Housing: a new philosophy

Two recent publications by the Economist Professor PJ Drudy of Trinity College have offered an interesting new approach to how Irish society view housing. In his paper at our 2005 *Social Policy Conference* and in a co-authored book with Michael Punch -entitled *Out of Reach* (2005) - he has outlined these views.

The essence of Professor Drudy's proposal is to view housing as a home rather than as a market commodity. In his conference paper Professor Drudy stated that we should "place the emphasis on housing as a home – shelter, a place to stay, to feel secure, to build a base, find an identity and participate in a community and society". Therefore he continued: "housing thus becomes a central feature of 'development' – a process not simply comprising increases in economic growth, but containing positive actions to improve the quality of life and wellbeing for all" (2005: 44).

In concluding his paper, Drudy suggested that Irish society now needs to address "a fundamental philosophical question: is it the purpose of a housing system to provide investment, speculative or capital gains for those with the necessary resources or should the critical aim be to provide a home as a right for all citizens?" (2004: 46). In his view it is time now for Ireland to move away from seeing housing as a commodity to be traded on the market like any other tradable commodity; and to accept the latter opinion that views housing as a social requirement like health services or education. CORI Justice strongly welcomes and endorses these views. We hope they lead to a debate on this issue and eventually to the adoption by Government, policy makers and society as a whole of this new philosophy.

NESC report on housing in Ireland

At the end of 2004 the National Economic and Social Council (NESC) published a major report on housing. Entitled *Housing in Ireland: Performance and Policy* the report spans over 230 pages and provides guidelines for the future direction of policy in this area.

In particular, the report makes important suggestions for policy initiatives focused on social housing (see table 3.29). Overall, NESC concluded that it was particularly concerned about two issues. These are:

- the quality of the neighbourhoods, villages, towns and cities being constructed in Ireland, and
- the provision of social and affordable housing

They also stress that adequately addressing these two issues will not be easy and that "the magnitude and significance of this challenge needs to be recognised". In reviewing the current situation of the Irish housing system the Council pinpointed three anxieties. These are:

*(i) **Stability**:* the stability of the housing sector in the next few years will be important. This sector is now a major employer in the economy and the projected declines in the number of house completions in the coming years needs to be managed. Simultaneously, the ongoing existence of unmet need for social housing threatens to produce instability.

*(ii) **Inequality**:* the housing sector has generated inequality through being unable to meet the housing needs of many of those on low incomes and a number of other social groups. Furthermore, recent changes in property prices have been the source of very significant changes in the distribution of wealth and income in Irish society.

*(iii) **Sustainability**:* the study also identified concerns about the patterns of settlement, neighbourhood design and density in the Irish housing system. NESC found that a strong case can be made that we are storing up significant social, environmental, budgetary and economic problems for the years to come.

Taking these three issues together NESC concluded that "the Irish housing system has been dynamic, but unbalanced". In conclusion the report identifies four key policy challenges:

- To achieve high quality, sustainable, development in both urban and rural areas
- To provide an effective range of supports to those households that fall below the affordability threshold
- To assist the market to continue to provide a high level of supply
- To ensure a tax and subsidy regime that supports these goals

2012 Social Housing target

A central conclusion of the NESC housing report is that the supply of social housing will have to rise dramatically if the needs of Irish society are to be addressed in the years ahead. The main recommendation of the council on the issue of social housing is outlined in table 3.29. It calls on Government to "create an expanded and more flexible stock of social housing – adding in the order of 73,000 permanent social housing units to bring the stock to 200,000 dwellings by 2012 – in a manner that is consistent with other public investment needs and sound public finances" (2004:221).

Table 3.29: The role of social housing in Ireland in 2012

	2012
Total number of dwellings	1,653,000
Social housing as a % of total	12.0
Number of social housing units	200,000
Population of Ireland	4,505,000
Social housing units per thousand	44.4

Source: Data are based on NESC projection (2004:152-153) and CSO (2004:26) projections for 2011 (assumption M1F1).

The figure of 200,000 social housing units has been calculated based on the projected increases in the Irish population over that period and in the context of limited responses to existing social housing needs (e.g. homelessness, community based accommodation for disabled and elderly persons). The scale of the challenge facing Irish society can be gauged from the fact that at the end of 2004 the total stock of social housing (including units managed by both local authorities and the voluntary and cooperative housing sector) stood at about 127,000.

NESC concluded that to achieve the target of 200,000 units over the eight year period between 2005 and 2012, an annual increase of in excess of 9,000 units is necessary. They also pointed out that an estimated capital investment of €1.4bn a year would be required to achieve a net increase of 73,000 units by 2012. Given the present level of capital expenditure this would mean an additional investment per annum of the scale of €500m to €600m on what is already projected.

CORI Justice welcomes the commitment in *Towards 2016* to provide 27,000 new social housing units by 2009. We also welcome the acknowledgement in that agreement of the 2012 NESC target of 73,000 new units. Reaching that target by 2012 is essential if Ireland is to achieve the goal of ensuring that everyone in the country has appropriate accommodation.

Waiting lists: how many and for how long?

The most recent assessment of local authority waiting lists occurred on the 31st of March 2005 and was partially reported in a Department of Environment, Heritage and Local Government publication in December 2005. It found that there was a total of 43,684 households on local-authority housing waiting lists (see table 3.30). This figure represents a decrease of 9.8 per cent since the 2002 assessment – a welcome improvement. However, since 1996 waiting lists have grown by 59.2 per cent and the 2005 figure indicates that across Ireland about 120,000 people are in need of accommodation.

Table 3.30: The Need for and Supply of Local Authority (LA) Social Housing, 1996- 2005			
Year	Households on LA Waiting Lists	Stock of LA Housing Units	Waiting List as % of Rental Stock
1996	27,427	98,394	28
1999	39,176	99,163	40
2002	48,413	104,688	46
2005	43,684	108,496	40

Source: Department of the Environment, Heritage and Local Government, *Housing Statistics Bulletin*, various issues and Department Housing Statistics as published on www.environ.ie

Developing a Fairer Ireland

The delay in releasing full details of the 2005 housing assessment study prevents a presentation of a detailed breakdown of these figures.[38] However, details of the 2002 examination are available and are presented in table 3.31 below. It shows that in 2002 the largest category of households on the lists is those labelled as being not able to meet costs of existing accommodation. This group accounted for 44 per cent of the waiting list or 21,452 households. The Housing *Statistics Bulletin* further indicates that since an earlier assessment in 1999 this group has grown from a situation where it accounted for 34 per cent of the list. This growth can be directly related to the excessive house price and rent increases over recent years. A comparison with the 1999 figures also reveals that all bar two of the categories experienced a growth in the number of households on the waiting lists. These are "existing accommodation unfit" and "elderly persons".

Analysis of these figures also reveals that 32 per cent (15,522) of all those households on the waiting lists consist of single-person households. Single-parent households, consisting of one adult and one child, make up a further 29 per cent (14,039) of the waiting list.

Table 3.31: Breakdown of the Local Authority Housing Waiting List by Major Categories of Need, 2002

Category of Need Households	Number of List	% of Waiting
Homeless	2,468	5.10
Travellers	1,583	3.27
Existing accommodation unfit	4,065	8.40
Existing accommodation overcrowded	8,513	17.58
Involuntarily sharing of accommodation	4,421	9.13
Young persons leaving institutional care	82	0.17
Medical or compassionate grounds	3,400	7.02
Elderly persons	2,006	4.14
Disabled or handicapped	423	0.87
Not able to meet costs of existing accommodation	21,452	44.31
Total	**48,413**	**100.00**

Source: Calculated from Department of the Environment, Heritage and Local Government, *Housing Statistics Bulletin,* September 2002:59

[38] CORI Justice will provide an update of these figures on our website (www.cori.ie/justice) once they become available.

When the 48,413 households on the 2002 waiting lists are classified by the length of time they have spent on the waiting list the figures reveal that 25 per cent of all households have been waiting for more than three years. A further 14 per cent are on the list for between 2-3 years while 22 per cent are waiting for between 1-2 years. The remaining 38 per cent have been waiting for less than a year (including those classified as first time).

In the context of all these figures it has to be acknowledged that more progress needs to be made. Achieving that progress requires a greater commitment to providing social housing. Implementing NESC's social housing recommendation (see table 3.29) will significantly address this problem and move Ireland closer to achieving CORI Justice's core policy objective of ensuring that appropriate accommodation is available for all.

House completions

Table 3.32 shows the rate of house completions in the various sectors between 1993 and 2004. During 2004 there was a major increase in total house completions with a growth since 2003 of almost 12 per cent; producing 76,954 new homes. However, in spite of the significant growth in the number of houses, the experience of the private and public sectors are very different

Table 3.32: House Completions, 1993–2004			
Year	Local Authority Housing	Voluntary/Non Profit Housing	Private Housing	Total
1993	1,200	890	19,301	21,391
1994	2,374	901	23,588	26,863
1995	2,960	1,011	26,604	30,575
1996	2,676	917	30,132	33,725
1997	2,632	756	35,454	38,842
1998	2,771	485	39,093	42,349
1999	2,909	579	43,024	46,512
2000	2,204	951	46,657	49,812
2001	3,622	1,253	47,727	52,602
2002	4,403	1,360	51,932	57,695
2003	4,516	1,617	62,686	68,819
2004	3,539	1,607	71,808	76,954

Source: Department of Environment, Heritage and Local Government, *Housing Statistics Bulletin Quarter3 2005* (2005:7); CSO (2003:54).

Developing a Fairer Ireland

In 2004 the vast majority of new houses (93 per cent) were built by the private sector. Local authorities built 3,539 new homes in 2004, a decrease of almost 1,000 since 2003 and the lowest number of new completions for five years. It is of some concern that the overall number of LA completions is falling particularly given the commitments given by Government in the National Development Plan. The figures for 2004 do reveal a sustained growth in voluntary/non-profit and co-op housing. These organisations built 1,607 houses during that year and they now account for well over one third of all publicly assisted housing completions. Currently they are managing a stock of approximately 18,000 dwellings. This trend is very welcome and underscores the growing role this sector is playing. CORI Justice believes this sector has a major contribution to make in addressing the current housing crisis and that government must give further assistance to facilitating its continued growth.

Table 3.33: Local Authority Completions and Acquisitions, 1995–2004			
Year	Local Authority Completions	Local Authority Acquisitions	Total
1995	2,960	882	3,842
1996	2,676	897	3,573
1997	2,632	585	3,217
1998	2,771	511	3,282
1999	2,909	804	3,713
2000	2,204	1,003	3,207
2001	3,622	1,400	5,022
2002	4,403	671	5,073
2003	4,516	456	4,972
2004	3,539	971	4,510

Source: Department of the Environment, Heritage and Local Government, *Housing Statistics Bulletin,* various issues and Department Housing Statistics as published on www.environ.ie

Table 3.33 further shows the inadequacy of local authorities' response. At a time of such need, the total number of local authority completions plus acquisitions is falling from 4,972 in 2003 to 4,510 in 2004. The fact that these figures report a decrease is a major disappointment. Clearly additional government investment in social housing is urgently required.

The Planning and Development (Amendment) Act, 2002.

CORI Justice considers the decision by the government to repeal section V of the Planning and Development Act 2000 as unacceptable. This u-turn changed the 20 per cent rule which required all developers to allocate 20 per cent of all housing built for social and affordable housing. This policy was worthwhile for two reasons. First it facilitated a more speedy provision of housing for those on our ever-growing waiting lists (see table 3.30) and second it opened up the prospect of Ireland developing as a more socially integrated nation. In response to this move Threshold (9th December 2002) indicated that the impact of these reforms will be that:

(i) the withdrawal of the two-year withering rule for planning permissions means that the Act will produce little social rented housing for at least two years, despite the fact that local authority waiting lists are climbing ever higher

(ii) the Act's ability to promote social integration in new residential developments is being sacrificed. Developers will in future manoeuvre to buy off or sideline their social housing commitment to unattractive locations

(iii) the money that local authorities receive under the 20 per cent rule from developers seeking to avoid social integration is not properly ring-fenced to build additional social housing units, whether by local authorities or housing associations. Consequently the funds are likely to disappear without helping people in need of social housing.

In the context of Ireland's social housing crisis, the decision to repeal this section of the Act was wrong. One of the major achievements of the Fianna Fáil/PD coalition 1997-2002 was that it showed a long-absent willingness to address the social housing and societal integration issue. Therefore it is particularly sad that within six months of re-assuming office it chose to cancel one of its most noteworthy previous achievements.

The private rented sector

A study by McCashin (2000) of the private rental sector points out the circular and complex links between the structure and operation of the housing system and poverty and social exclusion.

The private rented sector is the "tenure of last resort for those unable to obtain local authority housing or not yet ready to enter owner-occupation"

(McCashin, 2000:43). Traditionally the private rental sector was the residual sector of the Irish housing system. It was characterised by poor-quality accommodation and non-secure tenure at the lower end of the housing market. Today, this sector is highly differentiated, with high-quality housing and relatively secure tenure at the upper end of the market, and low-quality housing and insecurity of tenure at the lower end. Both ends of the market have experienced dramatic increases in rent over the last decade.

Table 3.34: Percentage distribution of housing units by occupancy status, 1961-2002.

Occupancy Status	1961	1971	1981	1991	2002
LA Rented	18.4	15.9	12.7	9.7	6.9
Private Rented	17.2	10.9	8.1	7.0	11.1
Owner Occupied	53.6	60.7	67.9	80.2	77.4
Other	10.8	12.5	11.2	3.0	4.6
Total	100.0	100.0	100.0	100.0	100.0

Source: CSO, 2003:28.

The percentage of the population dependent on this sector to meet their housing needs declined from 17.2 per cent in 1961 to 7 per cent in 1991 (see table 3.34). This compares with an EU average of 21 per cent. The results of Census 2002 indicate that the composition of the sector changed dramatically during the last decade. A combination of a growing population, changing household structure, and the increasing cost of owner-occupation has seen the number of households in the private rented sector increase by more than 60 per cent. As table 3.34 shows the private rented sector now accounts for 11 per cent of households. In total in 2002 there were 141,459 households living in the private rented sector. Of these 25,883 rented unfurnished dwellings and 115,576 rented furnished or part-furnished dwellings. The average weekly rents paid were €125.68 for unfurnished and €169.16 for part/fully furnished dwellings (CSO, 2003: 87).

Rent supplement
At the lower end of the housing market an increasing number of households are in receipt of a Supplementary Welfare Allowance in the form of rent supplement. There have been substantial changes to the rent supplement programme over the past year. Following on the furore caused by the changes introduced as part of

Budget 2004, Government has now taken a number of initiatives to address the concerns raised by CORI Justice and others at that time.

Some of the most contentious initiatives, such as the imposition of a six-month rule, have been replaced by more user-friendly procedures. Of greater importance, however, is the recognition by Government that the rent supplement programme, originally designed as an emergency intervention, had expanded into a housing payment for a great many people who had spent several years in receipt of rent supplement. The introduction of the new Rental Accommodation Scheme (RAS) is a welcome move in the right direction.

Homelessness

It is possible to extract from the assessment of housing needs information about those most urgently in need of accommodation – the homeless. The data, from March 2005 show that the level of homelessness across the country has fallen from 2,468 in 2002 to 2,399 in 2005; a decline of 2.8 per cent. A study focused on Dublin entitled Counted in 2005 also reported earlier this year and recorded that there were 1,361 homeless households representing a total of 2,015 homeless people (1,552 adults and 463 children) in the capital city. This figure represents a 19 per cent decrease on the previous assessment in 2002. Among the 1,552 adults 61 per cent were male with the majority aged between 21-39 years (2006: 25-27).

Research has shown that there are three broad categories of homeless people. The first category consists of those who become homeless because of poverty combined with either eviction or a relationship breakdown. The second and growing category of homeless persons consists of those who have chronic disabilities or special needs as a result of alcoholism, mental illness or drug dependency. This group has multiple needs, of which housing is just one (Homeless Initiative, 1999). A report for the National Advisory Committee on Drugs in mid-2005 noted that the vast majority (87 per cent) of the homeless people they surveyed first used drugs before becoming homeless. It also noted that 74 per cent of homeless individuals reported lifetime use of an illicit drug (Lawless and Corr, 2005:95, 97). A third category of homeless persons has emerged in Ireland in recent years – this comprises asylum-seekers and refugees who have specific housing and other social-service needs. The association between homelessness and mental health problems was assessed in a recent study at the Mater Hospital in Dublin. It found that one-third of all referrals for psychiatric assessment from its A&E department were homeless people. In all it is estimated that about 40 per cent of Ireland's homeless have mental health difficulties. These facts underscore the vulnerability of the homeless and the need for ever greater efforts to solve this problem.

In 2005 approximately €51 million of State funding was allocated to addressing homelessness. Added to this amount are the contributions of other charities, agencies and volunteers. In the context of the progress being achieved in addressing homelessness, and given the scale of this funding, a value-for-money review of the effectiveness of the current approach to tackling homelessness is long overdue.

Traveller accommodation
Results from the 2002 Census of Population show that there were 23,700 members of the Travelling community in Ireland. The 2003 Annual Count of Travellers found there were 6,799 Traveller families in the State. As a minority group, Travellers have been very exposed to social exclusion and in particular have experienced continued problems with the provision of accommodation. Responding to the report of The National Traveller Accommodation Consultative Committee (published in January 2005) the Minister of State for Housing, Noel Ahern, admitted that the pace at which Traveller accommodation is provided is too slow. A similar view was expressed by the Council of Europe in May 2004.

Since 1998 all Local Authorities have been required to provide multi-annual Traveller accommodation plans. Traveller organisations have reported that between 2000 and 2003 no Local Authority delivered on its plan in full and that approximately one-third of the accommodation envisaged in these plans was delivered. However, some progress has been made and should be acknowledged. Since 1999 a total of 1,369 Traveller families have been accommodated and the number of families living on the roadside has decreased by one-third from 1,200 to 800. The increase in the Traveller accommodation budget by €5m to €45m is also welcome. CORI Justice welcomes this report and the progress made over recent years. However there remains much more to be achieved. We regret that the committee failed to agree to the establishment of a Traveller accommodation agency as recommended by the Task Force in its original report in 1995.

Housing and people with a disability

CORI Justice welcomes the recognition by NESC in its review of housing policy that "a particular gap is the lack of a strategic framework to support the provision of tailored housing and housing supports for people with disabilities" (2004:157). A feature of having a disability is additional housing costs. Primarily these costs are for adjustments to residences to ensure access and continued use. For some years local authorities have provided a disabled persons housing grant to assist in the cost of these changes. However, during 2002 the Irish Wheelchair Association reported that an estimated six thousand people with disabilities across the state were waiting for these grants. Little progress has been made since. Besides quality of life issues studies have shown that the cost of keeping people who are older or who have a disability in nursing care is almost eight times the cost of adapting and providing health care within their own homes.

Properly funding this scheme is a necessity and CORI Justice believes that the government should allocate more funding to reduce these unnecessarily long waiting lists. Furthermore, as the population ages the demands on this scheme will increase. Therefore we believe that the government should judge the value of this scheme broadly. Surely this is the most basic of social inclusion policies and the long waiting lists that exist need to be addressed urgently.

Children and housing

Living in housing that is overcrowded, damp, in disrepair or in a poor neighbourhood can be damaging to people of all ages. However, its impact on children's welfare tends to be very significant. A study produced for the Children's Research Centre at Trinity College Dublin by Simon Brooke found that between 1991 and 2002 the numbers of children living in these conditions doubled. According to the report entitled *Housing Problems and Irish Children* there are some 50,000 children living in such conditions. The report found that there is a concentration of these problems among children in one-parent families and among those living in rented accommodation. In response to this problem the report suggested that local authorities need to create a specific fund to provide regular maintenance of their dwellings. Furthermore the report called for the current minimum standards set for the private rented sector to be raised and that these be enforced by local authorities. Finally the report suggested that the National Children's Strategy be revised to included housing as a "basic need". CORI Justice welcomes the recommendations of this report. As we have previously highlighted Ireland has a serious problem with child poverty (1 in every 5 children live in households at risk of poverty).

Continually research has pointed out that low income and low accommodation standards are associated with poor health levels and poor future educational and life opportunities. More resources need to be allocated to this area.

Second homes – a problem?
While addressing Ireland's housing problem, the *National Development Plan Mid-Term Review* (2003) pointed out the growing problem of second homes. It noted that a quarter of all houses built in 2003 were second (holiday) houses and will have nobody living in them for nine months of the year.

What is often overlooked when this is being discussed is that the infrastructure to support these houses is substantially subsidised by the tax-payer. Roads, water, sewage and electricity infrastructure are just part of this subsidy which goes, by definition, to those who are already better off as they can afford these second homes in the first place. In addition, the authors of the review point out that the huge growth in demand for second houses is eating up resources and militating against balanced regional development. Consequently, they recommend that people purchasing second houses should have to pay the full infrastructural costs, much of which is currently borne by society through the Exchequer. A similar conclusion was reached by Indecon Economic Consultants in their report on the future of Local Authority financing commissioned by the Department of Environment, Heritage and Local Government (2005:183-186; 189-190).

There seems something perverse in the fact that the taxpayer is providing substantial subsidies to the owners of these unoccupied (mostly holiday) houses while so many people don't have basic adequate accommodation. In the context of the housing phenomenon outlined above the second house problems should be addressed so that priority can be given to supplying houses which people need and will be lived in all year round.

Property Rights
During 2003 CORI Justice made a submission to the All-Party Oireachtas Committee on the Constitution. Subsequently, an oral presentation of our submission was made. In making the submission CORI Justice approached the issue from: (i) a social justice perspective drawn from Catholic Social Thought; (ii) a rights-based perspective believing that every person has a range of human rights that incorporates civil, political, economic, cultural and social rights; and (iii) with a special concern for the issue of social housing, the lack of which is

now reaching crisis proportions in Ireland and has the potential to undermine much of the progress that has been made on a wide range of fronts over the past decade

In April 2004 the Committee published its report and provided a set of wide ranging suggestions to the government on how to handle issues concerning private property. As part of that process the Committee singled out CORI Justice for its clarity in presenting the level of social housing need and complemented CORI Justice for the energy with which it formulated solutions. We believe that it is essential that ongoing policy making in this area be informed by the latest information available on the scale of the accommodation problem faced by this country. Publications such as this review and our *Policy Briefing – Housing and Accomodation* (CORI Justice, 2005) play a part in informing all interested parties of that information and thereby fuel a necessary debate on this issue.

> **Among the commitments on housing and accommodation contained in the new social partnership agreement *Towards 2016* are the following:**
>
> **On social housing**
> - The total number of new commencements/acquisitions in the period 2007-2009 will be 27,000 units.
> - To further assist the voluntary and co-operative sector the Government will arrange through Local Authorities for additional land/units to be provided under this Agreement for the purpose of meeting identified housing need. Units/sites sufficient to supply some 3,000 dwellings will be identified and made available over the period 2007-2009.
> - Minimum standards regulations for the private rented sector will be updated by the Dept of Environment, Heritage and Local Government and effectively enforced by Local Authorieies.
> - As a result of the various social and affordable housing measures the accommodation needs of some 60,000 new households will be addressed over the period 2007-2009.
>
> **On homelessness**
> - The Government's Integrated and Preventative Homeless Strategies will be amalgamated and updated taking on board the recommendations of the recent independent review of the strategies.
> - The revised strategies will have as an underlying objective the elimination of such homelessness by 2010.
> - The involvement of the voluntary and co-operative housing sector will be strengthened through the establishment of a National Homelessness Consultative Committee including representatives of the C & V Pillar under the aegis of the Housing Forum.
>
> **On people with disabilities**
> - A National Housing Strategy for People with Disabilities will be developed in order to support the provision of tailored housing and housing support to people with disabilities. This will be progressed through the establishment of a National Group under the aegis of the Housing Forum.
>
> **On Travellers**
> - Implementation of the Local Authority Traveller accommodation programmes.

Policy Proposals on Housing and Accommodation

- Articulate an integrated and comprehensive national housing policy capable of meeting the needs of all people in Ireland as the population of the State is set to expand dramatically in the years immediately ahead.

- Implement the commitment in *Towards 2016* to provide 27,000 new social housing units by 2009.

- Develop and support policies focused on mixed housing, mixed communities, choice of tenure, and mix of different-sized housing units.

- Recognise affordable housing as a separate category aimed at a particular income group.

- Provide sufficient resources to implement the commitment in *Towards 2016* to eliminate homelessness by 2010.

- Continue to increase the budget allocation for local authority, co-op and voluntary/non-profit housing.

- Ensure that 20 per cent of building land is allocated for social and affordable housing with at least half of this being allocated for social housing.

- Provide new resources for the security and management of local-authority housing.

- Actively implement and enforce the legislation on the private rented sector of housing.

- Ensure that nobody remains dependent on rent supplement for more than 18 months. To this end ensure prompt delivery and adequate resourcing of the Rental Accommodation Scheme (RAS).

- Provide the resources required to ensure implementation of the local authorities Travellers' Accommodation programmes.

- Give priority to tackling ongoing issues concerning accommodation for refugees and asylum-seekers.

- Introduce a policy where people purchasing second houses (holiday homes) should pay the full infrastructural costs of these homes.

- Integrate housing policy with other social and care supports to enable vulnerable people (e.g. disability, elderly, homeless) to live independent lives.

- Ensure that sufficient funds are made available to reduce the waiting lists for the disabled persons housing grant.

3.6 Healthcare[39]

> **CORE POLICY OBJECTIVE: HEALTHCARE**
> To provide an adequate healthcare service focused on enabling people to attain the World Health Organisation's definition of health as a *state of complete physical, mental and social well-being and not merely the absence of disease or infirmity*

Healthcare is a social right that every person should enjoy. People should be assured that care in their times of vulnerability is guaranteed. The standard of care is dependent on the resources made available which in turn is dependent on the expectations of the society. The obligation to provide healthcare as a social right rests on all people. In a democratic society this obligation is transferred through the taxation and insurance systems to government and other bodies who assume/contract this responsibility.

Health inequalities in Ireland

A very welcome insight into the extent of health inequalities in Ireland has been provided by the Public Health Alliance Ireland (PHAI). This group, an alliance of non-governmental organisations, statutory bodies, community and voluntary groups, advocacy bodies and individuals who are committed to work together for a healthier society by improving health and tackling health inequalities, have published a detailed report entitled *"Health in Ireland – An Unequal State"*. The report gathered together the baseline information on health inequalities in Ireland and its findings are worthy of serious attention. These included:

- Between 1989 and 1998 the death rates for all causes of death were over three times higher in the lowest occupational class than in the highest
- The death rates for all cancers among the lowest occupational class is over twice as high for the highest class, it is nearly three times higher for strokes, four times higher for lung cancer, six times for accidents
- Perinatal mortality is three times higher in poorer families than in richer families

---

[39] CORI Justice acknowledges the input of CORI Healthcare in preparing this section

- Women in the unemployed socio-economic group are more than twice as likely to give birth to low birth weight children as women in the higher professional group
- The incidence of chronic physical illness has been found to be two and a half times higher for poor people than for the wealthy
- Men in unskilled jobs were four times more likely to be admitted to hospital for schizophrenia than higher professional workers
- The rate of hospitalisation for mental illness is more than 6 times higher for people in the lower socio-economic groups as compared with those in the higher groups
- The incidence of male suicide is far higher in the lower socio-economic groups as compared with the higher groups
- The 1998 and 2002 National Health and Lifestyle Surveys (SLAN) found that poorer people are more likely to smoke cigarettes, drink alcohol excessively, take less exercise, and eat less fruit and vegetables than richer people. Poorer people's lifestyle and behavioural choices are directly limited by their economic and social circumstances
- On average 39 per cent of people surveyed in 2003 identified financial problems as the greatest factor in preventing them from improving their health.

The report also found that some groups experience particularly extreme health inequalities. These include:

- Members of the Traveller community live between 10 and 12 years less than the population as a whole
- The rate of sudden infant deaths among Travellers is 12 times higher than for the general population
- Research has found that many expectant mothers in direct provision suffer malnutrition, babies in these communities suffer ill-health because of diet, many adults experience hunger
- Homeless people experience high incidence of ill-health – a 1997 report found that 40 per cent of hostel dwellers had a serious psychiatric illness, 42 per cent had problems of alcohol dependency, 18 per cent had other physical problems
- The incidence of injecting drug use is almost entirely confined to people from the lower socio-economic groups.

The PHAI also compared the health of people in Ireland against that of the 15 other EU states (pre-enlargement) They found that Irish people compare badly with the experience of citizens in other EU counties. These findings included:

- Mortality rates in Ireland are worse than the EU average for a range of illnesses, particularly diseases of the circulatory system, breast cancer and death from smoking related illnesses
- Irish women have almost twice the rate of death from heart disease as the average European woman
- The incidences of mortality for Irish women for cancers of the breast, colon, larynx and oesophagus and for ischaemic heart disease are among the highest in the EU
- At the age of 65 Irish men have the lowest life expectancy in the EU.

(PHAI, 2004:3-4).

Life expectancy and infant mortality

In 2003 Irish people had one of the lowest life expectancies of all the EU countries for both males and females. The figures for Ireland, outlined in table 3.35, show that Irish males can expect to live 75.8 years while Irish females live 4.9 years longer to 80.7 years.

The story behind these figures incorporates many of the findings of the PHAI report and the earlier poverty figures. Ireland's growing poverty problem has serious implications for health in light of the fact that there is a clear link between poverty and ill health. This relationship has been well supported by international research. Poverty limits access to affordable healthcare and reduces the opportunity for those living in poverty to adopt healthier lifestyles. Thus, those in lower socio-economic groups have a higher percentage of both acute and chronic illnesses. In the NAPS, the Government has committed itself to reducing the gap in premature mortality between the lowest and highest socio-economic groups by 10 per cent for certain diseases by the year 2007 (2002:12). Achieving this target through various anti-poverty and health measures is an essential first step in addressing Ireland's life expectancy problems.

Table 3.35: EU-25 life expectancy at birth by sex in 2002, in years.

Country	Males	Females	Sex Difference
Spain	75.8	83.5	7.7
France	75.8	83.0	7.2
Italy	76.8	82.9	6.1
Sweden	77.7	82.1	4.4
Austria	75.8	81.7	5.9
Luxembourg	74.9	81.5	6.6
Finland	74.9	81.5	6.6
Germany	75.4	81.2	5.8
EU-25	*74.8*	*81.1*	*6.3*
Belgium	75.1	81.1	6.0
Cyprus[51]	76.1	81.0	4.9
Malta	75.9	81.0	5.1
Greece	75.4	80.7	5.3
Netherlands	76.0	80.7	4.7
Portugal	73.8	80.5	6.7
Slovenia	72.7	80.5	7.8
United Kingdom	75.9	80.5	4.6
IRELAND (2003 figures)	**75.8**	**80.7**	**4.9**
Denmark	74.8	79.5	4.7
Czech Republic	72.1	78.7	6.6
Poland	70.4	78.7	8.3
Slovak Republic	69.9	77.8	7.9
Lithuania	66.3	77.5	11.2
Estonia	65.3	77.1	11.8
Hungary	68.4	76.7	8.3
Latvia	64.8	76.0	11.2

Source: CSO 2005:51; CSO 2006:51

Statistics on infant mortality also provide an insight into the health of a countries population. Using data from 2001, Eurostat found that Ireland had the third highest infant mortality rate in the EU-15. The infant mortality rate is defined as the number of infants who die within the first year of life per 1,000 live births. Across the EU the average number is 4.6 while the corresponding Irish figure is 5.8. The highest figure in the EU was for Greece (5.9) and the lowest in Finland and Sweden with 3.2 deaths per 1,000 live births (Eurostat, 2004:94).

Health expenditure

Healthcare must be seen as a social right for all people. For this to be upheld governments need to provide funding to ensure this occurs. In table 3.36 we see that Ireland spends 7.4 per cent of GDP on health. Less is spent on public and private health as a proportion of GDP than most other OECD countries. In GNP term this expenditure translated in a figure of 8.8 per cent. In comparison Germany spends 11.1 per cent and Portugal 9.6 per cent Ireland has the sixth lowest expenditure on health (measured as a percentage of GDP) according to OECD data. Healthcare costs tend to be higher in countries which have a higher old age dependency ratio. This is not yet so significant an issue for Ireland as the old age dependency ratio is extremely low (16.6 per cent 65 and over) compared to the EU average (24.3 per cent 65 and over). This level of funding must be seen as inadequate in light of the fact that waiting lists, bed closures, shortage of staff and long-term care requirements are issues in the health service today.

Table 3.36: Health expenditure as a percentage of GDP, 2003

Country	%	Country	%
United States	15.0	Hungary#	8.4
Switzerland#	11.5	Italy	8.4
Germany	11.1	New Zealand	8.1
Iceland#	10.5	Japan#	7.9
Norway#	10.3	Spain	7.7
France#	10.1	United Kingdom★	7.7
Canada#	9.9	Austria	7.5
Greece	9.9	Czech Republic	7.5
Netherlands	9.8	Finland	7.4
Belgium	9.6	**IRELAND % GDP**	**7.4**
Portugal	9.6	Turkey#	7.4
Sweden	9.4	Luxembourg	6.9
Australia★	9.3	Poland	6.5
Denmark	9.0	Mexico	6.2
IRELAND % GNP	**8.8**	Slovak Republic	5.9

Source: OECD (2005) and CSO (2005:3)
Note: ★ these figures are for 2002 ; # these figures are an OECD estimate for 2003

Primary care

Primary Care has been recognised as one of the cornerstones of the health system. This was given recognition by the publication of a strategy *Primary Care – A New Direction* (2001). Between 90 and 95 per cent of the population are treated by the primary care system. The model of a primary care team presented in the document must be viewed in its most flexible form so that it can respond to the local needs assessment. The principle underlining this model should be a social model of health. This is in keeping with the World Health Organisation's definition on health. Universal access is needed to ensure that a social model of health as outlined in the document becomes a reality. For the development of *Primary Care – A New Direction* there is a clear need for the allocation of more resources. This would need an increase in the percentage of the healthcare budget being allocated for primary care.

The General Medical Service (GMS) system was first introduced in 1972 and it gave a commitment that 40 per cent of the population would be covered by this system. By 1977 some 39 per cent of the population were eligible for medical cards on income grounds. By 2003 this figure had decreased to approximately 27 per cent of the population. For families just over the eligibility level a visit to the GP and a prescription could cost some 25 per cent of their total weekly income. The implications of this for many individuals and families are that they cannot afford to access appropriate care at the time needed. This reduction must be viewed in the light of failed government commitments contained in, for example, the Department of Health and Children's document *Quality and Fairness – A Health System for You* (2001). In that document Action 38 states that "income guidelines for the medical card will be increased". This Government commitment has not been honoured. Accessibility is one of the factors in ensuring equity. Among other things equity is about outcomes. To achieve parity in outcomes requires recognition of the social determinants of health. The World Health Organisation (WHO) makes the following observation:

> "Community participation is a programmatic necessity. Without the close involvement of the community, and its families and individuals in health promotion, disease prevention and care of the sick, there is little likelihood that health services will have a durable impact on the health of the community."

The importance of paying attention to local people's own perspective on their health and to understand the impact of the conditions of their lives on their health is essential to community development and to community orientated approaches to primary care. There needs to be a community development approach to ensure that the community can define its own health needs, work out how these needs can best be met collectively and decide on a course of action to achieve the outcomes in partnership with service providers. This will ensure greater control over the social, political, economic and environmental factors that determine the health status of any community.

The Government's own Primary Care Strategy acknowledges the need for "community involvement" as a key factor in addressing health issues and recognises the need for partnership in both the planning and evaluation of all services. Community participation is an "essential component of a more responsive and appropriate care system which is truly people-centred" (Chief Medical Officers Report). CORI Justice welcomes the funding announced as part of Budget 2006 which allocated €28.5m to developing primary care in 2007. Commitments contained in *Towards 2016* are also welcome Further developing this area of Healthcare must remain a key priority in the years to come.

Medical cards

The introduction of 30,000 new medical cards and 200,000 'doctor visit only' cards in Budget 2005 was a small step in the right direction. However, a great deal more needs to be done before the 1996 level of provision is regained. In 1996 1,252,384 people on low incomes were covered by full medical cards. After Budget 2005 1,069,934 people will be similarly covered. An additional 111,065 people over 70 years of age have medical cards but would not qualify on low income grounds. The eligibility threshold for 'doctor-only' cards was raised in mid-2006 to a level 50 per cent above the standard medical card thresholds. This is likely to see an increase in the take-up for doctor-only cards.

What is required is full medical card coverage for all people in Ireland who are vulnerable. Currently, the income threshold for accessing a medical card is far below the poverty line. This in effect creates an employment trap as parents are often afraid to take up a job and, consequently, lose their medical card even though their income remains low. The 'doctor visit only' cards are an improvement on the present situation only if they are upgraded to full medical cards in due course. At present they will create new problems as many people will now find themselves in the most unenviable situation of knowing what is wrong with them but not having the resources to purchase the medicines they need to be treated.

Mental health

The National Health Strategy entitled *Quality and Fairness* (2001) identifies mental health as an area to be developed. The Expert Group on Mental Health Policy invited written submissions and held consultation days with all relevant stakeholders. We welcome the publication of the report *Vision for Change - Report of the Expert Group on Mental Health Policy* and look forward to the inclusion of the findings in the development of future policy.

There is an urgent need to address this whole area in the light of the World Health Report (2001) *Mental Health: New Understanding, New Hope* where it is estimated that, in 1990, mental and neurological disorders accounted for 10 per cent of the total Disability-Adjusted Life Years (DALYs) lost due to all diseases and injuries. This was 12 per cent in 2000. By 2020, it is projected that these disorders will have increased to 15 per cent. This has serious implications for services in all countries in the coming years.

Areas of concern

There is a need for effective outreach and follow-up programmes for people who have been in-patients in institutions upon their discharge into the wider community. These should provide:

- Sheltered housing (high, medium and low supported housing)
- Monitoring of medication
- Retraining and rehabilitation
- Assistance with integration into community

A stronger emphasis on the development of community services for all levels of mental health is urgently required. People with an intellectual disability who require a mental health service frequently find they do not have a psychiatric service available to them. Furthermore, there is a lack of appropriate mental healthcare for all who need it, especially vulnerable groups including children, the homeless, prisoners, Travellers, asylum seekers and refugees and other minority or vulnerable groups. People in these and related categories have a right to a specialist service to provide for their often-complex needs. A great deal remains to be done before this right could be acknowledged as being recognised and honoured in the healthcare system.

When the social determinants of health (housing, income, childcare support, education etc.) are not met the connection between those who are

Healthcare

disadvantage and ill health is well documented. This is also true where mental health issues are concerned.

Suicide

A related problem to mental health is suicide. For many years the topic of suicide was one rarely discussed in Irish society and as a consequence the healthcare and policy implications of its existence were limited. Data show that the numbers of suicide in Ireland has climbed over the last decade. In 1993 327 suicides were recorded and by 2004, the latest year for which data is available, the number of suicides had increased to 457. Over time Ireland's suicide rate has risen from 6.3 suicides per 100,000 people in 1980 to 11.3 suicides per 100,000 people in 2004 (OECD, 2005 and CSO, 2005:69).

The age and sex distribution of suicides provides an important insight into what groups in Irish society are most prone to suicide. Table 3.37 provides a breakdown for 2002 when there were 478 suicides. It shows that suicide is predominantly a male phenomenon with almost 81 per cent of suicide victims being male. When assessed by age group the data suggest that young people, and in particular young males, are the groups most at risk. Young males aged between 15 and 34 account for over 40 per cent of all suicides in 2002. Among this age-group in the population, suicide is one of the largest killers.

Table 3.37: Suicides in Ireland in 2002, by age group and gender.			
Age group	Male	Female	Total
less than 4 years	-	-	-
5-14 years	1	2	3
15-24 years	90	15	105
25-34 years	106	21	127
35-44 years	62	15	77
45-54 years	55	19	74
55-64 years	41	11	52
65-74 years	24	4	28
75-84 years	6	4	10
85 years+	2	-	2
All ages	387	91	478

Source: CSO (2005:58)

The growth and scale of suicides in Ireland is a significant healthcare and societal problem. Of course the statistics in table 3.37 only tell one part of the story. Behind each of these victims are families and communities devastated by these tragedies. Likewise, behind each of the figures is a personal story which leads to victims taking their own life. CORI Justice believes that further attention and resources need to be given to addressing and researching Ireland's suicide problem. In that light, we welcome recent moves by the HSE to establish a national office of suicide prevention. Resources are also required for the support systems that must be provided for such vulnerable groups. As a society we need to become more aware of this issue and more aware of methods to prevent it.

Older people
Mental health issues affect all groups in society. A particularly vulnerable group are older people with dementia as they often fall between two stools. i.e. mental health versus general medical care. Therefore there needs to be a co-ordinated service provided for this group.

There is a need for adequate ancillary services to be put in place (psychotherapy, counselling etc.) in an effort to move away from the purely medical model of care. If a comprehensive mental health framework is to be established then the above areas of concern must addressed. It is important that this service be needs based and service-user-led and should be in keeping with international human rights standards and best practice in line with the principles in the World Health Organisation's 2001 annual report. The recommendations of the NESF report on care for older people should also be resourced and implemented.

Research and development in all areas of mental health is needed to ensure a quality service is delivered. Providing good mental health services should not be viewed as a cost but rather as an investment for the future. Public awareness needs to be raised to ensure a clearer understanding of mental illness so that the rights of those with mental illness are recognised.

Disability
We welcomed the government's approach in Budget 2004 to the funding of the Disability Services over a five-year period. This development will enable a more co-ordinated and strategic approach to the planning and delivery of

services. There are many areas within the Disability Sector which are in need of further development and core funding and these need to be supported.

The health system reform process

It is a recognised fact that there was a need to restructure the Health System as the last major re-organisation occurred some thirty years ago. The Reform Programme needs to be in keeping with the commitments and the vision of the National Health and Primary Care Strategy "a Health System that supports and empowers you, your family and community to achieve your full health potential. A Health System that is there when you need it, that is fair and that you can trust". The Reform Process has identified the HSE (Health Services Executive) as the Executive Arm of the Health Service. Within this process there is a clear democratic deficit which has not been addressed to date. There is a need to recognise that community participation and involvement is key in the planning, delivery and evaluation of services to ensure that the vision of the Strategy is achieved. In that context, the commitment in *Towards 2016* to establish a new mechanism for consultation with the Community and Voluntary pillar is very welcome.

Future healthcare costs

A number of the factors highlighted elsewhere in this review will have implications for the future of our healthcare system. The projected increases in population by the CSO imply that there will be many more people living in Ireland in 10-15 years time, many of whom will be of different nationalities. One clear implication of this will be additional demand for more healthcare and more healthcare facilities. In the context of our past mistakes it is important that Ireland begin to plan for this additional demand and begin to train staff and construct facilities to cope.

As we indicated in section 3.2, on taxation, the ageing of the population over the next four decades will be an additional challenge to the provision of healthcare. Again, planning and investment is required.

Poverty and health status

The link between poverty and ill health has been well established by international and national research. The poor get sick more often and die younger than those in the higher socio-economic groups. Poverty directly affects the incidence of ill health; it limits access to affordable healthcare and reduces the opportunity for those living in poverty to adopt healthy lifestyles. Healthcare exclusion is a major dimension of poverty and social exclusion.

In the Government's National Anti-Poverty Strategy it has committed itself to "reduce the gap in premature mortality between the lowest and highest socio-economic groups by at least 10 per cent for circulatory diseases, for cancers and for injuries and poisoning by 2007". This is a welcome target but achieving it will require targeted resources. Some work has begun in identifying gaps in the data available to assist in the monitoring of the targets and how awareness can be raised with all stakeholders.

Among the commitments on healthcare contained in the new social partnership agreement *Towards 2016* are the following:

On primary care
- Developing primary care services drawing on the Primary Care Strategy. This will entail ongoing investment to ensure integrated, accessible services for people within their own community with a target of 300 primary care teams by 2008, 400 by 2009 and 500 by 2011.
- Further developing, as a priority, out-of-hours GP services with a view ultimately to having those services available to the whole population;

On mental health
- Delivering one child and adolescent community mental health team (CMHT) per 100,000 of the population by 2008 and two CMHTs per 100,000 of the population by 2013.

On consultation with the Community and Voluntary Pillar
- The C & V Pillar will be consulted on the health aspects of this agreement and on their perspectives on the ongoing reform of the health system and the HSE. It is envisaged that this structured consultation will involve quarterly meetings between the C & V Pillar, the Department of Health and Children, the HSE and other Departments as relevant.

On suicide
- Implementation of the National Strategy for Action of Suicide Prevention, 2005-2014.

On palliative care
- Further developing palliative care throughout Ireland, with particular reference to the Baseline Study on the provision of Hospice/Specialist Palliative Care Services.

On accessibility
- Develop specific community and sectoral initiatives to encourage healthy eating and access to healthy food and physical activity among adults, with a particular focus on adults living in areas of disadvantage.

Policy Proposals on Healthcare

- Recognise the considerable health inequalities present within the Irish healthcare system and provide sufficient resources to tackle them.

- Give far greater priority to community care and restructure the healthcare budget accordingly. Overall, government should ensure that at least 35 per cent of the non-capital healthcare budget is allocated to community care. In the process care should be taken to ensure that the increased allocation does not go to the GMS or the drug subsidy scheme.

- Develop and implement targets on health status within the National Anti-Poverty Strategy.

- Increase the percentage of the health budget allocated to health promotion and education in partnership with all relevant stakeholders.

- Provide the childcare services with the additional resources necessary to effectively implement the Child Care Act.

- Develop nursing care of older people in their own community on the model of hospice care.

- Establish monitoring procedures that will ensure the criteria for admission to continuing care for the elderly in receipt of state subvention for such services are administered in a manner, which is flexible and sensitive to the needs of the population.

- Provide additional respite care for elderly people and people with disabilities.

- Implement the commitment in *Towards 2016* to provide 500 primary care teams by 2011.

- Promote equality of access and outcomes to services within the Irish healthcare system.

- Ensure that structural and systematic reform of the health system reflects the key principles of the Health Strategy aimed at achieving high performance, person centred, quality of care and value for money in the health service.

- Develop and resource mental health services, in particular by implementing the *Towards 2016* commitment and by recognising that this will play a key factor in the health status of the population.

- Facilitate and fund a campaign to give greater attention to the issue of suicide in Irish society. In particular, focus resources on educating young people.

- Raise the eligibility threshold for the medical card.

- Implement the recommendations of the CEOs report on 'The Medical Card Scheme'.

- Monitor and evaluate the National Health Reform Programme to ensure equity, people-centeredness, quality and accountability for all.

- Enhance the process of planning and investment so that the healthcare system can cope with the increases in population and the aging of the population projected to happen over the next few decades.

- Work toward universal access to primary care.

3.7 Education[40]

> **CORE POLICY OBJECTIVE: EDUCATION**
> To provide relevant education for all people throughout their lives, so that they can participate fully and meaningfully in developing themselves, their community and the wider society

Education can be an agent for social transformation. CORI Justice believes that education can be a powerful force in counteracting inequality and poverty while recognising that, in many ways, the present education system has quite the opposite effect. Recent studies confirm the persistence of social class inequalities which are seemingly ingrained in the system. Even in the context of increased participation and economic boom, the education system continues to mediate the vicious cycle of disadvantage and social exclusion between generations. While there are a number of programmes and initiatives to tackle educational disadvantage, many of these initiatives simply involve providing additional resources for disadvantaged schools. Our policy approach in this area is based on a belief that early school leaving is a particularly serious manifestation of wider inequality in education, which is embedded in and caused by structures in the system itself.

Expenditure on Education

Ireland's expenditure on education, as a share of both GDP and GNP, increased over the period from 1995 to 2002. Compared to other OECD countries, Ireland's expenditure on education equalled 5.3 per cent of GDP (6.0 per cent of GNP) in 2002. This compares to an OECD average of 6.1 per cent in 2002.[41] The details are in table 3.38.

---

[40] CORI Justice acknowledges the input of CORI Education in preparing this section.
[41] The most recent EU-25 figures suggest a European average for 2001 of 5.1 per cent of GDP.

Table 3.38: OECD expenditure on education as a % of GDP, 1995 & 2002

Country	1995	2002	Country	1995	2002
Iceland	7.4	n/a	Portugal	5.8	5.3
United States	7.2	7.2	Austria	5.7	6.1
Denmark	7.1	6.3	Hungary	5.6	5.5
Korea	7.1	n/a	**IRELAND % GNP**	**5.4**	**6.0**
Norway	6.9	7.1	Germany	5.3	5.4
Sweden	6.9	6.2	Netherlands	5.1	4.9
New Zealand	6.8	n/a	Italy	4.9	n/a
Belgium	6.4	n/a	Spain	4.9	5.4
Mexico	6.3	5.6	Japan	4.7	4.7
Switzerland	6.2	n/a	Czech Republic	4.4	5.4
Poland	6.1	n/a	**IRELAND % GDP**	**4.4**	**5.3**
France	6.1	6.3	Slovak Republic	4.2	4.7
Finland	6.0	6.3	Greece	4.1	3.2
Australia	6.0	5.7	Turkey	3.8	2.3
United Kingdom	5.9	5.5	Canada	n/a	7.0

Source: OECD (2005:30 and Education Statistics Database) and CSO (2005:153).

Using Irish data we can analyse public non-capital education expenditure per student in Ireland over the 1998-2003 period. It shows that there have been real increases at all three education levels. Table 3.39 shows that these increases have been 42.6 per cent in first level, 38.1 per cent for second level students and a more modest 5.2 per cent at third level. These trends are partly explained by the trend in student numbers. Between 1993/94 and 2002/03 the numbers of students in Ireland decreased by 12.3 per cent at first level and by 7.7 per cent at second level. However, over the same period, the number of third level students increased by around 50 per cent (CSO: 2005:45). It should also be noted, however, that Ireland's young population as a proportion of total population is large by EU standards and, consequently, a higher than average spend on education might be expected.

Developing a Fairer Ireland

Table 3.39: Ireland's non-capital public expenditure on education 1998-2003, expressed at 1995 prices				
Year	First level	Second level	Third level	Total expenditure €m
1998	2,053	3,066	5,661	2,748.6
1999	2,144	3,145	5,849	2,836.6
2000	2,220	3,301	5,544	2,896.1
2001	2,393	3,623	5,920	3,123.1
2002	2,673	3,934	6,047	3,391.6
2003	2,928	4,234	5,958	3,623.9

Source: CSO, 2005:45.

When viewed in an international context, the most striking feature of investment in education in Ireland, relative to other OECD countries, is our comparative under-investment in primary education relative to international norms (not to mention our almost complete neglect of public funding for early childhood education). Irish investment in third-level education, which is widely regarded as inadequate, is approximately at the OECD average. However, our public investment at second level and, in particular, at primary level is substantially below the OECD average and is among the lowest of all OECD countries when the expenditure is standardised as a percentage of GDP[42].

The importance of investment in education is widely acknowledged. For individuals, the rewards from education are clear. Those with higher qualifications earn, on average, far more over their lifetime than those with lower qualifications. However, for those who do not assign great value to improving education levels in themselves, a recent study published by Statistics Canada shows a clear and significant association between pro-active investment in education in any period and a country's subsequent growth and labour productivity (Coulombe et al, 2004). This study, which looked at adult literacy skills of people in 14 countries who entered the labour force in the period 1960 to 1995 identified a clear and significant association between investments in human capital in each period an a country's subsequent growth and labour productivity. Specifically, a rise of 1 per cent in literacy scores relative to the international average is associated with an eventual 2.5 per cent relative rise in labour productivity and a 1.5 per cent rise in GDP per head.

---

[42] See OECD (2004: 216).

Educational disadvantage: literacy, early school leaving, and unemployment

The issue of literacy has been contentious in recent times. Some years ago an OECD survey found that a quarter of the Ireland's adult population performed at the very lowest level of literacy. More recently, the OECD found that Ireland's fifteen-year olds have the fifth best literacy rates out of 27 OECD countries. The reality appears to be that the literacy levels among Ireland's school-going population is much higher than among the population generally. But this hides a more telling fact.

A 2004 report prepared for the Department of Education examined literacy standards in disadvantaged primary schools. This report by the Education Research Centre at St Patrick's College, Drumcondra found that more than 30 per cent of children in those schools suffer from severe literacy problems. Furthermore, it concluded that only a small minority of 12-year olds from these areas take a positive view of their own reading achievement (Eivers et al, 2004). A similar report by the same authors published in late 2005 reaffirmed these findings and also noted that in some poorer areas up to 50 per cent of pupils have literacy difficulties (Eivers et al, 2005).

Both reports highlight the two-tier pattern of Ireland's educational outcomes. Many do very well. But it is also clear that a great many are being left behind. As identified in a 2003 report by the Department of Education and Science, "the worrying tendency for educational disadvantage to cluster in specific schools/areas and to be reproduced across generations raises serious equity issues and highlights the need for effective educational interventions"(2003:7).

Published statistics on school-completion rates help to clarify the overall situation. Table 3.40 shows that more than 86 per cent of persons aged 20-24 in 2004 had completed second level education or higher. This figure decreased for older age groups down to 40.2 per cent of persons aged 55-64. Women of all ages in Ireland are more likely than men to have completed at least upper secondary education. However, the other side of this situation is that almost 14 per cent of those aged 20-24 have not completed second level education. This has serious implications for the future. Early school-leavers, for example, are far more likely to be unemployed (see table 3.41) and, ironically, are less likely to participate in further and continuing education and training.

Developing a Fairer Ireland

Table 3.40: Proportion of Ireland's population aged 20-64 with, at least, upper secondary education, 2004

Age group	Persons	Males	Females
20-24	86.2	83.1	89.4
25-34	80.1	76.6	83.6
35-44	68.9	65.3	72.6
45-54	54.4	51.8	57.1
55-64	40.2	38.8	41.6

Source: CSO, 2005:49

Socio-economic background is closely linked to early school leaving, with a high proportion of early school leavers coming from semi-skilled and unskilled manual backgrounds. Employment opportunities and earning power are linked generally to level of education attained. People with no qualifications are more likely to be unemployed and if employed are less likely to get promotion. Even in the context of increased participation and economic boom, the education system continues to mediate the transmission of disadvantage and social exclusion between generations.

Table 3.41: Early school leavers by labour force status and sex, 2004 (%)

Labour force status	Persons	Males	Females
In employment	33.0	24.8	8.2
Unemployed	9.2	6.1	3.1
Unemployment rate of early school leavers	21.8	19.7	27.4

Source: CSO, 2005:49

The unemployment rate for persons in Ireland aged 18-24 with, at most, lower second level education (and not in further education or training) was 21.8 per cent in 2004. This contrasts with an unemployment rate for all persons in the same age group of 7.9 per cent in 2004. If this situation is not rectified there will be a substantial group of people permanently excluded from the benefits of Irish society in the decades ahead. According to the CSO the proportion of persons aged 18-24 who left school with, at most, lower second level education in Ireland, was 12.9 per cent in 2004 (CSO 2005:49).

Retention to upper second level is currently roughly 83 per cent through schooling (therefore there are some 17 per cent of early school leavers). The CSO figures quoted above suggest that further education and training opportunities are bringing a further 4-5 per cent of the cohort up to a level of or equivalent to 'at least upper second level' by the time they reach 20 to 24 years old, which is encouraging but serves to illustrate the scale of the problem that remains.

Government has invested heavily in trying to secure a school-based solution to this problem. It may well be time to try alternative approaches aimed at ensuring that people in this cohort attain the skills required to progress in the future.

Key issues: Early childhood education and lifelong learning

In the past the issue of early childhood education has not had a high profile within Ireland's policy development processes. This situation is changing in recent years with the growing realisation of the importance of early education for children. Nowadays the benefits of early education are acknowledged as studies show that it helps to determine how long children stay in school and how quickly they will find employment after leaving school. This requires a greater emphasis and additional resources within the Irish education system if the high non-completion rates outlined above are to be addressed successfully.

One of the basic principles that should underpin lifelong learning is the democratic one of equality of status as people. Access in adult life to desirable employment and choices is closely linked to level of educational attainment. Equal political rights cannot exist where some are socially excluded and educationally disadvantaged. The lifelong opportunities of those who are educationally disadvantaged are in sharp contrast to the opportunities for meaningful participation of those who have completed a second or third level education. Therefore, lifelong education should be seen as a basic need. In this context, second chance education and continuing education are vitally important and require ongoing support.

Access to educational opportunity and meaningful participation in the system together with access to successful outcomes is central to the democratic delivery of education. This is not to suggest a one-menu approach for everyone; rather it posits a variety of channels leading to parity of esteem. Equally it does not suppose a similar timeframe for the completion of a particular phase of education for everyone. Such a vision mirrors the stated policy of the White Paper on Adult Education and Lifelong Learning (2000), which sought to develop a strategic and targeted response which is co-ordinated within itself and with other sectors. This strategy would also enable progressive movement between education/home/work as a prelude to the development of mass provision. However, certain priority groups would be targeted initially and in the future in the interests of social inclusion and economic efficiency.

Within this context it is important to emphasise that people should not be seen as failures if they choose not to progress to third level on successful completion of second level education. This is a fundamentally different issue to the failure to complete second level education. It should be acknowledged that it is perfectly acceptable for young people to take alternative pathways to adult self-reliance and participation in the labour market. However, this suggests that people who take this approach should have access (for education and training purposes) to the resources that would otherwise have been spent on them by the state if they had gone into full-time third level education directly from school. An initiative along these lines is required. The exchequer invests 2.5 times more money per capita in the education of those who complete three years of third-level education than it does for those who leave school before the completion of post-primary education. In the light of the barriers to educational participation of the more disadvantaged people, especially at post-school level, a basic educational allowance for full-time and part-time education should be available to each person between the ages of eighteen and forty who does not proceed to third level from school. Eligible parties seeking re-entry to second chance education at all levels could draw upon such monies on demand for educational courses. Such an initiative could serve to increase access over an extended period for people currently disadvantaged by financial constraints and third-level structures. In this way, a culture of access to continuing lifelong educational opportunity might become the norm. The right to equality of educational opportunity has long been accepted both by individuals and by the state. This concept of equality of educational opportunity implies equality of educational funding by the state for its citizens. Such funding is, in fact, an issue of rights, of equality, of social inclusion and of citizenship. It should be additional to funding for educationally disadvantaged, socially excluded and marginalised people. Also, it should be additional to funding provided to respond to educational disadvantage through the home and the community.

There is widespread acknowledgement of the fact that both early childhood and adult education are critically importance for Ireland's future. They require substantial creative development and additional resourcing in the years ahead.

Additional resources required

The Irish public has consistently favoured a situation where government meets all the costs of first and second level education. There is also strong support for government supporting additional educational spending on children with learning difficulties. Likewise there is strong support for government providing the necessary support to ensure there are alternative pathways for those who fail to complete second level education. Government should act on this support and provide the required financing on condition that it can be shown that value is being got for the money invested.

There is also a need, which may not be accepted by all of the Irish public, that funding should be secured for early childhood education and for lifelong education. It is clear that substantial additional funding will be required to support these areas in the years ahead. This additional funding would be a good investment for the future and a good use of the resources being made available as a result of the economic growth of recent years.

Education is widely recognised as crucial to the achievement of our national objectives of economic competitiveness, social inclusion and active citizenship. However, the overall levels of public funding for education in Ireland are out-of-step with our social and economic aspirations. This under-funding is most severe in the early years of education and in the area of second-chance education - the very areas that are most vital in terms of the promotion of greater equity and fairness.

Among the commitments on education contained in the new social partnership agreement *Towards 2016* are the following:

- The number of children per classroom teacher at primary level will be reduced to 28:1 in 2006/2007 and 27:1 in 2007/2008 and will continue to improve as a result, in particular, of the application of resources in respect of special needs pupils.
- There will be an extra 550 language support teachers by 2009 and the current limit of two additional teachers per school will be reformed.
- An additional 100 posts in total will be provided for the National Educational Welfare Board and the National Educational Psychological Service by 2009.
- Development of special educational needs services in the framework of the Education for Persons with Special Educational Needs Act.
- Adult Literacy will be prioritised. Having regard to the implementation plan of the national adult literacy advisory group published by NALA and the role of the VECs, consideration will be given to the appropriate support structures in this area.
- The general national literacy service delivered by the Vocational Education Committees will be significantly increased by the provision of an extra 7,000 places by 2009.
- A Family Literacy project will also be put in place under the DEIS initiative.
- A targeted fund will be put in place to alleviate the fees in public institutions for part-time courses at third level by employees who have not previously pursued a third level qualification.
- Providing additional supports for students from disadvantaged backgrounds, students with disabilities and mature students to enhance access to further and higher education.
- Formulating a National Skills Strategy which will put in place a strategic framework for the implementation of a skills and training strategy into medium term.

Policy Proposals on Education

Make access to ongoing educational opportunity the norm. To this end:

- Ensure quality childcare and pre-school education, preferably in a community setting.

- Ensure meaningful participation in education up to the end of second level.

- Prioritise access to education for those outside the formal school system by the provision of user friendly structures and systems which enable success.

- Increase the resoursces available for adult education.

- Establish and resource an appropriate structure to underpin delivery of adult literacy services.

- Provide the necessary resources to ensure relevant education is available to migrants, Travellers, people with a disability and other vulnerable groups.

- Ensure right to self-realisation and equal participation in society by
  - widening access to back-to-education initiatives
  - improved student support for the educationally disadvantaged
  - the provision of a basic educational investment allowance
  - work-linked and full-time literacy initiatives.

3.8 Migration and Interculturalism

> **CORE POLICY OBJECTIVE:**
> **MIGRATION & INTERCULTURALISM**
> To ensure that all people can contribute to developing the underpinning values and meaning of society and can have their own cultures respected in this process, and to ensure that Ireland is open to welcoming people from different cultures and traditions in a way that is consistent with our history, our obligations as world citizens and with our current economic status

Respect for and recognition of their culture represents an important right of people within every society. Culture is defined by UNESCO as "the whole complex of distinctive spiritual, material, intellectual and emotional features that characterise a society or social group. It includes not only the arts and letters, but also modes of life, the fundamental rights of the human being, value systems, traditions and beliefs".

Many people in Ireland today – particularly Travellers, immigrants, refugees and asylum-seekers among others – do not experience a society where the majority population respects their cultures. In fact, as we become more racially diverse, it becomes evident that Irish society is capable of being as racist as any of our European neighbours who live in mixed racial societies. Government policy should encourage the creation of a multi-racial, inclusive society.[43]

Worldwide the number of refugees forced to flee from their own countries in order to escape war, persecution and abuses of human rights is declining. The United Nations High Commission for Refugees (UNHCR) cared for about 27 million people in the mid 1990s. This was the highest level of demand for its services ever. In 2004, the latest year for which comprehensive statistics are available, the overall number of people in need of help declined to 17.56 million (2005:14).

---

[43] Issues concerning migrant workers are dealt with in section 3.3.

Irish people have a long tradition of solidarity with peoples facing oppression within their own countries, but that tradition is not reflected in our policies towards refugees and asylum-seekers. Ireland should use its position in international forums to highlight the causes of the displacement of peoples. In particular Ireland should use these forums to challenge the production, sale and free access to arms and the implements of torture.

Table 3.42 shows how the number of asylum-seekers in Ireland increased between 1992 and 2005. Since then the numbers declined reaching 7,900 in 2003, 4,766 in 2004 and 4,323 in 2005. The main countries of origin of the 2005 applicants were Somalia (11.5 per cent), Nigeria (10.4 per cent), DR Congo (9.4 per cent), Zimbabwe (7.7 per cent), Romania (5.2 per cent) and Cameroon (5.2 per cent). Of the 5,682 applications for asylum who received a decision on their initial application during 2005 455 (8 per cent) were recognised as refugees. During the year there were 393 deportations and 208 transfer orders (to other EU Member States). An additional 336 persons who would otherwise have been removed from the State returned home voluntarily. To facilitate these deportations there were 6 charter plane flights during the year, 4 to Nigeria and 2 to Romania and Moldova.

Table 3.42: Applications for asylum in Ireland, 1992-2005

Year	Number	Year	Number
1992	39	1999	7,724
1993	91	2000	10,938
1994	362	2001	10,325
1995	424	2002	11,634
1996	1,179	2003	7,900
1997	3,883	2004	4,766
1998	4,626	2005	4,323

Source: Office of the Refugee Applications Commissioner Monthly Statistics (Feb, 2006).

The figures for asylum-seekers in 2002 represented the highest number of applications on record. In response the government amended the 1996 Refugee Act and created two independent statutory offices for the processing of asylum applications: the Refugee Applications Commissioner and the Refugee Appeals Tribunal. Additional staff and resources have been allocated to speed up the processing times for asylum applications; however the delay for some applicants is still considerable. The Refugee Legal Service has also been given more staff and resources.

While asylum-seekers are assigned initial accommodation in Dublin, most are subsequently allocated accommodation at locations outside Dublin, pending completion of the asylum-seeking process. The Reception and Integration Agency (RIA) was established to perform this task. By the end of 2005 there were sixty four direct-provision accommodation centres spread across twenty four counties in Ireland accommodating approximately 3,500 people. The November 2005 statistical report of the RIA indicates that these were from 95 different countries, including 7 per cent of these recipients who are Irish born children. The policy of "direct provision" employed in these centres results in these asylum-seekers receiving accommodation and board, together with €19.10 per week per adult and €9.60 per child.[44] CORI Justice believes that this is an inadequate amount of money and should be increased immediately to at least €50 a week for an adult and €25 for a child.

Asylum-seekers are not the only foreigners who have come to Ireland in substantial numbers over recent years. Many Irish companies have also recruited staff from abroad and recent economic assessments of the performance of the Irish economy have identified the input of these workers as of importance to the achievement of our recent growth. In the last year thousands of people from the 10 new EU states have been among those who have come to work in Ireland. Without this increased number of skilled workers from outside Ireland, our economy would not have sustained its high growth rates. In that context CORI Justice welcomes the *National Action Plan Against Racism: Planning for Diversity* (2005). Its implementation will play an important role in forming a cohesive, comprehensive policy to ensure that the new diversity of cultures and ethnic minorities within Ireland is respected as an enrichment of our society. This approach needs to integrate immigration policy with refugee and asylum-seeking policy. It also requires a recognition and acceptance of the importance of equality of respect and esteem in this area.

---

[44] These sums have not even been adjusted from inflation over the last number of years.

Ireland has both a moral and legal responsibility towards refugees and asylum-seekers. As a nation whose own people have themselves experienced the pain of emigration in the past, we should be to the forefront in implementing our obligations under the 1951 UN Geneva Convention relating to the Status of Refugees. The non-governmental organisations (NGOs), already playing a major role in addressing the many issues that arise in this context, should be resourced to continue and develop their work.

Asylum-seekers are among the most excluded and marginalised in Ireland, yet they are treated in a very unjust way by Irish society. The single most important issue in this context is the fact that they are denied access to employment. Consequently we propose that asylum-seekers who currently are not entitled to take up employment should be allowed to do so with immediate effect. Removing this restriction would have a major impact on reducing their poverty and exclusion. In this context we regret the ending of the FAS asylum seekers project with no replacement giving entry to the labour market.

Despite the fact that we have focused principally on the problems facing refugees and asylum-seekers, it is important to recognise that other groups, such as Travellers, also require their culture to be respected as of right.[45] Implementation of the recommendations of the Task Force on the Travelling People has progressed with the establishment of the structures recommended by the report. However, it is now very important to ensure that the recommendations of the report are fully implemented.

---

[45] We have addressed other issues concerning Travellers in a number of other sections of this review.

> **Among the commitments on migration and interculturalism contained in the new social partnership agreement *Towards 2016* are the following:**
>
> - A new framework will be finalised to address the broader issue of integration policy.
> - The Government will develop a comprehensive strategy for all legally resident immigrants following consultation with relevant stakeholders including the social partners which will build on and be linked with progress already achieved in the areas of social inclusion and anti-racism.
> - Appropriate co-ordinating mechanisms to implement such a strategy will be developed and the scope for a role for civil society organisations will also be explored.
> - A range of strategies will also be pursued as part of the National Action Plan Against Racism.
> - Racism in the workplace will be proactively addressed in the context of the Anti Racist Workplace Week in keeping with best international practice in this area.
> - See also section 3.3 which outlines the commitments on migrant workers.

Policy Proposals on Migration and Interculturalism

- **Develop and resource a cultural policy which involves a dynamic conserving of traditions and beliefs, while also developing a vision for the future which incorporates hope, confidence and involvement.**

- **Recognise the right to work of all asylum-seekers whose application for asylum is at least six-months old (and who are not entitled to take up employment).**

- **Provide fully resourced language training for asylum-seekers.**

- **Give special consideration to gender and cultural sensitivities of asylum-seekers.**

- Ensure proper protection and care of minors, while safeguarding their rights and the integrity of the asylum process.

- Give to asylum-seekers on 'direct provision' who are more than six months awaiting the processing of their application, equal rights to accommodation and other social welfare provision, in line with the rights enjoyed by other Irish residents.

- Immediately increase the weekly allowance allocated to asylum-seekers on 'direct provision' to at least €50 a week for an adult and €25 for a child.

- Increase the winter and summer clothing allowance for asylum seekers to €200 paid twice a year (€400 in total).

- Put sufficient resources into the Refugee Legal Service to ensure that the service is available on a daily basis at all centres where asylum-seekers are located.

- Fully implement the *National Action Plan Against Racism: Planning for Diversity*

- Ensure that the asylum process treats all nationalities and ethnic groups with fairness and equality.

- Ensure that the carrier sanctions will not further jeopardise the health and safety of people wishing to seek asylum in Ireland.

- Increase financial supports for voluntary organisations which care for refugees and asylum-seekers.

- Provide special labour-market integration measures that address the special needs of refugees.

- Provide access to free full-time education, certified courses and public health education for asylum-seekers.

- Provide that the trans-national Protocol on Organised Crime is adopted in full into Irish law, especially the section and definitions relating to the trafficking of women and children for sexual exploitation.

- Recognise that prostitution is violence in its own right.

- Government should argue that the production and sale of arms and instruments of torture be curtailed and should lobby for the elimination of child soldiers.

3.9 Participation

> **CORE POLICY OBJECTIVE: PARTICIPATION**
> To ensure that all people have a genuine voice in shaping the decisions that affect them and to ensure that all people can contribute to the development of society

The changing nature of democracy has raised many questions for policy-makers and others concerned about the issue of participation. Decisions often appear to be made without any real involvement of the many affected by the decisions' outcomes. Voter apathy is widespread and as chart 3.9 shows turnout has been falling at every election. The 2002 turnout, at 63 per cent, is the lowest voter turnout recorded for a general election and considerably below the average turnout achieved by other European countries at 72 per cent (CSO, 2003:36).[46]

Chart 3.9: Percentage turnout in Irish General Elections, 1973-2002.

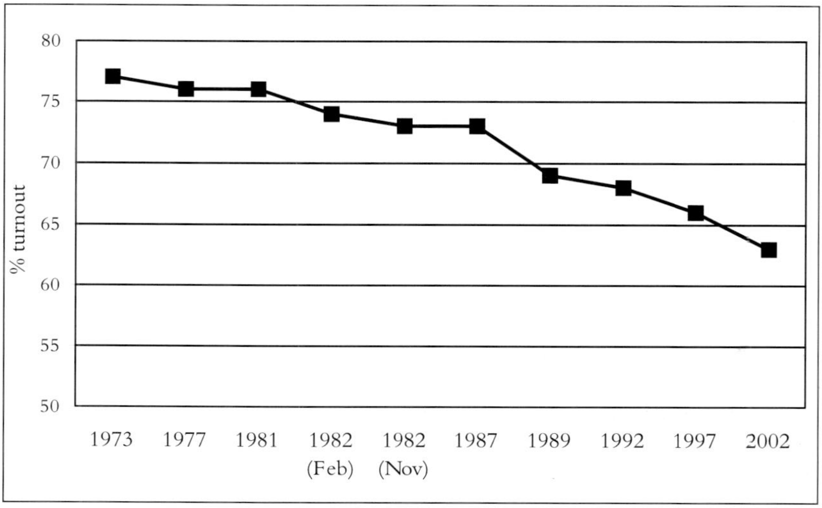

Source: CSO (2003:36)

---

[46] The 2006 review of the accuracy of the electoral register may suggest that these official figures are somewhat understated.

An insight into how people regard the electoral process was revealed by the results of a CSO quarterly national household survey module on voter participation and abstention issued in April 2003. It examined participation in the May 2002 general election and found high levels of non-participation among young people. Just over 40 per cent of those aged 18-19 and only 53 per cent of those aged 20-24 years voted in the 2002 election. This contrasts with participation figures of well above 80 per cent for older voters aged over 65.

The survey also examined why people did not participate in the election and found that 20.4 per cent of non-voters said they had "no interest"; 10.6 per cent were "disillusioned" with politics; 3.7 per cent felt that their "vote would make no difference"; and 2.9 per cent were "lacking understanding/ information" and so did not vote. Other reasons for not voting were: *not registered* (21.8 per cent); *away* (15.6 per cent); *too busy* (8.5 per cent); *illness/disability* (6 per cent); *no polling card* (3.8 per cent); and *lack of transport* (1.3 per cent). Across the age groups young people were more likely to be *not registered* and *not interested* (CSO, 2003:5). Finally the survey also found that it is those people who participate least in other areas of society (employment, voluntary groups, organisations) that do not participate in elections.

The implications of these findings suggest that many people, especially young people, have little confidence in the political process. They are disillusioned because the political process fails to involve them in any real way, while also failing to address many of their core concerns. Transparency and accountability are demanded but rarely delivered. A new approach is clearly needed to address this issue.

An agreed forum and structure for argument on issues on which people disagree is a need that is becoming more obvious as political and mass communication systems develop. Most people are not involved in the processes that produce plans and decisions which affect their lives. They know that they are being presented with a *fait accompli*. More critically, they realise that they and their families will be forced to live with the consequences of the decisions taken. A lack of structures and systems to involve people in the decision-making process result in the exclusion and alienation of large sections of society. It causes and maintains inequality.

Any exclusion of people from debate on the issues that affect them is suspect. Such exclusion leaves those responsible for it open to charges concerning the arbitrary use of power. Some of the decision-making structures of our society and of our world allow people to be represented in the decision-making process. However, almost all of these structures fail to provide genuine participation for most people affected by their decisions. Our society and the world in which we live need decision-making structures that enable participation.

Real participation by all is essential if society is to develop and, in practice, to maintain principles guaranteeing satisfaction of basic needs, respect for others as equals, economic equality, and religious, social, sexual and ethnic equality. Modern means of communication and information make it relatively easy to involve people in dialogue and decision-making. It is a question of political will – will the groups who have the power share it with others?

Some progress has been made in recent years. At local government level the development of Community Forums, Strategic Policy Committees and County/City Development Boards are moves in this direction. So also are developments in social partnership at national level, most importantly the creation in 1996 of the fourth pillar of social partners to represent the community and voluntary sector. This was a welcome initiative and much appreciated by the groups concerned. However, much remains to be done in this area and deeper issues need to be addressed.

A Task Force on Active Citizenship was established in 2006. It has been asked to recommend measures which could become part of public policy to facilitate and encourage a greater degree of engagement by citizens in all aspects of life and the growth and development of voluntary organisations as part of a strong civic culture. The new national agreement contains a commitment that, arising from the work of this Task Force, consideration will be given to the development of appropriate measures and indicators of social capital, and to future approaches in relation to citizenship education and voter participation.

A forum for dialogue on civil society issues
An issue that is contributing to disillusionment with the political process concerns the range of civil society issues that are of major concern to large numbers of people. These are issues that many people feel are not being addressed adequately; insofar as a discussion or debate does take place, they feel that they are not allowed to participate in any real way.

Social partnership, as we have pointed out, is one process aimed at improving the participation of various sectors in Ireland. However, it is in danger of being overloaded. The various social partners in the four pillars of social partnership –employers, trades unions, farmers and the community and voluntary pillar – represent large segments of Irish society. However, they do not represent, nor do they claim to represent, all of Irish society. In fact the case is made, with some legitimacy, that none of these social partners represents their own entire sector.

The development of a new forum within which a civil society debate could be conducted on an ongoing basis would be a welcome addition to the political landscape in Ireland. Such a forum could make a major contribution to improving participation by a wide range of groups in Irish society.

Establishment of such a forum would ensure that civil society issues were not being loaded onto the already extensive work of social partnership in the socio-economic area. It would also be complementary to the work of the National Economic and Social Forum and the National Economic and Social Council, both of which already have extensive agendas.

CORI Justice proposes that government authorise and resource an initiative to identify how a civil society debate could be developed and maintained in an ongoing way in Ireland, and to examine how it might connect to the growing debate at European level around civil society issues.

There are many issues such a forum could address. One such issue that comes to mind, given recent developments in Ireland, is the issue of citizenship, its rights, responsibilities, possibilities and limitations in the twenty-first century. Another topical issue is the shape of the social model Ireland wishes to develop in the decades ahead. Do we follow a European model or an American one? Or do we want to create an alternative – and, if so, what shape would it have and how could it be delivered? The issues a civil society forum could address are many and varied. Ireland would benefit immensely from having such a forum.[47]

---

[47] For a further discussion of this issue see Healy and Reynolds (2003:191-197).

Impact on the democratic process

Would a civil society forum and a new social contract against exclusion take from the democratic process? Democracy means "rule by the people". This implies that people participate in shaping the decisions that affect them most closely. What we have, in practice, is a highly centralised government in which we are "represented" by professional politicians. The more powerful a political party becomes, the more distant it seems to become from the electorate. Party policies on a range of major issues are often difficult to discern. Backbenchers have little control over, or influence on, government ministers, opposition spokespersons or shadow cabinets. Even within the cabinet some ministers seem to be able to ignore their cabinet colleagues.

The democratic process has certainly benefited from the participation of various sectors in other arenas such as social partnership. It would also benefit from taking up the proposals to develop a new social contract against exclusion and a new forum for dialogue on civil society issues.

The decline in participation is exacerbated by the primacy given to the market by so many analysts, commentators, policy-makers and politicians. Many people feel that their views or comments are ignored or patronised, while the views of those who see the market as solving most if not all of society's problems are treated with the greatest respect.

Markets have a major role to play. But it needs to be honestly acknowledged that markets produce very mixed results when left to their own devices. In terms of many policy goals, they are extremely limited. Consequently other mechanisms are required to ensure that some re-balancing, at least, is achieved. The mechanisms proposed here are simply two that would be positive in improving participation in a twenty-first century society.

Among the commitments on participation contained in the new social partnership agreement *Towards 2016* are the following:

On active citizenship and voter participation
The agreement states:
- Future policy will take account of the work of the Task Force on Active Citizenship which has been asked to recommend measures which could be taken as part of public policy to facilitate and encourage a greater degree of engagement by citizens as part of a strong civic culture.
- Arising from the work of the Task Force, consideration will also be given to the development of appropriate measures and indicators of social capital, and to future approaches in relation to citizenship education and voter participation.

On funding the Community and Voluntary Sector
The agreement states that:
- The Government is committed to appropriately resourcing the sector into the future as part of this agreement. The Government remains committed to reviewing the funding mechanisms for the C & V sector, to identify areas of overlap or gaps. The Government also remains committed to the White Paper principle of providing multi-annual statutory funding.
- The Sector's important role in service provision will continue to be funded appropriately where it is delivering services on behalf of the State. This will be reflected through an increase in funding as part of the ongoing expansion in overall expenditure on service delivery in the course of the agreement.
- As well as this, the Government will provide the following specific additional supports to the sector:
  - The Community Services Programme + €30m by 2009.
  - Increased funding of €5m per annum to support volunteering.
  - Increased funding of €10m per annum to support the C & V Sector, including the costs arising from contributing to evidence based policy making, over and above normal activities and programmes.

On volunteering

The agreement states that:
- The Government will continue to develop policies on volunteering arising from the package of measures initiated in February 2005. A key principle underlying the Government's approach is that volunteering finds meaning and expression at a local level and that supports and funding should seek, as far as possible, to recognise this reality.
- The Government remains committed to further developing policy to support volunteering, drawing on the experience in delivering these measures and informed by the recommendations of the Task Force on Active Citizenship.

Policy Proposals on Participation

- **Establish and resource a forum for dialogue on civil society issues. This initiative should identify how a civil society debate could be developed and maintained in an ongoing way in Ireland and should examine how it might connect to the growing debate at European level around civil society issues.**

- **Ensure that Strategic Policy Committees (SPC) and Community Forums strengthen participation at local level.**

- **Resource the ongoing participation of the community and voluntary sector in both the CDB and SPC structures.**

- **Resource the participation in national social partnership of social partners within the community and voluntary sector as outlined in** *Towards 2016*.

- **Develop a mechanism to provide ongoing funding for NGOs working across traditional sectors and boundaries.**

- **Implement the recommendations contained in the Report on the National Committee on Volunteering entitled** *Tipping the Balance*.

- **Ensure that there is real and effective monitoring of policy implementation. Involve a wide range of perspectives in this** process, thus ensuring inclusion of the experience of those currently excluded.

- Resource voter education programmes for young people and socially excluded people.

- Government should use the findings of the 2003 CSO study on voter participation to identify methods by which electoral participation can be increased and to target those groups who are not participating.

- To assist the achievement of higher voter turnout, a commitment should be given to holding all elections and referenda on Saturdays, with polls open from 7am and 10pm.

3.10 Sustainability

> **CORE POLICY OBJECTIVE: SUSTAINABILITY**
> To ensure that all development is socially, economically and environmentally sustainable

Sustainability is a crucial issue for people and the environment in the 21st century. Too often, however, sustainability is defined in terms that are too narrow. Sustainability is about a range of issues including environmental, economic and social. To complement the economic and social analysis elsewhere in this publication, this section focuses first on promoting sustainable development before then turning to assess environmental issues.

(a) Promoting Sustainable Development

The search for a humane, sustainable model of development has gained momentum in recent times. After years of people believing that markets and market forces would produce a better life for everyone, major problems and unintended side-effects have raised questions and doubts. There is a growing awareness that sustainability must be a constant factor in all development, whether social, economic or environmental.

This fact was reiterated by Kofi Annan, the Secretary-General of the United Nations, at the opening of the World Summit on Sustainable Development in Johannesburg, South Africa (September 2002). There he stated that the aim of the conference was

> to bring home the uncomfortable truth that the model of development that has prevailed for so long has been fruitful for the few, but flawed for the many.

And he further added that

> the world today, facing the twin challenges of poverty and pollution, needs to usher in a season of transformation and stewardship – a season in which we make a long overdue investment in a secure future.

Sustainable development has been defined in many different ways. Perhaps the best-known definition is that contained in *Our Common Future* (World Commission on Environment and Development, 1987:43):

> development that meets the needs of the present without compromising the ability of future generations to meet their own needs.

It is crucial that the issues of environmental, economic and social sustainability be firmly at the core of the decision making process.

The need for shadow national accounts

Conventional economic models of development or progress fail to meet the needs of millions and millions of people on this planet today. This failure is evident even within better-off countries such as Ireland. These conventional economic models also compromise the ability of future generations to meet their needs. As this becomes more evident, there is a growing demand worldwide to find new models that will conserve the planet and its resources and empower people to meet their own needs and the needs of others.

Central to any model of development which has sustainability at its core must be a realisation of the need to move away from money-measured growth, as the principal economic target and measure of success, towards sustainability in terms of real-life social, environmental and economic variables. Already within mainstream decision-making, this realisation has begun to have some impact. This can be seen, for example, in the growing awareness that environmental taxation should be recognised as a key policy instrument in dealing with environmental concerns. Public concern in the area of genetically modified (GM) food stands as another example. In the context of income and social welfare policy, the increasing recognition of the benefits of a basic income are a further example of the same search for policies that will be sustainable into the future (see section 3.1(d)). The growing demand for the recognition of unpaid work being done in society stands as yet another example. As can be seen from these examples, however, there is a long way to go before Ireland or the EU can claim to have placed sustainability at the centre of their development models.

A central initiative in this context should be the development of "satellite" or "shadow" national accounts. Our present national accounts miss fundamentals such as environmental sustainability. Their emphasis is on GNP/GDP as scorecards of wealth and progress. These measures, which came into widespread use during World War II, more or less ignore the environment, and completely ignore unpaid work. Only money transactions are tracked. Ironically, while environmental depletion is ignored, the environmental costs of dealing with the effects of economic growth, such as cleaning up pollution or coping with the felling of rain forests, are added to, rather than subtracted from, GNP/GDP. New scorecards are needed.

Already a number of alternative scorecards exist, such as the United Nations' Human Development Index (HDI), former World Bank economist Herman Daly's Index of Sustainable Economic Welfare (ISEW) and Hazel Henderson's Country Futures Index (CFI). A 2002 study by Wackernagel et al presented the first systematic attempt to calculate how human demands on the environment are matched by its capacity to cope. It found that we currently use 120 per cent of what the earth can provide sustainably each year.

In the environmental context it is crucial that dominant economic models are challenged on (among other things) their assumptions that nature's capital (clean air, water and environment) are essentially free and inexhaustible; that scarce resources can always be substituted; and that the planet can continue absorbing human and industrial wastes which most economists tend to downplay as externalities.

Some governments have picked up on these issues, especially in the environmental area. They have begun to develop "satellite" or "shadow" national accounts, which include items not traditionally measured. *Towards 2016* commits the Irish government to examine the application of satellite accounts in the area of environmental sustainability. CORI Justice welcomes this development.

Principles to underpin sustainable development

Principles to underpin sustainable development have been suggested in a report for the European Commission prepared by James Robertson in May 1997. Entitled *The New Economics of Sustainable Development*, the report argues that these principles would include the following:

- systematic empowerment of people (as opposed to making and keeping them dependent) as the basis for people-centred development

- systematic conservation of resources and environment as the basis for environmentally sustainable development
- evolution from a "wealth of nations" model of economic life to a "one-world" economic system
- evolution from today's international economy to an ecologically sustainable, decentralising, multi-level one-world economic system
- restoration of political and ethical factors to a central place in economic life and thought
- respect for qualitative values, not just quantitative values
- respect for feminine values, not just masculine ones.

At first glance, these might not appear to be the concrete guidelines that policy-makers so often seek. Yet they are principles that are relevant to every area of economic life. They also apply to every level of life, ranging from personal and household to global issues. They impact on lifestyle choices and organisational goals. If these principles were applied to every area, level and feature of economic life they would provide a comprehensive checklist for a systematic policy review.

It is also important that any programme for sustainable development should take a realistic view of human nature, recognising that people are altruistic and selfish, co-operative and competitive. Consequently it is important to develop the economic system to reward activities that are socially and environmentally benign (and not the reverse, as at present). This in turn would make it easier for people and organisations to make choices that are socially and environmentally responsible. A simple example is the tax on plastic bags. It shows how quickly people can and will change. In just one week some retail outlets were reporting a 90 per cent reduction in the use of plastic bags. Overall the Department of Environment and Local Government estimated that usage had declined by 95 per cent (approximately one billion bags) in 2002. Since then there has been some increase in usage. This highlights the need to sustain the effort required in relevant areas to ensure the need for sustainable development is recognised and pursued.

Any programme for sustainable development has implications for public spending. In addressing this issue it needs to be understood that public expenditure programmes and taxes provide a framework which helps to shape market prices, rewards some kinds of activities and penalises others. Within this framework there are other areas which are not supported by public expenditure or are not taxed. This framework should be developed to encourage economic efficiency and enterprise, social equity and environmental sustainability. Systematic reviews should be carried out and published on the sustainability effects of all public subsidies and other relevant public expenditure and tax differentials. Such reviews could then lead to the elimination of subsidies that favour unsustainable development. Systematic reviews should also be carried out and published on the possibilities for re-orienting public spending programmes, with the aim of preventing and reducing social and environmental problems.

EU sustainability strategy

Sustainable development is a fundamental objective of the EU. Its importance is reflected in the EU Treaty and taken up in the proposed Constitution, which challenges the EU "to work for the sustainable development of Europe based on balanced economic growth and price stability, a highly competitive social market economy, aiming at full employment and social progress, and a high level of protection and improvement of the quality of the environment".

In early 2005 the EU Commission set about reviewing its Sustainable Development Strategy which contains the following components. First, it set out a broad vision of what is sustainable. The strategy's basic message was that, ultimately, the economic, social and environmental dimensions of sustainability must go hand–in–hand and mutually reinforce one another: Second the strategy, sought to improve the way the EU and member state Governments make policies. Third, the strategy addressed a limited number of trends that are clearly not sustainable, such as the issues of climate change, threats to public health, poverty and social exclusion, ageing societies, natural resources, and land use and transport. Finally, a global dimension focused on some of the international goals and objectives identified in the EU contribution to the World Summit on Sustainable Development.[48]

Monitoring sustainable development: some problems

Two recent studies have highlighted the lack of socio-economic and environmental data in Ireland required to assess trends in sustainable development. A chapter by Carrie in the Feasta review (2005) focused on the lack of long-run socio-economic data on issues such as education participation, crime and healthcare. Another paper by Scott (ESRI, 2005) outlined the empirical and methodological gaps which continue to impede the incorporation of sustainable development issues into public policy making and assessment.

---

[48] The full report is available on our website www.cori.ie/justice

(b) Environmental Issues
Our environment is a priceless asset. Its protection is of major importance not just to current times but also to the generations that will follow us. However, the environment is regularly taken for granted; it is often mistreated and excessively exploited. The following are environmental issues that are of concern at this time.

(i) Waste disposal and recycling
Reports by the Environmental Protection Agency (EPA, 2001 & 2004) and the CSO (2005) present insightful overviews of the state of Ireland's environment. Unfortunately the statistics they contain are far from good news. On waste they show that household's and commercial waste has increased by over 11 per cent in volume between 2001 and 2003. Currently Ireland produces almost 2.8 million tonnes of waste each year.

Table 3.43: EU Municipal waste collected and landfilled in kg's per person, 2003

Country	Collected	Landfilled	% landfilled
Netherlands	599	16	2.7
Denmark	675	34	5.0
Belgium	446	56	12.6
Sweden	471	64	13.6
Germany	638	127	19.9
Luxembourg	658	149	22.6
Austria	610	183	30.0
France	561	214	38.1
Spain	609	361	59.3
Italy	523	323	61.8
Finland	450	285	63.3
Estonia	418	274	65.6
Latvia	362	248	68.5
Slovakia	319	222	69.6
Ireland	**643**	**461**	**71.7**
Czech Republic	280	201	71.8
Portugal	452	338	74.8
United Kingdom	610	460	75.4
Slovenia	451	344	76.3
Hungary	463	390	84.2
Cyprus	724	653	90.2
Greece	428	393	91.8
Poland	260	251	96.5
Lithuania	263	263	100.0
Malta	549	549	100.0
EU 25	**534**	**261**	**48.9**

Source: CSO, 2005:67

The management of this waste remains a problem. In 2003 28.3 per cent of our waste is recycled, while the remaining 71.7 per cent was going to landfill (EPA, 2002: 25-27). At this rate of growth it is of no surprise that our landfill capacity will soon be reached. While our recycling rates are steadily increasing, and this is long overdue, they still remain very low. Furthermore Ireland has agreed to an EU obligation to recycle 50 per cent of our waste by 2006. If we are to meet this target this year then immediate and major changes are required.

A welcome innovation during 2005 was the production for the first time of a performance league table of local authority waste management by the Local Government Management Services Board (LGMSB). Table 3.44 sets out the results for the 5 best and 5 worst local authorities. Galway city council topped the league table by recycling 49.5 per cent of their waste. This compares to the very poor performances recorded for Mayo (2.5 per cent of waste recycled) and Cork City (2.55 per cent of waste recycled). Ireland has quite a distance to travel if we are to reach the EU recycling target, and even further to match some Scandinavian countries and the US city of San Francisco who have set targets to eliminate all landfill by 2020.

Table 3.44: League table of local authority waste management – best and worst

	% Landfill	% Recycling
5 Best		
Galway city	43	49.5
Waterford city	53	47
Longford	56	44
Cork county	63	37
Clare	63	37
5 Worst		
Mayo	97.5	2.5
Cork city	97.45	2.55
Kildare	92.8	7.2
Cavan	80	8
Roscommon	90	10

Source: LGMSB, 2005: 142-145

Both industry and households need to change their attitude towards recycling. Industry in all sectors will have to use fewer material inputs and emit fewer wastes. To facilitate this, government needs to move towards making material inputs and waste disposal far more expensive, and towards making increasing demands for the durability, repairability and recyclability of goods. The recent highly successful Waste Electrical & Electronic Equipment directive marks considerable progress in the right direction. Further EU directives which will force car companies to take back their products at the end of their useful lives are also a necessary step in this direction. However, more needs to be done. Households will also have to change their behaviour. Sustained campaigns to encourage and facilitate recycling are necessary, while incentives to recycle rather than landfill need to be put in place.

(ii) Greenhouse gases and air pollution

Over time, Ireland's air has become more and more polluted. Between 1990 and 2004 the Environment Protection Agency (EPA) reported that Ireland's greenhouse gas emissions grew by 23.1 per cent. Total combined Irish emissions of the three main greenhouse gases regarded as having global warming potential amounted to 68.46m tonnes of CO_2 equivalent in 2004, up from 55.6m tonnes in 1990 (EPA, 2006). Despite two successive years of reductions – 2002 and 2003 – the 2004 figures mark a marginal increase of 0.15 per cent. A breakdown of the 2004 pollution figures show that agriculture is the single largest contributor to the overall emissions, at 29 per cent of the total, followed by energy (generation and oil refining) at just over 23 per cent and transport at 18.4 per cent.

The most recent figures indicate that the current levels of emissions now exceed the limits agreed under the Kyoto protocol. The Irish government and the European Commission agreed a target of an 8 per cent reduction in European CO_2 emissions on their 1990 level by 2012. Within this agreement, Ireland agreed to limit its increase of CO_2 emissions to 13 per cent between 1990 and 2012. CORI Justice welcomes Ireland's ongoing commitment to this protocol, despite the refusal of some countries, including the USA, to ratify its implementation. However, these emissions are a major cause of climate change, and it is in all our interests to ensure that the limits agreed in the Kyoto protocol are met. Major changes are required if we are to reduce our emissions towards this target. Central to this is the need for full implementation of the National Climate Change Strategy. However, the decision in 2004 to allow Ireland's 100 largest industrial companies to maintain their current levels of emissions does not assist in progressing towards these aims.

The National Climate Change Strategy proposed to impose (unspecified) taxes on oil, gas, coal and other fossil fuels to be phased in from 2002. However, in spite of a few budgetary innovations, there has been limited progress in implementing this proposal. Furthermore we believe that all the proposals outlined in the National Climate Change Strategy should be acted upon with increased urgency, because the issue of climate change is critical. These proposals include

- the conversion of the coal-fired power station at Moneypoint,
- reductions in methane emissions from agriculture by reducing the national herd,
- the provision of an option for industry to participate in "emissions trading" and voluntary agreements,
- changes in the grant scheme for new-house purchases to promote energy efficiency,
- changes in vehicle registration tax to favour more fuel-efficient transport.

A further significant issue relating to air quality is the deterioration recorded in urban air quality by the EPA (2002:31; 2004:24-37). Its report directly ties this phenomenon to the 60 per cent increase in the number of vehicles on the road in Ireland during the 1990s. In Ireland, the growth in traffic on our roads has been one of the more visible elements of our recent economic growth. However, the lack of an extensive public transport system has resulted in enormous growth in car usage. Irish cars now cover more kilometres each year than the cars of any EU country – 24,400 km for Ireland versus 16,300 for the UK, 8,200 for Spain and an EU-average of 12,800km.[49] Given that we are a small island, these figures are amazing and underscore a significant problem. Consequently, the EPA state that "road traffic is now the primary threat to urban air quality in Ireland" (2004:25). Therefore the EPA concludes that "there is a need to bring about a shift in transport use from the private vehicle to public transport in particular. An integrated, efficient public transport system is urgently required. Infrastructure to divert heavy vehicles away from city and town centres is also essential" (2002: viii).

(iii) Climate change: international and Irish implications

A 2003 report prepared for the EPA by the Department of Geography at the NUI, Maynooth, presented an assessment of the magnitude and likely impacts of climate change in Ireland over the course of the current century. Entitled *Climate Change: scenarios & impacts for Ireland* (Sweeney et al, 2003) the report first sets out the international implications of climate change as found by the Third Assessment Report of the Intergovernmental Panel on Climate Change (IPCC, 2001). Produced by several hundred leading scientists in various areas of climate studies this report is considered the most authoritative assessment of

---

[49] These figures are outlined in our July 2005 *Policy Briefing* on Sustainability.

global climate change to date and its principal conclusions include the following:

- Global average temperature has increased by 0.6 ± 0.2°C since 1860 with accelerated warming apparent in the latter decades of the 20th century. A further increase of 1.5–6.0°C from 1990 to 2100 is projected, depending on how emissions of greenhouse gases increase over the period.
- The 20th century was the warmest of the last millennium in the Northern Hemisphere, with the 1990s being the warmest decade and 1998 the warmest year. Warming has been more pronounced at night than during the day.
- Reductions in the extent of snow cover of 10 per cent have occurred in the past 40 years, with a widespread retreat also of mountain glaciers outside the Polar Regions. Sea-ice thickness in the Arctic has declined by about 40 per cent during late summer/early autumn, though no comparable reduction has taken place in winter. In the Antarctic, no similar trends have been observed. One of the most serious impacts on global sea level could result from a catastrophic failure of grounded ice in West Antarctica. This is, however, considered unlikely over the coming century.
- Global sea level has risen by 0.1–0.2 m over the past century, an order of magnitude larger than the average rate over the past three millennia. A rise of approximately 0.5 m is considered likely during the period 1990–2100.
- Precipitation has increased over the land masses of the temperate regions by 0.5–1.0 per cent per decade.
- Frequencies of more intense rainfall events appear to be increasing also in the Northern Hemisphere. In contrast, decreases in rainfall over the tropics have been observed, though this trend has weakened in recent years. More frequent warm-phase El Niño events are occurring in the Pacific Basin. Precipitation increases are projected, particularly for winter, for middle and high latitudes in the Northern Hemisphere and for Antarctica.

The specific findings of the report for Irish climate change suggest that:

- Current mean January temperatures in Ireland are predicted to increase by 1.5°C by mid-century with a further increase of 0.5–1.0°C by 2075.

- By 2055, the extreme south and south-west coasts will have a mean January temperature of 7.5–8.0°C. By then, winter conditions in Northern Ireland and in the north Midlands will be similar to those currently experienced along the south coast.
- Since temperature is a primary meteorological parameter, secondary parameters such as frost frequency and growing season length and thermal efficiency can be expected to undergo considerable changes over this time interval.
- July mean temperatures will increase by 2.5°C by 2055 and a further increase of 1.0°C by 2075 can be expected. Mean maximum July temperatures in the order of 22.5°C will prevail generally with areas in the central Midlands experiencing mean maxima of up to 24.5°C.
- Overall increases of 11 per cent in precipitation are predicted for the winter months of December–February. The greatest increases are suggested for the north-west, where increases of approximately 20 per cent are suggested by mid-century. Little change is indicated for the east coast and in the eastern part of the Central Plain.
- Marked decreases in rainfall during the summer and early autumn months across eastern and central Ireland are predicted. Nationally, these are of the order of 25 per cent with decreases of over 40 per cent in some parts of the east.

(Sweeney at al, 2003)

Finally the report proceeds to identify the specific implications of these findings for agriculture, water resources, forestry, sea-levels and eco-systems in Ireland. Overall the reports findings suggest that there are considerable implications of climate change for Ireland and it underscores the necessity to adequately address this issue in the immediate future.

(iv) River water quality

Slowly the quality of Ireland's surface waters is improving. The EPA (2002:vii, 2004:39-57) has recorded an improvement in water quality for the first time since surveys began. However, it is of concern that over 30 per cent of river channels are still classified as polluted to some extent. The EPA cites agriculture as the main source of this problem and claims it is responsible for the largest inputs of phosphorus and nitrates to waters and suggests that there is a need to promote better farmyard management, to reduce the over-application of fertilisers and to expand the system of nutrient management planning. It is of significance that the improvements achieved came in areas that have had intensive management programmes implemented in the past three to five years. Their success underscores a need to further expand these programmes.

Groundwater quality is also of concern. Bacteriological contamination rates remain high. In 2001 the EPA found that groundwater in counties Carlow, Cork, Kerry, Louth and Waterford were polluted or susceptible to pollution by nitrates from agricultural sources (2002: vii).

Given the extent of pollution it is clear that existing legislation to protect our inland watercourses from pollution is neither adequate nor effective. This will have to be improved if these problems are to be adequately addressed and if the EU water framework directive is to be fully implemented.

(v) Genetic engineering (GE)

Genetic engineering refers to a set of technologies that artificially move genes across species boundaries to produce new organisms. The techniques involve the manipulation of genetic material and other biologically important chemicals. The resultant organisms have new combinations of genes, and therefore new combinations of traits that are not found in nature and, indeed, are not possible through normal breeding techniques. Proponents of the technology, mainly multinational agribusiness corporations, argue that genetically engineered crops are necessary to feed a growing world population.

By contrast, opponents of agricultural biotechnology claim that genetic engineering will not feed the hungry people in our world. Only sustainable agriculture and equitable social and economic policies at local and global level can effectively tackle malnutrition, hunger and poverty.

Critics of genetic engineering maintain that it is hazardous to human health and the environment, and that it will undermine biodiversity. Given the risks to human health and the environment, and the complex ethical, economic and social issues involved, we believe that a moratorium should be placed on the deliberate release of genetically engineered organisms.

(vi) Environmental taxation and poor households

The extent of Ireland's pollution problem is clear from the studies outlined above. Furthermore, it is also clear that if we are to seriously address this problem then new environmental taxes are necessary. In particular, the commitments in the National Climate Change Strategy to introduce some form of carbon taxation must be met. In that context, the decision in mid-2004 to abandon the commitment to introduce these taxes in Budget 2005 was regrettable.

These taxes should focus on increasing the excise duty on all fuels. One of the objections presented to the introduction of these taxes is that they would substantially damage the economic position of poor households. Indeed research by the ESRI has confirmed this. However, a series of research papers by the ESRI has shown that it is possible to insulate poorer households from the effects of these new taxes (see Bergin et al 2002:25; Scott and Eakins, 2002). Scott and Eakins have suggested that a proportion of the revenue generated by new carbon taxes should be transferred to the Department of Social and Family Affairs and used by them to increase payments (in particular fuel allowances) given to poor households. Such an increase in these payments would therefore compensate poorer households for the effect of the new tax and consequently ensure that Ireland's poorest households do not suffer.

CORI Justice believes that environmental taxes should be introduced and that the compensation mechanism proposed for poorer households should be simultaneously implemented. In these circumstances the argument that these carbon taxes would substantially damage the economic position of poor household cannot be justified or used as an objection to the policy.

Sustainability

> Among the commitments on sustainability contained in the new social partnership agreement *Towards 2016* are the following:
>
> **On satellite national accounts**
> - Examination of the feasibility of the application of satellite accounts in the area of environmental sustainability (2007).
>
> **On strategies to be published and implemented**
> - Publication of Consultation Paper on the Review of the Climate Change Strategy by June 2006.
> - Publication of an updated Climate Change Strategy by end 2006.
> - Investment in environmental infrastructure, especially in relation to waste water treatment, rural water supplies and recycling facilities.
> - Implementation of further EU and domestic environmental legislation, taking due account of regulatory impact assessments.
> - Additional impetus to enforcement measures.
> - Utilisation of economic instruments as circumstances require.
> - Assessment of the appropriateness of the range of environmental policy responses.
> - A renewed National Sustainable Development Strategy to be published by mid-2007.
>
> **On COMHAR**
> Strengthening the role of COMHAR in the ongoing process of policy development in the context of environmental sustainability.

Policy Proposals on Sustainability

- **Sustainability-proof all public policy initiatives and provision.**

- **Develop 'satellite' national accounts that include the value of all unpaid work and the costs of all environmental damage and resource consumption.**

- **Restructure the tax system in favour of environmentally benign development and high levels of employment and useful work.**

- **Terminate subsidies and other public-expenditure programmes that encourage unsustainable development.**

- Introduce public purchasing policies that encourage contractors to adopt sustainable practices.

- Develop more self-reliant local economies.

- Develop and implement a programme of accounting, auditing and reporting procedures to establish the sustainability performance of businesses and other organisations.

- Introduce demand-reduction policies in areas such as energy and transport, and tackle the implications of such reduction.

- Fully introduce the National Climate Change Strategy, including the introduction of new taxes on oil, gas, coal and other fossil fuels.

On waste
- Develop a policy for resource management, and achieve waste-reduction targets by implementing relevant sections of the Waste Management Act, 1996.

- Provide households with incentives to recycle rather than landfill their waste.

- Allocate substantial resources to the development of recycling facilities.

- Meet the EU target of recycling 50 per cent of household waste by 2006.

- Put in place appropriate mechanisms to address the issue of the cost of waste disposal for those on low incomes.

On pollution
- Put mechanisms in place to ensure that the Kyoto targets of an 8 per cent CO_2 reduction by 2012, agreed by the Irish Government and the European Commission, are met.

- Continue to pursue strategies to achieve the reduction of activities at Sellafield.

On water
- Review the Water Pollution Acts and increase the level of statutory fines with a scale from €6,348 to a maximum of €150,000.

- Implement a nutrient-management plan on a national basis as one effective measure to protect against agricultural pollution of watercourses.

- Review water-pricing policies and introduce a water charge, which is equitable and is levied on high-consumption water-users, to ensure conservation of our water supplies.

On genetic engineering (GE)
- Introduce a five-year moratorium on the deliberate release of GE organisms. During this period
    - promote public debate about the desirability of genetic engineering and fund independent research into the health and environmental risks associated with GE,
    - insist that there be segregation at the source of all genetically engineered organisms,
    - reform the way the Environmental Protection Agency (EPA) deals with applications to release GE organisms into the environment.

- Facilitate a full-scale public debate on both the benefits and risks involved in GE, based on comprehensive scientific knowledge and a full airing of the economic, social and ethical implications of biotechnology.

- Fund appropriate research in parallel with such a consultative process.

- Introduce legislation that protects the consumer and the environment, rather than the interests of multi-national corporations.

On the Environmental Protection Agency (EPA)
- **Review the interface between the EPA and An Bord Pleanála to ensure that the environmental impact and sustainability of industrial developments are thoroughly assessed in an integrated way.**

3.11 Rural Development

> **CORE POLICY OBJECTIVE:
> RURAL DEVELOPMENT**
> To secure the existence of substantial numbers of viable communities in all parts of rural Ireland where every person would have meaningful work, adequate income and access to social services, and where infrastructures needed for sustainable development would be in place

Rural Ireland continues to change dramatically. The 1996 census recorded that 46 per cent of Ireland's population lived in small villages and in the open countryside. This figure declined to 40.4 per cent (1,582,921 people) according to the results of census 2002 (CSO, 2003:53). A factor in that reduction is the sustained decline in farm numbers. Agriculture, forestry and fishing now account for only 5.8 per cent (115,300 people) of the overall labour force (QNHS, February 2006:8). At present those in farming comprise one-quarter of the rural labour force, and are a minority of the rural population. Furthermore fewer farm children seek a future in farming.

This section addresses a variety of issues relevant to rural Ireland and to its long-term development. A central and persistent theme is that rural Ireland is currently in transition from an agricultural to a rural development agenda.

Farm incomes

Among its many characteristics rural Ireland has high dependency levels, increasing out-migration and many small farmers living on very low incomes. Only a minority of farmers are at present generating an adequate income from farming and, even on these farms, income lags considerably behind the national average. An important annual insight into the income of Irish farmers is provided by Teagasc in their National Farm Survey.

The latest survey, reporting income for 2004 and published in 2005, collected data from a representative sample of 1,194 farm households nationwide. Its results indicate that the average family farm income (FFI) (excluding off-farm income) was €15,557 in 2004, an increase of 5.4 per cent from the figure of €14,765 recorded in 2003. Amongst full-time farmers the average income was

€30,650 while among part-time farmers FFI equalled an average of €6,407 (Teagasc, 2005:4-5).

The survey also noted great variations in income depending on the size of the farm and the type of farming pursued. Farmers involved in cattle rearing had an average income of €7,286 while those in dairying had an average from farm income of €34,421. Farmers in tillage and sheep farming had average incomes of €24,012 and €10,966 respectively. An examination of the distribution of farm income reveals that 10 per cent of farmers had an income exceeding €40,000 while 40 per cent of farmers had a 'from farm' income of less than €6,500. Teagasc found that 86 per cent of average family farm incomes in 2004 were comprised of direct payments or subsidies (2005:2).

Off-farm income is extremely important among farm families, especially in the western region. The National Farm Survey indicates that on 52 per cent of farms the farmer and/or spouse had an off-farm job and that overall on over 78 per cent of farms the farmer and/or spouse had some source of off farm income be it from employment, pension or social assistance. The results of the Household Budget Survey (CSO, 2002:89) further indicate that only 43.8 per cent of farm-household income came from farming. This situation is likely to intensify in the coming years, thus increasing the importance of additional off-farm income being available if rural poverty and social exclusion are to be addressed.

Table 3.45 presents an interesting analysis from the National Farm Survey which assesses the real value of FFI over the period 1995-2004. It reveals a marked decline in farm income in real terms. Measuring in real terms removes the effect of inflation (price increases) and essentially represents the buying power of agricultural earnings. The same method is used to assess national income figures such as GDP/GNP whose growth rates are also recorded in real terms. Therefore the table shows that the buying power of family farm incomes in 2004 is equivalent to €11,822 in 1995 terms. More simply, FFI is 17 per cent lower in real terms in 2004 than it was in 1995.

Table 3.45: Family Farm Income in cash and buying power terms, 1995-2004			
	Cash value	Buying power (1995 terms)	% change in buying power since 1995
1995	€14,236	€14,236	0.0
1996	€13,866	€13,634	-4.2
1997	€14,042	€13,607	-4.4
1998	€13,442	€12,717	-10.7
1999	€11,088	€10,324	-27.5
2000	€13,499	€11,903	-16.4
2001	€15,840	€13,322	-6.4
2002	€14,917	€11,991	-15.8
2003	€14,765	€11,467	-19.5
2004	€15,557	€11,822	-17.0

Source: Calculated from Teagasc (2005:5)

The decline of agriculture

A key element in the evolution of any developed world society/economy has been a noticeable shift away from dependence on agriculture. That natural phase of economic development has been slowly occurring in Ireland over the past few decades. As Ireland develops, the size of its agricultural sector and the numbers employed in that sector continue to decline. The focus of that sector has also shifted from being producer driven to being consumer driven.

Two insights into the future shape of Irish agriculture have been provided over recent years. The first published in November 2004 is that of the Government appointed Agri-vision 2015 committee. In their report the committee concluded that:

> "The number of Irish farms is expected to decline by 23%, from 136,000 in 2002 to 105,000 in 2015. By 2015, one third of the farm population will be classed as economically viable, another third of farms will be economically unviable with the operators working primarily off the farm and the remaining third will be transitional farms characterised by adverse demographic features, such as having an elderly farm operator and/or lacking an identified heir.
>
> Of the third of farms that will remain economically viable by 2015,

75% will be farmed on a part-time basis, with the on-farm enterprise providing a return sufficient to remunerate the labour and capital used. Of those farms that are operated on a full time basis, and which are economically viable, the vast majority are expected to be dairy enterprises" (2004:37).

During the last year a second major report set out the expected future direction of rural Ireland up to 2025. Funded by the Department of Agriculture and Food and a number of other Government bodies it was compiled by some of the leading experts on rural Ireland at Teagasc, NUI Maynooth and University College Dublin. The report is entitled *Rural Ireland 2025: Foresight Perspectives* (2005) and it indicates a further sizeable change in the shape of rural Ireland over the next two decades.

Looking to the future of agriculture the expert group concluded that "it is unlikely that by 2025 that Ireland will have appreciably more than 10,000 full-time commercial farmers, comprising predominantly dairy farmers, a thousand or so commercial dry stock farmers, with roughly a similar number of sheep producers and a few hundred pig enterprises" (2005:10). This conclusion was reached on the basis of there being no unexpected major policy changes (nationally and at EU level) between now and 2025. The report also projected that the remainder of farmers (a further 30,000 full time equivalent jobs implying approximately 60,000 part-time workers) will be working part-time (2005: 10-11). Overall the report projected that many of these part-time farmers as well as a number of the projected 10,000 full-time commercial farmers will be involved in producing green energy fuels, such as wood biomass, as an important component of their farming enterprises.

Rural development
As agriculture declines there is need for a more comprehensive set of rural development policies. Long-term strategies to address the failures of current policies on critical issues such as infrastructure development, the national spatial imbalance, local access to public services, public transport and local involvement in core decision-making are urgently required. Recognition that current development policies are largely city-led is also necessary and this approach needs to be re-balanced.

The 1999 White Paper on rural development was welcome in that it provided an outline of a vision to guide rural development policy as we have advocated for over a decade. In so doing, it accepted that the statement of a vision is a necessary first step in moving forward. CORI Justice also welcomed the identification by the White Paper of much that is already being done under a variety of headings in all areas of rural development. However, there was little in terms of new and imaginative policies proposed for the implementation of the vision, and no commitment of new and measurable resources to attain the objectives set out.

The context of current rural development policy, however, is one where

- EU policies in particular ensure that production is concentrated among larger producers, and where regulations, policies and financing all militate against small local producers,
- direct payments favour large volume, higher income farmers,
- there is a dominance of the agri-model of rural development,
- there is very limited progress in achieving balanced regional development. Areas such as the western region have been losing ground to the rest of the country in recent years.

It is clear that the scale of the infrastructure and investment deficit in rural Ireland is unacceptably high. In recent years there have been major spatial changes and there are major spatial disparities as well. The failure of current policies in so many crucial areas requires that long-term strategies be developed to address these failures.

The *Rural Ireland 2025* report succinctly summarises the objectives for rural development contained within government policies. It states that "government policy for rural areas aims to build a rural economy where enterprises will be commercially competitive without damaging the environment. It seeks to have vibrant sustainable communities, with a quality of life that will make them attractive places in which to work and live. It aspires for equity of opportunity between rural and urban areas, and for balanced development between the regions. These initiatives are underpinned by EU policy for rural areas, which subscribes to the attainment of 'living countrysides' within the context of balanced regional development across the Union" (2005: *v*).

To successfully move rural Ireland closer to these policy goals the *Rural Ireland 2025* report suggests a series of rural development strategies which should be immediately pursued (2005:*v-vi*). These include taking action on:

- The National Spatial Strategy, implemented in conjunction with successive regionally focused national plans, would result in a more balanced distribution of population and economic activity throughout the country.
- Rapid communications and supporting infrastructure would provide greater accessibility throughout all parts of the country.
- The rural economy could sustain more competitive enterprises through the development of additional entrepreneurial and management skills, as well as further innovation in products, business organisation and marketing.
- The agri-food industry could have more developed business, technological and innovative capacities, with a widely differentiated product portfolio selling in international markets.
- Forestry and the ocean economy could be sizeable suppliers to the energy sector and provide valued public goods.
- Maintenance of an attractive rural environment could be secured by compliance with EU Directives and payment for public goods, as well as better management systems nationally.
- A knowledge-based bio-economy could emerge built on the comparative advantage of Ireland's natural resources.
- 'Old economy' enterprises could be upgraded, and manufacturing small and medium sized enterprises (SMEs) could increase their contribution to the rural economy.
- Tourism could be a vibrant sector of the rural economy, providing knowledge-based environmental goods and services, focused on Ireland's unique landscapes and culture.
- Clusters of internationally oriented companies could exploit the full potential of natural resources in food, the marine, forestry and tourism.

Over recent years there have been many welcome initiatives aimed at rural development. For example, Budget 2004 made provision for a new Rural Social Scheme (RSS) "to help improve rural services in a more efficient way and at the same time to provide an income for small farmers with a working week compatible with farming" (Department of Finance Budget 2004: A16). In 2006 it is estimated that there would be 2,500 places on this scheme which is receiving government funding of €36.32m for the year and which is run by the Department of Community, Rural and Gaeltacht Affairs. The decision to further increase funding to this scheme in all recent Budgets is welcome. Similarly, the CLAR programme is going a little way towards addressing these problems.

However, far more is required if rural Ireland is to be viable in the twenty-first century. As of now, Ireland has a long way to go before it could be said that it is meeting the requirement of balanced sustainable regional development.

Policies that prioritise people

CORI Justice believes that it is clear that the future development of rural Ireland now depends on moving to adopt policies that prioritise people. In that regard a recent proposal from Irish Rural Link (IRL) deserves consideration. The proposal, made as part of its submission to the Department of Community, Rural & Gaeltacht Affairs and the Department of Agriculture & Food on preparation for Ireland's Rural Development Strategy Plan 2007-2013, suggested a template for the percentage division of future funds towards rural Ireland over that period. Table 3.46 presents IRL proposed distribution of future government funding divided across four 'axis' or areas of policy focus.

Table 3.46: Irish Rural Link proposed % distribution of future Government rural funding

Axis	Policy area	% allocation
Axis 1	Improving competitiveness of the agricultural and forestry sector	20%
Axis 2	Improving the environment and the countryside	30%
Axis 3	The quality of life in rural areas and the diversification of the rural economy	40%
Axis 4	Leader programmes	10%

Source: Irish Rural Link (2005:13)

The thrust of IRL's proposal is that greater focus now be given to axis 3 and axis 4. CORI Justice strongly welcomes this proposal and encourages government to adopt it.

Other rural development issues

As the rural development agenda moves to the fore, there are a series of other issues that deserve consideration. To complete this section of our review, we highlight a number of these issues.

Rural transport

The availability of transport as a means of access to both public and private services is a major issue for people living in rural areas and one that we have addressed earlier (see section 3.4). Progress towards this goal is not helped by the continued centralisation of public services. When rural schools closed there was no account taken of the transport costs of bringing children to the larger schools. Despite the recent transport initiatives, many communities in rural areas are not well served. Some of the difficulties faced by these initiatives have stemmed from the lack of regulation and the constant debate on who should have the profit orientated routes. There are also considerable problems associated with providing a service in areas where the population is scattered over a large area. CORI Justice believes that we are now reaching a crucial juncture that requires key decisions in ensuring that rural communities receive the public transport infrastructure and services that it is entitled to. It is also worth mentioning that it is vital that a quality public transport infrastructure is put in place if the government is to meet its commitment to sustainable balanced regional development. In that regard we support the call from Irish Rural Link to establish a National Rural Transport Office (NTRO), perhaps within the Department of Transport, which links and supports the development of rural transport within the overall auspices of developing public transport in general.

Accessibility of transport for older people is vital in terms of accessing health and other services, social networks and remaining active. *Towards 2016* supports the further development of the Rural Transport Initiative (RTI) which is making a very important contribution to supporting community-based living. The agreement states that in developing proposals for the roll-out of the RTI from 2007, particular attention will be paid to the transport needs of rural communities that do not currently have access to public transport, having particular regard to the special transport needs of older people with disabilities. Funding for the RTI will be doubled by 2007 (based on the 2005 allocation of €4.5m). Thereafter, funding for rural transport services will be steadily increased; ultimately to a cash level of about four times the 2005 allocation. We welcome these commitments.

Rural public services
Section 3.4 of this review has already addressed issues associated with current and future regulation of public services. One key element of policy in this area which is relevant to rural Ireland is the current and sustained existence of so-called 'public service obligations'. These require services to be made available on a nationwide basis and as a policy play an important role in ensuring the possibility and sustainability of rural communities. For service providers, be

they public or private, there are additional costs associated with adhering to these obligations and therefore there is a clear incentive for them to seek their removal. Government policy should ensure that these obligations remain and that permanent residents of rural areas are not disadvantaged through their removal.

Sustaining rural communities

As a contribution to the process of sustaining rural communities the National Economic and Social Council (NESC) has proposed the establishment of service centres where public or essential local facilities could be located together in a single complex (New Approaches to Rural Development, NESC 1995). NESC suggests that the practicality of such an approach could be explored on a pilot basis. It emphasises that, given the vertical organisation of public administration, integration at local level can only happen if there is commitment to such an approach at the highest level. CORI Justice believes that pilot funding should be provided to develop and assess such an initiative.

Social Exclusion

Many rural areas continue to loose population as highlighted in the Audit of Innovation report (2005) prepared by the BMW regional assembly. This is occurring despite overall national population growth. Such a loss means that there is an increasing dependant population, including a higher cohort of older people and others requiring care. Because of such dependency social exclusion, including the incidence and risk of poverty, becomes more associated with remoteness and rurality. Indeed the CLAR initiative based on areas with most population decline demonstrates this danger. This pattern will worsen unless population growth is significantly distributed throughout the regions.

Settlement Patterns

Housing has become a controversial topic because of the once off house debate. However this masks many issues in terms of settlement that need attention. Many rural villages are victims of poor planning and design in terms of long life tenure. Social housing provision according to the Local Authority Assessment of Social Housing Needs is particularly low in towns and villages around the country (Department of Environment, Heritage and Local Government, 2005). While many experts continue to argue against the practice of one off housing in terms of the social and economic benefits to the community, the lack of any serious alternative is detrimental to the needs of many people who cannot afford basic housing within their own community.

There is a huge need to ensure that local authorities, organisations involved in housing provision, and local communities are resourced to ensure that rural villages can be the focus of long life housing design.

Retrieving energy from agricultural sources

Two issues raised over this and that last section of this review are worth reflecting on. The decline in the number of people employed in farming (outlined above) and the increasing challenges posed by environmental targets that Ireland must meet (as considered in section 3.10b). CORI Justice believes that both of these issues could be simultaneously addressed by focusing on the development of energy focused on bio-fuels, biomass and bio-gas. Earlier this year we outlined these views in a joint government submission with Irish Rural Link.

The EU recently published a Green Paper which clearly set out a European determination that renewable energy must be central to policy for the foreseeable future. The section on EU financial support for biomass energy states:

> *"Many regions assisted by structural and cohesion funds have high potential to pursue economic growth and employment creation through biomass. Supporting the development of RE and other alternative energy sources such as the production of biomass, is therefore an important objective of these funds. The funds can be used to support re-training farmers, the provision of equipment for biomass producers, investment in facilities to produce bio fuels and other materials, fuel switching to biomass by electricity and district heating providers. The Commission calls on member states when preparing National strategic Reference frameworks and operational programmes to ensure potential benefits of biomass are thoroughly taken into account".*

To date, Ireland is far from fully utilising its ability to take advantage of the direction that EU policy is taking on the production of renewable energy. The EU policy has set an objective that consumption of energy from renewable sources will be over 20% by 2020 - at present Ireland consumes only 1.9%. The intention of the EU is to add a million jobs in the Union by adopting a range of renewable energy targets.

Our joint proposal envisages the establishment of a commission to address these issues and to identify the measures required to ensure a smooth and swift development of alternative energy from agricultural sources. The outcome of this commission's work would simultaneously halt the decline of farming in Ireland and significantly increase the supply of renewable energy available

Overall, CORI Justice believes that the establishment of such a body would be very timely. Ireland has the advantage of an agriculture sector undergoing radical transition, and therefore it is a sector that is extremely receptive to new ideas that build on existing skills. Within a short period of time this potential might well have disappeared. Via this development Ireland can align itself with EU policy while simultaneously establishing social and economic stability in rural areas.

Among the commitments on rural development contained in the new social partnership agreement *Towards 2016* are the following:

On strategy
- The allocation of the funding under the National Rural Development Programme to individual measures will reflect the need to underpin the competitiveness and sustainability of the agriculture and forestry sectors while, at the same time, acknowledging and supporting the key contribution being made to rural areas by the wider rural economy. Engagement between local development agencies and the co-operative movement will be encouraged, to ensure their familiarity with the co-operation option, particularly where incorporation is a condition of funding for applicants.
- In the context of the preparation of the next National Development Plan (NDP), an inter-Departmental Group on the development of the Rural Economy will prepare a draft chapter for inclusion in the NDP covering, inter alia, the main challenges specific to the rural economy, issues critical to its future development and existing and planned sectoral measures from across Departments that significantly support or impact on the rural economy.

On the National Spatial Strategy (NSS)
Among the high level outcomes on the NSS sought within the longer-term 10-year framework agreement are:
- Substantial and faster growth evident in all of the Gateways;

- Gateways both individually and collectively providing alternative locations for investment and economic activity complementing Dublin
- Hub Towns extending the impact of Gateways more widely within their regions.
- Enhanced quality of life through more balanced development of the Gateways and their wider regions, the co-ordinated delivery of infrastructure and amenities and improved connectivity between urban and rural areas.

On rural transport
- There will be a doubling of the cash funding available to the Rural Transport Initiative (RTI) by 2007. Thereafter, a steady increase in funding will be provided for rural transport services, ultimately to a cash level about four times the 2005 allocation.
- The Public Transport Partnership Forum will continue to provide a means for consultation with the Social Partners on matters relating to public transport.

On bio-energy
- Government will put in place high-level co-ordinated arrangements, to deliver a cohesive policy approach, across all elements of the Bio-Energy value chain (i.e. producer, processor and consumer) to optimise the potential sectoral benefits across the agriculture, enterprise, transport and energy sectors, including an appropriate forum for engagement with the social partners.

Policy Proposals on Rural Development

- **Transform the decoupled direct payment into a basic income for each person.**

- **Reappraise the concept of work. In doing this, the potential of the social economy should be incorporated, the range of activities of the Farm Relief Service broadened, and the facilitation of family-farm inheritance should be ensured.**

- **Ensure the provision of basic infrastructure and services, based more on principles of equity and social justice, than on cost effectiveness, and take particular account of rural disadvantage.**

Rural Development

- Ensure the provision of a reliable and appropriate transport system, by providing resources for the development of local-transport strategies and initiatives tailored to meet the needs of the local community.

- Reverse the trend of centralising services away from local communities in areas such as healthcare, education, post offices, etc.

- Structure housing lists to reflect rural needs. In particular, in rural areas, develop a framework to guide planning policy, which is focused on supporting and sustaining viable rural communities and protecting and enhancing the rural environment.

- Ensure that public-service bodies take steps to inaugurate an effective and ongoing consultative process with all rural people.

- Overhaul the model for development in agriculture to take effective account of the difficulties of smaller farmers.

- Reappraise programmes to create employment for part-time farmers with a view to targeting effectively the needs of smaller farmers.

- Develop policies, which encourage alternative farm enterprises through the promotion of quality (including organic) food production and processing.

- Conduct a high level review of the training and education available to those willing to remain in rural areas. This would examine the role played by Teagasc agricultural colleges, the Institutes of Technology and FAS.

- Support additional special outreach education programmes in rural areas, particularly those where no major third-level colleges are located.

- Promote research on initiatives that will develop information systems and technologies in a manner that will enhance, rather than detract from, the viability of rural communities.

- Adopt the suggestions of the Rural Ireland 2025 report.

- Refocus government funding to rural areas in a way that is consistent with the approach outlined in table 3.46.

- Ensure that policy protects the sustained existence of public service obligations.

- Finance a pilot project to establish service centres (one-stop shops) in rural areas.

- Begin to rural-proof all policies to ensure that their adoption does not further isolate rural communities or undermine rural development.

- Investigate the use of farm land as a means of meeting Ireland's renewable energy requirements by maximising the retrieval of energy from agricultural sources.

3.12 The Developing World

> **CORE POLICY OBJECTIVE:**
> **THE DEVELOPING WORLD**
> To ensure that Ireland plays an active and effective part in promoting genuine development in the developing world and to ensure that all Ireland's policies are consistent with such development

Globally, the scale and extent of underdevelopment and inequality remains large. An indication of the size of this problem is outlined annually in the United Nations Human Development Report (UNDP, 2005). Table 3.44 (a) and (b) presents an insight into the scale and extent of these problems using the latest UN data.

Table 3.47 (a) shows that today almost 1.1 billion people live in absolute poverty on less than one dollar a day. This equates to approximately one fifth of the world's population. Future projections suggest that by 2015, this figure will increase to 1.7 billion people. In Africa alone, over 90 per cent of the population lives in abject poverty. Overall, the vast majority of those who experience this level of poverty live in the South (the Third World).

Coupled with poverty is the ongoing problem of malnourishment. Worldwide some 831 million people have a less than basic food supply and as a consequence their health and survival is continually compromised. One manifestation of this is the very high level of child mortality, measured as the number of deaths per thousand children aged under 5 years. In 2002 10.5 million children died with these figures concentrated in Sub-Saharan Africa and South Asia.

Table 3.47(a): United Nations development indicators by region and worldwide.			
Region	No's living on less than a $1 a day	No's who are under-nourished*	Child mortality: no's of under-5 deaths
Sub-Saharan Africa	313m	185m	4.8m
Arab States	7m	34m	0.6m
East Asia & the Pacific	271m	212m	1.2m
South Asia	431m	312m	3.5m
Latin America & the Caribbean	50m	53m	0.4m
Central & Eastern Europe and the CIS	21m*	33m	0m
Worldwide total	**1,093m**	**831m**	**10.5m**

Source: UNDP (2005:43-45); UNDP (2004:129-131)
Notes: * Data for 2000 all other data for 2002

Table 3.47(b): United Nations development indicators by region and worldwide.			
Region	No's without access to clean water	No's without access to adeq. sanitation*	No's of primary aged children not enrolled
Sub-Saharan Africa	278.2m	299m	45.5m
Arab States	46.7m	51m	8.8m
East Asia & the Pacific	419.0m	1,004m	10.0m
South Asia	232.6m	944m	42.3m
Latin America & the Caribbean	55m	121m	3.3m
Central & Eastern Europe and the CIS	29m*	0m	3m
Worldwide total	**1,066m**	**2,742m**	**113m**

Source: UNDP (2005:43-45); UNDP (2004:129-131)
Notes: * Data for 2000 all other data for 2002

The extent of the underdevelopment problem being experienced in poorer regions is further revealed by the figures in table 3.47(b). In 2002, 1.066 billion people worldwide did not have access to clean water while 2.7 billion people did not have access to adequate sanitation. The lack of these basic facilities once again undermines the health and survival of people living in less developed regions. Finally, the fact that 113 million children of primary school age are not enrolled in, and therefore not attending, school is worrying. The lack of basic education levels for future generations must be a concern.

UN millennium development goals

In response to these problems the UN Millennium Declaration was adopted in 2000 at the largest-ever gathering of heads of state. It committed countries – both rich and poor- to doing all they can to eradicate poverty, promote human dignity and equality and achieve peace, democracy and environmental sustainability. World leaders promised to work together to meet concrete targets for advancing development and reducing poverty by 2015 or earlier. Emanating from the Millennium Declaration, a set of Millennium Development Goals was agreed. These bind countries to do more in the attack on inadequate incomes, widespread hunger, gender inequality, environmental deterioration and lack of education, health care and clean water. They also include actions to reduce debt and increase aid, trade and technology transfers to poor countries. These goals and their related targets are:

Goal 1: Eradicate extreme poverty and hunger

Target 1: Halve, between 1990 and 2015, the proportion of people whose income is less than $1 a day.

Target 2: Halve, between 1990 and 2015, the proportion of people who suffer from hunger.

Goal 2: Achieve universal primary education

Target 3: Ensure that, by 2015, children everywhere, boys and girls alike, will be able to complete a full course of primary schooling.

Goal 3: Promote gender equality and empower women

Target 4: Eliminate gender disparity in primary and secondary education, preferably by 2005 and in all levels of education no later than 2015.

Goal 4: Reduce child mortality

Target 5: Reduce by two-thirds, between 1990 and 2015, the under-five mortality rate.

Goal 5: Improve maternal health

Target 6: Reduce by three-quarters, between 1990 and 2015, the maternal mortality ratio.

Goal 6: Combat HIV/AIDS, malaria and other diseases

Target 7: Have halted by 2015 and begun to reverse the spread of HIV/AIDS.

Target 8: Have halted by 2015 and begun to reverse the incidence of malaria and other major diseases.

Goal 7: Ensure environmental sustainability

Target 9: Integrate the principles of sustainable development into country policies and programmes and reverse the loss of environmental resources.

Target 10: Halve by 2015 the proportion of people without sustainable access to safe drinking water.

Target 11: Have achieved by 2020 a significant improvement in the lives of at least 100 million slum dwellers.

Goal 8: Develop a global partnership for development

Target 12: Develop further an open, rule based, predictable, nondiscriminatory trading and financial system (includes a commitment to good governance, development, and poverty reduction—both nationally and internationally).

Target 13: Address the special needs of the least developed countries (includes tariff- and quota free access for exports, enhanced program of debt relief for and cancellation of official bilateral debt, and more generous official development assistance for countries committed to poverty reduction).

Target 14: Address the special needs of landlocked countries and small island developing states (through the Program of Action for the Sustainable Development of Small Island Developing States and 22nd General Assembly provisions).

Target 15: Deal comprehensively with the debt problems of developing countries through national and international measures in order to make debt sustainable in the long term

Target 16: In cooperation with developing countries, develop and implement strategies for decent and productive work for youth.

Target 17: In cooperation with pharmaceutical companies, provide access to affordable essential drugs in developing countries.

Target 18: In cooperation with the private sector, make available the benefits of new technologies, especially information and communications technologies.

(UNDP, 2003: 1-3)

To date progress on these goals and targets has been mixed with some regions doing better than others. In particular the UN suggests that East Asia and the Pacific are progressing satisfactorily but that overall "human development is proceeding too slowly" (2004:132). The UN note that the pace of development is so slow in Sub-Saharan Africa that "at the current pace Sub-Saharan Africa will not meet the goal for universal primary education until 2129 or the goal for reducing child mortality by two-thirds until 2106 – 100 years away, rather than the 11 called for by the goals. In three of the goals – hunger, income poverty and access to sanitation – no date can be set because the situation in the region is worsening, not improving" (2004:132). CORI Justice believes that the international community needs to play a more active role in assisting less developed countries achieve these goals. Central to this will be the provision of additional financial support (see ODA below).

Poverty and its associated implications remains the root cause of regional conflicts and civil wars in many of these poor countries. States and societies that are poor are prone to conflict. It is very difficult for governments to govern adequately when their people cannot afford to pay taxes, and industry and trade are almost non-existent. Poverty is also a major cause of environmental degradation. Large-scale food shortages, migration and conflicts lead to environmental pressures.

Clearly poverty in the southern world threatens the very survival of all peoples. It is the major injustice in a world that is not, as a unit, poor. Now more than ever, as Ireland becomes more prosperous, the Irish government must exercise its voice within the European Union and in world institutions to ensure that the elimination of poverty becomes the focus of all policy development.

Trade and debt

A further implication of table 3.47 (a) and (b) above is to underscore the totally unacceptable division that currently exists between rich and poor regions of the world. The fact that this phenomenon persists is largely attributable to unfair trade practices and to the backlog of unpayable debt owed by the countries of the South to other governments, to the World Bank, the International Monetary Fund (IMF) and to commercial banks.

The effect of trade barriers cannot be overstated; by limiting or eliminating access to potential markets the Western world is denying poor countries substantial income. At the 2002 UN Conference on Financing and Development Michael Moore, the President of the World Trade Organisation, stated that the complete abolition of trade barriers could "boost global income by $2.8 trillion and lift 320 million people out of poverty by 2015". Research by Oxfam (2002) further shows that goods from poor countries are taxed at four times the rate of goods from rich countries and that 120 million people could be lifted out of poverty if Africa, Latin America and Asia increased their share of world markets by just 1 per cent. It is clear that all countries would gain from trade reform. Such reform is now long overdue.

The high levels of debt experienced by Third World countries have disastrous consequences for the populations of indebted countries. Governments that are obliged to dedicate large percentages of their country's GDP to debt repayments cannot afford to pay for health and educational programmes for their people. In 1997, Third World debt totalled over $2.2 trillion. In the same year nearly $250 billion was repaid in interest and loan principal. Africa alone spends four times more on interest on its loans than on healthcare. For every €1 given in aid by rich countries, poor countries pay back nearly €4 in debt repayments. It is not possible for these countries to develop the kind of healthy economies that would facilitate debt repayment when millions of their people are being denied basic healthcare and education and are either unemployed or earn wages so low that they can barely survive.

A process of debt cancellation has been argued for over a number of years and should be implemented. CORI Justice welcomes recent moves in this direction and in particular we welcome the commitment during 2002 by the Irish government to support such a move. This is a major policy shift, following entrenched opposition to the move by the Department of Finance. It is now important that Ireland campaign on the international stage to see this process implemented. Progress to date on debt cancellation has been slow.

CORI Justice believes that Ireland's representatives at the World Bank and the IMF should be more critical of the policies adopted by these bodies. The Department of Finance annual reports on Ireland's involvement in these organisations reveal an alarming degree of unconditional support. According to these reports Ireland has unconditionally supported the World Bank's positions in all of the following areas: poverty reduction, gender issues, private-sector development, governance issues and corruption, military spending, post-conflict initiatives and environmentally sustainable projects. This level of support does not match Irish public opinion. NGOs, such as the Debt and Development Coalition, which have done much work on these issues, are very critical of the World Bank in its policies on issues such as poverty reduction, gender and the environment. We believe that this criticism of government is well founded.

Ireland's commitment to ODA

The international challenge to significantly increase levels of Overseas Development Assistance (ODA) was recently set out by the UN Secretary General Kofi Annan when he stated that:

> "We will have time to reach the Millennium Development Goals — worldwide and in most, or even all, individual countries — but only if we break with business as usual. We cannot win overnight. Success will require sustained action across the entire decade between now and the deadline. It takes time to train the teachers, nurses and engineers; to build the roads, schools and hospitals; to grow the small and large businesses able to create the jobs and income needed. So we must start now. And we must more than double global development assistance over the next few years. Nothing less will help to achieve the Goals".

These comments lay down a clear challenge to the international community and CORI Justice believes that Ireland can lead the way in responding to that challenge. We welcome the announcement by the Taoiseach that Ireland will reach the UN target of 0.7% of GNP on overseas aid by 2012. We also welcome the re-iteration of this commitment in *Towards 2016*. Although this is two years later than we suggested in our contribution to the 2005 Department of Foreign Affairs consultation process, the detailed nature of that commitment is welcome. In particular we welcome the accompanying funding timetable announced by the Department of Foreign Affairs. Our submission called for such a set of programmed funding increases to accompany any Government commitment. It is important that the Government, Development Co-operation Ireland and Irish society generally are aware of the scale of these ODA allocations.

In 2005 a total of €545m (0.4% of GNP) was allocated to ODA. Budget 2006 allocated €675m, equivalent to 0.466% of GNP. This increase is a welcome endorsement of the Taoiseach's commitment to ODA at the UN. It is important that Government stay focused on reaching 0.7% of GNP by 2012. The interim commitment to reach 0.5% of GNP must be met in 2007. Based on the Department of Finances own figures, published in the Budget 2006 documentation, in Budget 2007 an additional €104m must be allocated to ODA bringing that Budget to €779m (see table 3.48). Such an increase will achieve the interim target and, as table 3.48 shows, it will underscore that over time Ireland has achieved sizeable increases in our ODA allocation.

Table 3.48: Ireland's net overseas development assistance, 1993-2007.		
Year	€m's	% of GNP
1993	69.4	0.18
1994	95.5	0.23
1995	122.0	0.26
1996	142.3	0.28
1997	157.6	0.27
1998	177.3	0.26
1999	230.3	0.30
2000	254.9	0.29
2001	320.1	0.33
2002	422.1	0.41
2003	446	0.40
2004	475	0.39
2005★	545	0.40
2006★	675	0.46
2007★★	779	0.50

Source: CSO, 2003:37, Budget 2006 (2005:D5).
Notes: ★ from Budget 2006 documentation, ★★ calculated from Budget 2006 documentation

In reviewing previous (missed) ODA targets the OECD's development assistance committee expressed the opinion that Ireland's aid programme was being hindered by a failure to set out "programmed funding increases" into the future. As this remains the case for the period to 2012, CORI Justice lays out here a proposed set of programmed funding increases to be implemented in the exchequer Estimates and Budgets for the period 2007-2012 (six budgets). Table 3.49 first presents GNP figures based on Department of Finance Budget documentation data for 2006, 2007 and 2008 and projected growth rates from the ESRI (adjusted for an annual inflation rate of 2 per cent) for the period 2009-2012.

Table 3.49: Ireland's GNP, 2006-2012.

	2007	2008	2009	2010	2011	2012
Nominal GNP growth rate	7.7%	7.4%	6.7%	6.6%	6.4%	5.5%
Value of GNP, €ms	155,800	167,350	178,562	190,348	202,530	213,669

Source: Calculated from Budget 2006 (2005: D5); and ESRI (2005:43).
Notes: The 2009-2012 nominal GNP growth rates incorporate an assumed 2 per cent inflation rate for these years.

Table 3.50 then proposes a set of programmed funding increases to be implemented in the exchequer Estimates and Budgets for 2007, 2008, 2009, 2010, 2011 and 2012. Adopting these proposed increases would result in the ODA as a percentage of GNP figure growing from 0.46 per cent in 2006 to the target of 0.7 per cent in 2012. The proposed increases from the interim 2007 target are the same for each of the years: +0.04 of a percentage of GNP annually. Table 3.50 and chart 3.10 outline the implications of following this path. By 2012, Irish ODA should amount to almost €1,500m.

Table 3.50: Proposed Irish ODA programmed funding increases, 2007-2012

	2007	2008	2009	2010	2011	2012
Annual increase	–	+0.04	+0.04	+0.04	+0.04	+0.04
Path to 0.7% GNP	0.50%	0.54%	0.58%	0.62%	0.66%	0.70%
ODA, €ms	€779	€903.7	€1,036.7	€1,180.2	€1,336.7	€1,495.7
Year-on-year increase, €ms		+€104.0	+€124.7	+€132.0	+€144.5	+€156.5	+€159.0

Chart 3.10: Ireland's ODA as a % of GNP, 1993-2012 (including CORI Justice's proposed programmed funding increases 2008-2012)

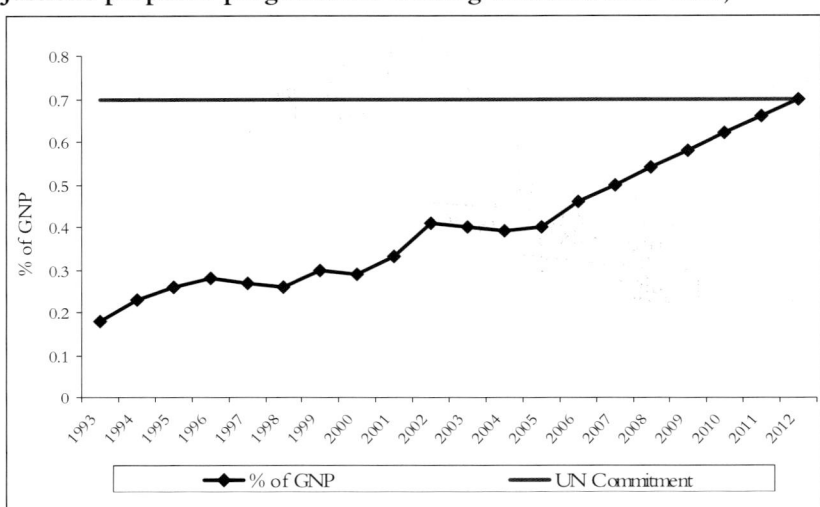

A further essential element of the transition to this target is need for the Department of Foreign Affairs, Ireland Aid and the aid agencies to begin detailed planning on how to use these additional resources. CORI Justice believes that this would be best achieved through the appointment of a senior civil servant within the Department who would have specific responsibility for this planning process.

By 2012, it is crucial that the Irish government be seen to finally honour the very public commitment it made to achieve this UN target. Not only would its achievement be a major success for government, and an important element in the delivery of promises made in the national agreement, but it would also be of significance internationally. Ireland's success would not only provide additional assistance to needy countries but would also provide leadership to those other European countries who do not meet the target.

HIV/AIDS

The recent UNAIDS report (2005) revealed that there are now 40.3 million people worldwide with HIV/AIDS. This figure comprises approximately 38 million adults and 2.3 million children. Predominantly, the crisis is concentrated in poorer African and Asian countries. Of the total, 25.8 million

(64 per cent) of the infected are in sub-Saharan Africa. In 2005 there were 4.9 million new HIV/AIDS infections and 3.1 million deaths (UNAIDS, 2004: 2-6). These figures imply that there are almost 8,500 deaths and 13,500 new infections each day, such that almost 6 deaths and 9 new infections occur every minute.

Kofi Annan, the UN Secretary-General, has described this epidemic as "an unparalleled nightmare" whose health, social, economic and family consequences are far beyond any ever previously experienced. In the worst-suffering African countries, over 30 per cent of the adult population have HIV/AIDS. In the least infected countries around 7 per cent of the adult population have contracted the disease. To date there is no cure for HIV/AIDS and progress towards identifying an appropriate vaccine for the African and Asian strains has been a slow and seriously under-funded process.

The UN also notes that beyond sub-Saharan Africa, more recent epidemics continue to grow - in China, Indonesia, Papua New Guinea, Vietnam, several Central Asian Republics, the Baltic States, and North Africa. Its leading expert on AIDS has suggested that currently the disease is "only in its infancy".

To address this epidemic the UN has estimated that €10 billion is needed annually. In recent years there has been a sea-change in the global AIDS response with global funding increasing from roughly US$2.1 billion in 2001 to an estimated US$6.1 billion in 2004. However, this is still not enough and governments worldwide need to allocate additional resources.

CORI Justice welcomes the commitment by the Irish government to spend at least €30m a year on combating HIV/AIDS in the developing world. This is a welcome start and an action that should be matched by many more governments worldwide. We also welcome the commitment in *Towards 2016* to "spending a significant proportion of the expanding ODA budget on the fight against HIV/AIDS and other communicable diseases" (2006:37). In doing this Ireland should encourage other states to fund programmes and research aimed at resolving this growing crisis.

In concluding its 2005 report, UNAIDS note the complexity of challenges that face the international community as we address this epidemic. It suggests that "bringing AIDS under control will require tackling with greater resolve the underlying factors that fuel these epidemics - including societal inequalities and injustices. It will require overcoming the still serious barriers to access that take the form of stigma, discrimination, gender inequality and other human rights violations. It will also require overcoming the new injustices created by AIDS, such as the orphaning of generations of children and the stripping of human and institutional capacities. These are extraordinary challenges that demand extraordinary responses" (2005: 5).

Among the commitments on the Developing World contained in the new social partnership agreement *Towards 2016* **are the following:**

On overseas development aid
- The Government is committed to reaching the United Nations target for spending 0.7% of our GNP on official development assistance (ODA) in 2012. As an interim step towards reaching the target, our ODA spending will reach 0.5% of GNP in 2007.

On HIV/AIDS
- The Government is committed to spending a significant proportion of the expanding ODA budget on the fight against HIV/AIDS and other communicable diseases.

Policy Proposals on the Developing World

- **Ensure the Irish government has a consistent policy on Overseas Development Assistance and adheres to that policy.**

- **Take a far more proactive stance at government level on ensuring that Irish and EU policies towards countries in the South are just.**

- **Adopt a more critical perspective towards the policies of the World Bank and the IMF.**

- **Ensure that Ireland delivers on its promise to meet the United Nations target of contributing 0.7 per cent of GNP to Overseas Development Assistance by 2012. In doing so, the Government** should adopt a set of programmed funding increases for the ODA budget to be implemented in the exchequer Estimates and Budgets from 2007-2012.

- Continue to support the international campaign for the liberation of the poorest nations from the burden of the backlog of unpayable debt and take steps to ensure that further progress is made on this issue.

- Continue to support the implementation of the Millenium Goals.

- Government should live up to the commitments it signed up to at the World Earth Summit in Johannesburg in 2002.

- Work for changes in the existing international trading regimes, to encourage fairer and sustainable forms of trade. In particular, resource the development of Ireland's policies in the WTO to ensure that this goal is pursued.

- Ensure that the government takes up a leadership position within the European and international arenas to encourage other states to fund programmes and research aimed at resolving the AIDS/HIV crisis.

4. VALUES

Economic growth has triggered reflection and new questions such as: "Where did the wealth go?" "When we had the resources what did we as a society 'fix' other than reduce unemployment". "If people did so well why do we meet so many anxious faces on our streets?" "Why are so many people experiencing stress in meeting their commitments, be they financial, social, family, etc?" "Why do so many parents have a struggle to find the resources necessary to keep their children in school?" "Why are so many people homeless or living in overcrowded accommodation?" "Why is there so much fear and anxiety in our communities? As the pace of change escalates, those who have the economic and social resources acquire the equipment necessary to ride the crest of the wave, while a large minority lives in fear of being submerged. Those on the crest of the wave have anxieties about staying there. This anxiety fuels the tendency to accumulate more and more to the point where "greed is good". Meanwhile, those who struggle to "hang on" are feeling their grip loosening, and the prospect of being part of this society becoming more remote.

This reflection brings to the fore the issue of values. Our fears are easier to admit than our values. Do we as a people accept a two-tier society in fact, while deriding it in principle? This dualism in our values allows us to continue with the status quo, which, in reality, means that it is okay to exclude almost a quarter of the population from the mainstream of life of the society, while substantial resources and opportunities are channelled towards other groups in society. This dualism operates at the levels of individual people, communities and sectors.

Christian Values
CORI's concerns in this area are deeply rooted in Christian values. Christianity subscribes to the values of both human dignity and the centrality of the community. The person is seen as growing and developing in a context that includes other people and the environment. Justice is understood in terms of relationships. The Christian scriptures understand justice as a harmony that comes from fidelity to right relationships with God, people and the environment. A just society is one that is structured in such a way as to promote these right relationships so that human rights are respected, human dignity is protected, human development is facilitated and the environment is respected and protected (Healy and Reynolds, 2003:188).

VALUES

As our societies have grown in sophistication, the need for appropriate structures has become more urgent. While the aspiration that everyone should enjoy the good life, and the goodwill to make it available to all are essential ingredients in a just society, the good life will not happen without the deliberate establishment of structures to facilitate its development. In the past charity, in the sense of alms-giving by some individuals on an arbitrary and ad hoc basis, was seen as sufficient to ensure that everyone could cross the threshold of human dignity. Calling on the work of social historians it could be argued that charity in this sense was never an appropriate method for dealing with poverty. Certainly it is not a suitable methodology for dealing with the problems of today. As recent world disasters have graphically shown, charity and the heroic efforts of voluntary agencies cannot solve these problems on a long-term basis. Appropriate structures should be established to ensure that every person has access to the resources needed to live life with dignity.

Few people would disagree that the resources of the planet are for the use of the people – not just the present generation, but also the generations still to come. In Old Testament times these resources were closely tied to land and water. A complex system of laws about the Sabbatical and Jubilee years (Lev 25: 1-22, Deut 15: 1-18) was devised to ensure, on the one hand, that no person could be disinherited, and, on the other, that land and debts could not be accumulated or the land exploited.

These reflections raise questions about ownership. Obviously there was an acceptance of private property, but it was not an exclusive ownership. It carried social responsibilities. We find similar thinking among the leaders of the early Christian community. St John Chrysostom, speaking to those who could manipulate the law so as to accumulate wealth to the detriment of others, taught that "*the rich are in the possession of the goods of the poor even if they have acquired them honestly or inherited them legally*" (Homily on Lazarus). These early leaders also established that a person in extreme necessity has the right to take from the riches of others what s/he needs, since private property has a social quality deriving from the law of the communal purpose of earthly goods (*Gaudium et Spes* 69-71).

In more recent times, Pope Paul VI said "*private property does not constitute for anyone an absolute and unconditional right. No one is justified in keeping for his/her exclusive use what is not needed when others lack necessities.... The right to property must never be exercised to the detriment of the common good*" (*Populorum Progressio*

No. 23). Pope John Paul II has developed the understanding of ownership, especially in regard to the ownership of the means of production. One of the major contributors to the generation of wealth is technology. The technology we have today is the product of the work of many people through many generations. Through the laws of patenting and exploration a very small group of people has claimed legal rights to a large portion of the world's wealth. Pope John Paul II questions the morality of these structures. He says "*if it is true that capital as the whole of the means of production is at the same time the product of the work of generations, it is equally true that capital is being unceasingly created through the work done with the help of all these means of production*". Therefore, no one can claim exclusive rights over the means of production. Rather that right "*is subordinated to the right to common use, to the fact that goods are meant for everyone*". (*Laborem Exercens* No 14). Since everyone has a right to a proportion of the goods of the country, society is faced with two responsibilities regarding economic resources: firstly each person should have sufficient to access the good life; and secondly, since the earth's resources are finite, and since "more" is not necessarily "better", it is time that society faced the question of putting a limit on the wealth that any person or corporation can accumulate.

Interdependence, mutuality, solidarity and connectedness are words that are used loosely today to express a consciousness which is very Christian. All of creation is seen as a unit that is dynamic – each part is related to every other part, depends on it in some way, and can also affect it. When we focus on the human family, this means that each person depends on others initially for life itself, and subsequently for the resources and relationships needed to grow and develop. To ensure that the connectedness of the web of life is maintained, each person is meant to reach out to support others in ways that are appropriate for their growth and in harmony with the rest of creation. This thinking respects the integrity of the person, while recognising that the person can achieve his or her potential only in right relationships with others and the environment.

Most people in Irish society would subscribe to the values articulated here. However these values will only be operative in our society when appropriate structures and infrastructures are put in place.

5. CONCLUSION

In this socio-economic review CORI Justice has presented its analysis of the present socio-economic situation in Ireland, paying special attention to the sectors that have not benefited much in recent years. We proposed a programme to ensure economic development, social equity and sustainability in the medium to long term. Within this programme we outlined and proposed a wide range of policy initiatives that should form the basis of any movement towards building for the future. In the areas covered these initiatives should form part of all policy development in the years immediately ahead. Economic forecasts suggest that sufficient resources will be available in the next few years to fund these policy initiatives. All our proposals are made within responsible fiscal parameters.

We do not claim to have all the answers. However, we make our proposals as a contribution to the public debate on what the key priorities in the socio-economic arena should be in the years ahead. All responses are most welcome.

REFERENCES

Agenda 21 (1993), *The Earth Summit's Agenda for Change*, Geneva, Centre for our Common Future.

Annan, K. (2002), *Speech to World Summit on Sustainable Development*, Johannesburg, South Africa, September.

Bacon and Associates (1998), *An Economic Assessment of Recent House Price Developments*, Dublin, Stationery Office.

Bacon, Peter (1998), *The Fiscal Treatment of Housing in Ireland: An Overview*, Foundation for Fiscal Studies Annual Conference.

Begg, D. (2003), "The Just Society – Can we afford it?" in Reynolds B. and S. Healy (eds.) *Ireland and the Future of Europe: leading the way towards inclusion?*, Dublin, CORI.

Bennett M., D. Fadden,. D. Harney, P. O'Malley, C. Regan and. L. Sloyan (2003) *Population Ageing in Ireland and its Impact on Pension and Healthcare Costs*. Report of Society of Actuaries Working Party on Population Studies. Society of Actuaries in Ireland.

Bergin A., Fitz Gerald J. and Kearney I. (2002), *The Macro-economic Effects of Using Taxes or Emissions Trading Permits to Reduce Greenhouse Gas Emissions*, paper presented to ESRI conference entitled "The sky's the limit: efficient and fair policies on global warming", December, Dublin.

Bergin, A., J. Cullen, D. Duffy, J. Fitzgerald, I. Kearney and D. McCoy (2003), *Medium-Term Review: 2003-2010*, Dublin, ESRI.

BMW Regional Assembly (2005), Audit of Innovation Report. Roscommon, BMW Regional Assembly.

Bradley, J. (2003) Article in the Irish Times, April 10th 2003.

Bristow, J. (2004). *Taxation in Ireland: an economist's perspective*, Dublin, Institute of Public Administration.

REFERENCES

Brooke, S. (2004), *Housing Problems and Irish Children*, Children's Research Centre, Trinity College Dublin.

Caring for Carers (2003). *Submission to the Oireachtas Joint Committee on Social and Family Affairs*.

Carrie, A. (2005) "Lack of long-run data prevents us tracking Ireland's social health" in *Feasta Review No 2 Growth: The Celtic Cancer*. Dublin, Feasta.

Central Statistics Office (2003), *Census 2002: Principal Socio-economic Results*, Dublin, Stationery Office.

Central Statistics Office (2003), *Census 2002: Volume 2: Ages and Marital Status*, Dublin, Stationery Office.

Central Statistics Office (2003), *Measuring Ireland's Progress (Volumes 1 and 2)*, Dublin, Stationery Office.

Central Statistics Office (2003), *Population and Migration Estimates*, Dublin, Stationery Office.

Central Statistics Office (2003), *Quarterly National Household Survey: Voter participation and abstention*, Dublin, Stationery Office.

Central Statistics Office (2004), *Population and Labour Force Projections 2006-2036*, Dublin, Stationery Office.

Central Statistics Office (2005), *EU Survey on Income and Living Conditions*, Dublin, Stationery Office.

Central Statistics Office (2005), *Measuring Ireland's Progress 2004*, Dublin, Stationery Office.

Central Statistics Office (2005), *Quarterly National Household Survey: Disability update*, Dublin, Stationery Office.

Central Statistics Office (2005), *Statistical Yearbook of Ireland - 2005*, Dublin, Stationery Office.

Central Statistics Office (2005), *Vital Statistics - 2002*, Dublin, Stationery Office.

Central Statistics Office (2005). *National Income and Expenditure Accounts*, Dublin, Stationery Office.

Central Statistics Office (2006), *Measuring Ireland's Progress 2005*, Dublin, Stationery Office.

Central Statistics Office (various), *Household Budget Survey*, Dublin, Stationery Office.

Central Statistics Office (various), *Industrial Earnings and Hours Worked*, Dublin, Stationery Office.

Central Statistics Office (various), *Quarterly National Accounts,* Dublin.

Central Statistics Office (various), *Quarterly National Household Survey,* Dublin.

Chambers of Commerce of Ireland (2004), *Local Authority Funding – Government in Denial,* Dublin.

Clark C.M.A. (2002), *The Basic Income Guarantee: ensuring progress and prosperity in the 21st century*, Dublin, Liffey Press and CORI Justice Commission.

Clark C.M.A. and J. Healy (1997), *Pathways to a Basic Income.* Dublin, CORI Justice Commission.

Collins, M.L. (2002), *A decomposition of Irish Household Income Inequality, 1994-2002*, paper presented to the Irish Economics Association Annual Conference, April.

Collins, M.L. (2004), "Taxation in Ireland: an overview" in B. Reynolds, and S. Healy (eds.) *A Fairer Tax System for a Fairer Ireland,* Dublin, CORI Justice Commission.

Collins, M.L. and C. Kavanagh (1998), "For Richer, For Poorer: The Changing Distribution of Household Income in Ireland, 1973-94", in Healy, S. and B. Reynolds, *Social Policy in Ireland: Principles, Practice and Problems,* Dublin, Oak Tree Press.

REFERENCES

Conroy, P. and A. Brennan (2003) *Migrant Workers and their experiences*, Dublin, Equality Authority, IBEC, Congress, CIF and Know Racism.

CORI Justice Commission (2003), *Submission to the All-Party Oireachtas Committee on the Constitution on Property Rights*, Dublin, CORI.

CORI Justice Commission (2004), *Pathways to Inclusion — Socio economic review 2005*, Dublin, CORI.

CORI Justice Commission (2004), *Priorities for Fairness — Socio economic review 2004*, Dublin, CORI.

CORI Justice Commission (2005), *Budget 2006- Analysis and Critique*, Dublin, CORI.

CORI Justice Commission (2005), *Policy Briefing - Housing and Accommodation*, Dublin, CORI.

CORI Justice Commission (2005), *Policy Briefing - Sustainability*, Dublin, CORI.

CORI Justice Commission (2005), *Policy Briefing - Taxation*, Dublin, CORI.

CORI Justice Commission (2005), *Submission to Department of Finance Consultation Process on the Review of Tax Reliefs and High Earners 2005*, Dublin, CORI.

CORI Justice Commission (2006), *Securing Fairness and Wellbeing: Ireland in the coming years*, Dublin, CORI.

CORI Justice (2006), *Contact — Special Edition on the new social partnership agreement Towaeds 2016*, Dublin, CORI.

Coulombe, S. J. Tremblay and S. Marchand (2004) *Literacy scores, human capital and growth across 14 OECD countries* Statistics Canada, Canada.

Dail Eireann (2004) Report of *the All-Party Oireachtas Committee on the Constitution on Property Rights*, Dublin.

Delaney, L. and T. Fahey (2005), *Social and Economic Value of Sport in Ireland*. Dublin, ESRI.

Department of Agriculture and Food (1999), *White Paper on Rural Development*, Dublin, Stationery Office.

Department of Agriculture and Food (2005), *Agri Vision 2015 Committee Report*, Dublin, Stationery Office.

Department of Agriculture, Food and Rural Development (2001), *CLAR Programme on Rural Development*, Dublin, Stationery Office.

Department of Education and Science (2000), *Learning for Life: White Paper on Adult Education*, Dublin, Stationery Office.

Department of Enterprise, Trade and Employment (2004), *Enterprise Strategy Report*, Dublin, Stationery Office.

Department of Finance (1982), *Report of the Commission of Taxation*, Dublin, Stationery Office.

Department of Finance (2002), *Budget 2003*, Dublin, Stationery Office.

Department of Finance (2003), *Budget 2004*, Dublin, Stationery Office.

Department of Finance (2004), *Budget 2005*, Dublin, Stationery Office.

Department of Finance (2005), *Budget 2006*, Dublin, Stationery Office.

Department of Finance (2006), *Budget 2006 – Review of Tax Schemes Volumes I, II and III*. Dublin, Stationery Office.

Department of Finance (various), *Annual Report*, Dublin, Stationery Office.

Department of Health and Children (2001), *Primary Care A New Direction Health Strategy*, Dublin: Stationery Office.

Department of Health and Children (2001), *Quality and Fairness: A Health System for You*, Dublin: Stationery Office.

REFERENCES

Department of Health and Children (2003) *The Report of the Commission on Financial Management and Control Systems in the Health Service*, Dublin: Stationery Office.

Department of Health and Children (2003) *The Report of the National Task Force on Medical Staffing*, Dublin: Stationery Office.

Department of Justice, Equality and Law Reform (2005) *National Action Plan Against Racism: Planning for Diversity*, Dublin, Stationery Office.

Department of Social and Family Affairs (various), *Statistical Information and Social Welfare Services*, Dublin, Stationery Office.

Department of Social, Community and Family Affairs (2000), *Supporting Voluntary Activity*, Dublin, Stationery Office.

Department of the Environment and Local Government (2000), *National Climate Change Strategy*, Dublin, Stationery Office.

Department of the Environment and Local Government (2000), *Planning and Development Act 2000*, Dublin, Stationery Office.

Department of the Environment and Local Government (2002), *National Spatial Strategy*, Dublin, Stationery Office.

Department of the Environment and Local Government (2002), *Planning and Development (Amendment) Act 2002*, Dublin, Stationery Office.

Department of the Environment, Heritage and Local Government (2005), *Report of the National Traveller Accommodation Consultative Committee*, Dublin, Stationery Office.

Department of the Environment, Heritage and Local Government (2005), *Housing Needs Assessment*, Dublin, Stationery Office.

Department of the Environment, Heritage and Local Government (various), *Housing Statistics Bulletin*, Dublin, Stationery Office.

Department of the Taoiseach (1997), *Partnership 2000 for Inclusion, Employment and Competitiveness*, Dublin, Stationery Office.

Department of the Taoiseach (2000), *Programme for Prosperity and Fairness*, Dublin, Stationery Office.

Department of the Taoiseach (2001), *Final Report of the Social Welfare Benchmarking and Indexation Group*, Dublin, Stationery Office.

Department of the Taoiseach (2002), *Basic Income, A Green Paper*, Dublin, Stationery Office.

Department of the Taoiseach (2003) *Sustaining Progress - Social Partnership Agreement 2003-2005,* Dublin, Stationery Office.

Department of the Taoiseach (2004), *Better Regulation*, Dublin, Stationery Office.

Department of the Taoiseach (2006) *Towards 2016 - Ten-Year Framework Social Partnership Agreement 2006-2015,* Dublin, Stationery Office.

Dept of Education and Science (2003), *Supporting Equity in Higher Education,* Dublin, Stationery Office.

Dowthwaite, R. (2004), "Tradable Quotas: the fairer alternative to eco-taxation" in B. Reynolds, and S. Healy (eds.) *A Fairer Tax System for a Fairer Ireland,* Dublin, CORI Justice Commission.

Drudy, P.J (2005) "Housing: the case for a new philosophy" in B. Reynolds and S. Healy (eds.) *Securing Fairness and Wellbeing in a Land of Plenty,* Dublin, CORI Justice Commission.

Drudy, PJ and M. Punch (2005) *Out of Reach: Inequalities in the Irish Housing System*, Dublin, Tasc at New Island.

Dublin City Council (2002), *Profile of Households Accommodated by Dublin City Council*, Dublin.

Dunne, T. (2004), "Land Values as a Source of Local Government Finance" in

REFERENCES

B. Reynolds, and S. Healy (eds.) *A Fairer Tax System for a Fairer Ireland*, Dublin, CORI Justice Commission.

Economist Magazine (2005), *World in Figures −2006*. London.

Eivers, E., Shiel, G., and Shortt, F. (2005), *Literacy in disadvantaged primary schools: Problems and solutions*. Dublin: Educational Research Centre, 2005.

Environmental Protection Agency (2002), *Environment in Focus 2002: key environmental indicators for Ireland*, Dublin, EPA.

Environmental Protection Agency (2004), *Irelands Environment - 2004*, Dublin, EPA.

Environmental Protection Agency (2006), *Ireland's Emissions of Greenhouse Gases for the Period 1990-2004*, Dublin, EPA.

ESRI (various), *Quarterly Economic Commentary (QEC)*, Dublin, ESRI.

European Union (1997), *Stability and Growth Pact*, EU Commission, Brussels.

Eurostat (2003), *European Social Statistics: social protection expenditure and receipts 1995!-2003*, Luxembourg.

Eurostat (2003), *Structures of the Taxation System in the European Union*, Luxembourg.

Eurostat (2004), *Living Conditions in Europe 1998-2002*, Luxembourg.

Eurostat (2004). *Structures of the Taxation System in the European Union, 1995-2002*. Luxembourg, Eurostat.

Eurostat (2006), *European Social Statistics: social protection expenditure and receipts 1991-2000*, Luxembourg.

Eurostat (various editions), *Statistics in Focus*, Luxembourg.

Feasta and New Economics Foundation (NEF) (2006), *The Great Emissions Rights Give-Away*. Feasta and NEF.

Fianna Fáil and Progressive Democrats (2002), *Programme for Government*, Dublin.

Fitzgerald, J. A. Bergin, I. Kearney, A. Barrett, D. Duffy, S Garrett and Y McCarthy (2005), *Medium-Term Review: 2005-2012*, Dublin, ESRI.

Flannery, Austin (1982), *Gaudium et Spes*: Pastoral Constitution on the Church in the Modern World (Second Vatican Council, December 7, 1964.

Focus Ireland (2003), *Annual Report 2002*, Dublin.

Government of Ireland, (2000) *Ireland: National Development Plan 2000-2006*, Dublin, Stationery Office.

Government of Ireland, (2004) *Ireland: National Development Plan Mid-Term Review*, Dublin, Stationery Office.

H.M. Treasury (2004). *Financial Statement and Budget Report, 2004*. London, H.M. Treasury.

Healy J (2004), *Fuel Poverty and Policy in Ireland and the European Union*, Dublin, The Policy Institute TCD.

Healy, S. and B. Reynolds (2003), "Christian Critique of Economic Policy and Practice" in J.P. Mackey and E. McDonagh (eds.) *Religion and Politics in Ireland at the turn of the millennium*, Dublin, Columba Press.

Healy, S. and B. Reynolds (2003), "Ireland and the Future of Europe – a social perspective" in in Reynolds B. and S. Healy (eds.) *Ireland and the Future of Europe: leading the way towards inclusion?*, Dublin, CORI.

Healy, S. and B. Reynolds (2004), "Towards a Fairer Tax System for the 21st Century" in B. Reynolds, and S. Healy (eds.) *A Fairer Tax System for a Fairer Ireland*, Dublin, CORI Justice Commission.

Homeless Agency (2004), *Making it Home: an action plan on homelessness in Dublin 2004-2006*, Dublin, Homeless Agency.

Homeless Agency (2006), *Counted in 2005*, Dublin, Homeless Agency.

REFERENCES

Indecon (2005), *Indecon Review of Local Government Funding – Report commissioned by the Minister for Environment, Heritage and Local Government.* Dublin, Stationery Office.

IPCC (2001), *Climate Change 2001: The Scientific Basis: Contribution of Working Group 1 to the Third Assessment Report of the Intergovernmental Panel on Climate Change.* Cambridge University Press, UK.

John Paul II (1981), *Laborem Exercens,* Encyclical Letter of the Supreme Pontiff John Paul II on Human Work, Catholic Truth Society, London.

Lawless, M. and C. Corr (2005), *Drug Use Among the Homeless Population in Ireland.* Dublin, National Advisory Committee on Drugs.

Local Government Management Services Board (2005), *Service Indicators in Local Authorities in 2004.* Dublin, LGMSB.

McCashin A (2000), *The Private Rented Sector in the 21st Century – Policy Choices.* Dublin, Threshold and St Pancras Housing Association.

McGovern, C. and D.A. Cusack (2004) "A Study of Suicides in Kildare, 1995-2002", *Journal of Clinical Forensic Medicine,* Vol.11 issue 6 p289-298.

McGowan, P. (2004), *Competitive Advantage – the challenge for financial services in Ireland.* Paper delivered to the Finance Dublin Conference, March 31st 2004.

Ministry of Social Development of South Africa (2002), *The Report of the Committee of Inquiry into a Comprehensive Social Security System for South Africa (The Taylor Committee),* South Africa.

Moore, M. (2002), Speech to *UN Conference on Financing and Development.*

National Action Plan against Poverty and Social Exclusion (2001). Dublin, Stationery Office.

National Action Plan against Poverty and Social Exclusion (2003). Dublin, Stationery Office.

National Anti-Poverty Strategy (1997), *Sharing in Progress*, Dublin, Stationery Office.

National Anti-Poverty Strategy Review (2002), *Building an Inclusive Society* Dublin, Stationery Office.

National Committee on Volunteering (2002), *Tipping the Balance*, Dublin, Stationery Office.

National Economic and Social Council (1995), *New Approaches to Rural Development,* Dublin, NESC.

National Economic and Social Council (2001), *Review of the Poverty Proofing Process,* Dublin, NESC.

National Economic and Social Council (2002), *National Progress Indicators*, Dublin, NESC.

National Economic and Social Council (2003), *An Investment in Quality: Services, Inclusion and Enterprise*, Dublin, NESC.

National Economic and Social Council (2004), *Housing in Ireland: performance and policy,* Dublin, NESC.

National Economic and Social Council (2005), *NESC Strategy 2006: People, Productivity and Purpose*, Dublin, NESC.

National Economic and Social Council (2005), *The Developmental Welfare State*, Dublin, NESC.

National Economic and Social Council (2006), *Creating a More Inclusive Labour Market*, Dublin, NESC.

National Economic and Social Forum (2003), *Labour Market Issues for Older Workers,* Dublin, NESF.

Nolan B., Gannon B., Layte R., Watson D., Whelan CT. and Williams J (2002) *Monitoring Poverty Trends in Ireland: Results from the 2000 Living in Ireland survey*. ESRI Dublin, Policy Research Series No. 45, July.

REFERENCES

NUI Maynooth, University College Dublin and Teagasc (2005). *Rural Ireland 2025 - Foresight Perspectives*. NIRSA NUI Maynooth, RERC Teagasc, UCD Dublin.

O'Shea, E. and B. Kennelly (2004), "Why does poverty persist in a land of plenty?" in Healy, S., B. Reynolds, and T. Jordan, (eds.) *Spirituality and Poverty in a Land of Plenty*. Dublin, CORI Justice Commission and Dominican Publications.

O'Sicchru, E. (2004), "Land Value Tax: unfinished business" in B. Reynolds, and S. Healy (eds.) *A Fairer Tax System for a Fairer Ireland,* Dublin, CORI Justice Commission.

OECD (2003), *Health Statistics*, Paris, OECD.

OECD (2003). *Revenue Statistics 1965-2002*, Paris, OECD.

OECD (2004), *Education at a Glance - 2004*, Paris, OECD.

OECD (2005), *Education at a Glance - 2005*, Paris, OECD.

OECD (2005), *Health Data 2005*, Paris, OECD.

OECD (2005), *Society at a Glance - 2005*, Paris, OECD.

OECD (2005). *Revenue Statistics 1965-2004*, Paris, OECD.

OECD (2006), *Ireland – Country Report*, Paris, OECD.

Office of the Refugee Applications Commissioner (2003), *Annual Report 2002*, Dublin, Stationery Office.

Office of the Refugee Applications Commissioner (2006) *Monthly Statistics – February 2006*, Dublin, ORAC.

Oxfam (2002). *Make Trade Fair Campaign*. www.maketradefair.com.

Pope Paul VI, (1967) *Populorum Progressio* No. 23, Vatican City, Rome.

Power, J. (2003) "After Strong Growth, Serious Problems" in J. Mulholland (ed.) *Why Not? Building a Better Ireland*, MacGill Summer School.

Public Health Alliance Ireland (2004), *Health in Ireland – An Unequal State*, Dublin, PHAI.

Rapple, C. (2004), "Refundable Tax Credits" in B. Reynolds, and S. Healy (eds.) *A Fairer Tax System for a Fairer Ireland*, Dublin, CORI Justice Commission.

Reception and Integration Agency (2006), *Monthly Statistics – November 2005*. Dublin.

Revenue Commissioners (2002), *Effective Tax Rates for High Earning Individuals*, Dublin, Stationery Office.

Revenue Commissioners (2003), *Statistical Report 2002*, Dublin, Stationery Office.

Revenue Commissioners (2004), *Statistical Report 2003*, Dublin, Stationery Office.

Revenue Commissioners (2005), *Effective Tax Rates for High Earning Individuals*, Dublin, Stationery Office.

Reynolds, B. and S. Healy (2004) *A Fairer Tax System for a Fairer Ireland*, Dublin, CORI Justice Commission.

Reynolds, B. and S. Healy (2005) *Securing Fairness and Wellbeing in a Land of Plenty*, Dublin, CORI Justice Commission.

Robertson, J. (1994), *Benefits and Taxes: A Radical Strategy*, London: The New Economics Foundation.

Robertson, J. (1997), *The New Economics of Sustainable Development*, report to the European Commission, Brussels.

Russell H., Smyth E., Lyons M. and O'Connell P. J. (2002), *Getting out of the House: Women Returning to Employment, Education and Training*, National Women's Council of Ireland and Dept of Justice, Equality and Law Reform, Dublin, The Liffey Press.

REFERENCES

Scott S. and Eakins J. (2002), *Distributive effects of carbon taxes*, paper presented to ESRI conference entitled "The sky's the limit: efficient and fair policies on global warming", December, Dublin.

Society of St Vincent De Paul (2005), *Annual Report 2004*. Dublin.

Society of St. Vincent de Paul, Combat Poverty Agency and Crosscare (2004), *Food Poverty and Policy*. Dublin, Combat Poverty Agency.

Sweeney, J., T. Brereton, C. Byrne, R. Charlton, C. Emblow, R. Fealy, N. Holden, M. Jones, A. Donnelly, S. Moore, P. Purser, K. Byrne, E. Farrell, E. Mayes, D. Minchin, J. Wilson and Jh. Wilson (2003). *Climate change: scenarios & impacts for Ireland*. Dublin, Environmental Protection Agency.

Sweeney, P. (2004), "Corporation Tax: leading the race to the bottom" in B. Reynolds, and S. Healy (eds.) *A Fairer Tax System for a Fairer Ireland*, Dublin, CORI Justice Commission.

Task Force on the Travelling Community (1995), *Final Report*, Dublin, Stationery Office.

Teagasc (2005), *National Farm Survey 2004*, Athenry, Teagasc.

The Irish Times (2002), Editorial on 5th September, 2002, Dublin.

Threshold (2002). *Government Rout on Social Housing*, press release 9 December.

UNAIDS (2004), *AIDS epidemic update December 2004*, UNAIDS/WHO, Switzerland.

UNAIDS (2005), *AIDS epidemic update December 2005*, UNAIDS/WHO, Switzerland.

United Nations Development Program (2003), *Human Development Report – 2003*, New York: United Nations Publications.

United Nations Development Program (2004), *Human Development Report – 2004*, New York: United Nations Publications.

United Nations Development Program (2005), *Human Development Report – 2005,* New York: United Nations Publications.

United Nations High Commission for Refugees (2005), *2004 Global Refugee Trends,* Geneva: United Nations Publications.

Vincentian Partnership for Social Justice (2004), *Low Cost But Acceptable Budgets for Three Households,* Dublin.

Wackernagel, M., Schulz N.B., Deumling D., Linares A.C., Jenkins M., Kapos V., Monfreda C., Loh J., Myers N., Norgaard R. and Randers J. (2002), Tracking the ecological overshoot of the human economy in *Proc. National. Academy of Science,* Vol. 99, Issue 14, 9266-9271.

Ward, S. (1994), "A Basic Income System for Ireland" in Reynolds, B. and Healy, S. (eds.) *Towards an Adequate Income for All,* Dublin, CORI.

Watson, D., C. Whelan, J. Williams, and S. Blackwell (2005), *Mapping Poverty: National, Regional and County Patterns.* Dublin, IPA and Combat Poverty Agency.

Whelan, C.T., R. Layte, B. Maitre, B. Gannon, B. Nolan, W. Watson, J. Williams (2003) *Monitoring Poverty Trends in Ireland: Results from the 2001 Living in Ireland Survey.* ESRI Dublin, Policy Research Series No. 51, December.

World Commission on Environment and Development (1987), *Our Common Future,* Oxford University Press.

World Economic Forum (2003). *Global Competitiveness Report 2003-04.* www.weforum.org.

World Economic Forum (2005). *Global Competitiveness Report 2005-06.* www.weforum.org.

World Health Organisation (2001), *Mental Health: New Understanding, New Hope* Geneva, Switzerland.

World Health Organisation (2002), *Annual Report 2001* Geneva, Switzerland.